Fikret Adaman (BA and MA in Economics at Boğaziçi University; PhD in Economics at the University of Manchester) is currently Professor of Economics at Boğaziçi University. His interests include political ecology, political economy of Turkey and methodology of economics. His recent work has been published in the *Journal of Peasant Studies, Development and Change, Antipode, Social Science and Medicine*, and *Conservation Letters*.

Bengi Akbulut (BA in Economics at Boğaziçi University; PhD in Economics at the University of Massachusetts, Amherst) is Assistant Professor of Ecological Economics in the Department of Geography, Environment and Planning at Concordia University. Her work focuses on political economy of development, political ecology, state-society relationships, and feminist economics. With Fikret Adaman she runs a biweekly radio programme, 'The End of Economics as We Know It', criticising the growth paradigm that disregards social and ecological costs. Her recent work has been published in the *Journal of Peasant Studies, Development and Change,* and *Cambridge Journal of Economics*.

Murat Arsel (BA in Economics and Government at Clark University, MA in Politics of the World Economy at the LSE, MPhil in Environment and Development and PhD in Human Geography at the University of Cambridge) is Associate Professor of Environment and Development at the International Institute of Social Studies (ISS) of Erasmus University Rotterdam. He is currently co-chair of the editorial board of *Development and Change* and held the Keyman Family Visiting Professorship in Modern Turkish Studies at Northwestern University in 2014. His recent work has been published in the *Journal of Peasant Studies*, the *European Journal of Development Research, Extractive Industries and Society,* and *Conservation Letters*.

'This is an exceptionally rich collection of papers that manages to successfully ground the familiar discourse on neoliberalism by addressing topics ranging from land use and housing to energy policy and environmental movements. I can think of no better scholarly guide to appreciate the social and cultural complexity of contemporary Turkish politics.'

Çağlar Keyder, Boğaziçi University, Istanbul

'The large-scale infrastructures and other energy, environmental and construction efforts of the AKP-led Turkish government of the past decade have been noteworthy. This volume serves as a careful and insightful guide to better understand these projects, while also providing context in terms of the political and economic backdrop that informs their design and implementation. It is essential reading for anyone interested in the ongoing contestation and negotiation over meanings of development, progress, justice and sustainability in contemporary Turkey.'

Leila Harris, University of British Columbia, Vancouver

'This is an outstanding book, offering a uniquely vibrant and refreshing analysis of neoliberal modernisation in AKP-led Turkey. The chapters review social transformations, economic development and environmental politics in the country, and their implications for construction and urban development, agriculture, the production of food and energy, and much else. They also examine in vibrant detail the routes of contestation emerging in the wake of the neoliberal takeover of nature and society, and their implications for social reproduction now, and in the future.'

Alfredo Saad Filho, School of Oriental and African Studies (SOAS), University of London

NEOLIBERAL TURKEY AND ITS DISCONTENTS

Economic Policy and the Environment under Erdoğan

EDITED BY
Fikret Adaman, Bengi Akbulut
and Murat Arsel

I.B. TAURIS
LONDON · NEW YORK

Published in 2017 by
I.B.Tauris & Co. Ltd
London • New York
www.ibtauris.com

Library of Modern Turkey 31

ISBN: 978 1 78453 872 9
eISBN: 978 1 78672 209 6
ePDF: 978 1 78673 209 5

A full CIP record for this book is available from the British Library
A full CIP record is available from the Library of Congress

Library of Congress Catalog Card Number: available

Typeset in Garamond Three by OKS Prepress Services, Chennai, India
Printed and bound by CPI Group (UK) Ltd, Croydon, CR0 4YY

MIX
Paper from responsible sources
FSC® C013604
FSC www.fsc.org

CONTENTS

FIGURES AND TABLES

Figures

Tables

ACKNOWLEDGEMENTS

We would like to thank Tomasz Hoskins, David Campbell and the rest of the I.B.Tauris staff for their support during the production process of the book. We also gratefully acknowledge the financial support of the International Institute of Social Studies and Erasmus University Rotterdam. Finally, Murat Arsel would like to thank Rita Koryan, the former executive director of the Keyman Modern Turkish Studies programme at Northwestern University.

INTRODUCTION

NEOLIBERAL DEVELOPMENTALISM IN TURKEY: CONTINUITY, RUPTURE, CONSOLIDATION

Fikret Adaman, Murat Arsel and Bengi Akbulut

The rise of the Justice and Development Party (the AKP in its Turkish acronym) to power more than a decade ago was accompanied by fears of social conflict in Turkey. Given the AKP's socially conservative and pious posture, anticipated conflicts mainly concerned the role of religion in public life and the future of socio-cultural modernisation. Although the lifting of the ban on religious garbs in public spaces, constraints on alcohol sale and consumption in public spaces as well as a few other similar measures did raise heckles in certain quarters, the remarkable feature of the AKP's rule has been that the most visible manifestations of state-society conflict were not over social or cultural values or even ideas of development. For while the AKP stuck closely to the decades-old script supported by the country's elites on the necessity and desirability of rapid and modernising economic growth, its particular brand of crony neoliberalism and the manifestation of these relationships in the energy and the construction sectors, which have been the main engines of growth, did most to unite disparate social and economic classes to challenge the AKP's rule.[1,2] These movements, from the uprising around Gezi Park in 2013 to the numerous much smaller but just as significant revolts in the countryside against micro-hydro power plants, rose up to defend life spaces, be they rural or urban, as well as the rights of communities to exercise power over whether and how rapidly their lives and livelihoods could be transformed by capitalist accumulation. This book focuses on their emergence, development and significance for just, equitable and sustainable development in Turkey.

The history of state-led economic growth in Turkey is replete with conflict, often arising from the top-down model of policy making and implementation, which aimed to 'civilize' a putatively 'backward' populace.[3] While the AKP era in many ways is a continuation of this approach to state-society relations, both the particular political economic conjuncture in which the AKP came to power and the socio-cultural identity of the party add a unique dimension to the struggles discussed in this volume. The AKP's rise took place as Turkey's post-1983 turn to neoliberal economic policies began to falter within a climate of political instability, causing widespread discontent across society. Domestic capitalists were dissatisfied with the slow pace of Turkey's integration with global finance and export markets, whereas the poorer segments of the urban population suffered from further socio-economic disenfranchisement after losing their modest benefits provided by the state or being displaced by gentrification processes without sharing the spoils of the new neoliberal economic climate. While rural communities did manage to fight off or dilute some World Bank-designed policies aiming to remove the protection of the state and expose them to global price speculations, it became clear that peasants and other smallholders would no longer enjoy the type of stability that had characterised their relationship with the state since the post-1923 era of the modern republic. Cutting across these issues, numerous identity-centred movements – Kurdish, Alevi as well as 'Islamist' – began to agitate more vigorously within the climate engendered by talk of eventual European Union integration. These movements found friends and allies within the country's liberal intelligentsia who could no longer excuse the actions of an inflexible state in the name of the Kemalist dream of secular modernity.

The AKP coalesced and came to power in this climate of dissatisfaction, representing a fundamental break from a political system whose violent reverberations at the surface – with periodic *coups d'état* and suppression of any and all diversion from officially sanctioned model of aggressively secular and nationalist Turkishness – belied a highly stable alliance between the military and the bureaucratic establishment. The upper echelons of the party were made up of political outsiders with little connection to Turkey's cultural, political or economic elite, and it was carried to power by a voting bloc that drew not only from the above mentioned disaffected groups but also a peasant base in the country's heartland fighting for rural survival and those engaged in often precarious – but sometimes lucrative – set of diverse economic activities in ever more dynamic urban centres. Early on, the AKP embraced the liberal promise of democratic individualism not only to deliver visible gains to its pious social base but also to shield itself from the seemingly limitless power of the army by endearing itself to both the EU and the US. This meant promises for greater individual freedom in the socio-cultural sphere matched by deeper neoliberalisation in the economic environment, and it was this two-pronged liberalisation as well as the resulting political stability that ensured its recurrent electoral victories.

As a matter of fact, the AKP's policies did not mark a fundamental divergence from the prevailing idea of development, which historically animated public policy in Turkey.[4] Motivated by nostalgia for the Ottoman Empire, which for the Islamists demonstrated the necessity of economic and military might for furthering the cause of Islam, the AKP and its more hard-line predecessors have gradually – but surely – come to embrace the necessity or desirability of an idea of development that is primarily defined in terms of material accumulation. Thus, Erdoğan came to power, first as prime minister and since 2014 as president, not to displace the prevailing neoliberal economic policy but to implement it 'better'. Chiefly, the AKP government ensured the independence of the central bank, reformed the banking system and exercised fiscal discipline – policies long advocated by the World Bank and the IMF but not implemented with sufficient rigour or determination by previous administrations. The AKP was rewarded with electoral gains that translated into much needed political stability at home, and Turkey emerged as one of the 'next 11', which, in Goldman Sachs-speak, meant that the country was ready for deeper integration with global financial flows.[5]

However, the continued electoral success of the AKP necessitated more than political stability and measures to liberalise the legal code to allow, among others, wearing of headscarves in universities and other public institutions or the lifting of the ban on Kurdish language broadcasts. Especially in light of the socio-economic turmoil created by its neoliberal policies, which went further and deeper than previous administrations, the AKP's continued success came to depend on rapid economic growth. This growth would have to assuage the fears and insecurities of the large group of (newly migrated) urban populations who had lost their livelihoods either to agricultural liberalisation programmes or to withdrawal of state support to various industries (not to mention the 'forced-migration' of the mid-1990s in the rural Kurdish settlements).

For much of the late Ottoman and modern republican history, the state had used land distribution as a paternalistic mechanism to demonstrate its benevolent attitude to social welfare and to smooth out (emerging) social problems. To that extent, Z. Umut Türem in Chapter 1, 'The State of Property: From the Empire to the Neoliberal Republic', demonstrates that the neoliberal climate under the AKP was no different and that the state continued to use land policy for a variety of socio-economic and political ends. Yet he also observes several characteristics that make the AKP years different, teasing out contrasts with a conventional reading of the relationship between the state, market and land under neoliberalism. For instance, he begins his chapter by noting that the Turkish State Treasury's share of land ownership in the country had increased by 20 per cent (230 billion square metres) between 2009 and 2014. Similarly, in Istanbul, without a doubt the setting in which Turkey's neoliberal transformation is most advanced and most visible, the Treasury owns 43.5 per cent of immovable property. What makes the current conjuncture different, or neoliberal, is the 'state's increasing approach to its land as property, as a commodity'.[6] Such a transformation, Türem concludes, is radical without marking a clear rupture from land's centrality in processes of state-making and legitimisation.

The increased commodification of land took different shapes in the urban and rural spheres. In the former, where, for decades, informal claims to land had been legalised in exchange for short-term electoral support for the governing political parties and long-term legitimacy for the state itself, a new dispensation emerged. Türem beautifully captures this as the 'jealousy' of the state in defending its claim to the land against the 'intruders' that until recently had been periodically accommodated (as the labour base for the post World War II industrialisation drive). This transition was not 'natural' in the sense that neither the governing logic of the AKP nor the legitimisation need of the state and, ultimately, not even the functioning of late modern capitalism truly necessitated it.

The necessity for rapid growth, combined with the global political economic climate in which Turkey emerged as a relatively safe haven for global capital flows, did of course make the country the target of and dependent on short-term international financial flows. But the lava-like flow of this 'hot money' onto urban and rural landscapes requires further explication.[7]

In Chapter 2, 'Two Crises, Two Trajectories: The Impact of the 2001 and 2008 Economic Crises on Urban Governance in Turkey', Tuna Kuyucu locates another piece of this complex puzzle by focusing on the relationship between economic crises and urban governance. He is particularly interested in understanding why the AKP's initial policy of administrative decentralisation of urban governance – which can be located within a broader set of democratisation and liberalisation policies implemented at the national level – was not just abandoned but reversed dramatically. By posing this question, Kuyucu makes an argument with far reaching significance, namely that neither the initial democratising decentralisation nor the later authoritarian centralism of the AKP (and by extension, Erdoğan) can be explained by reference to intrinsic qualities of the party (and its leader) or in terms of the corrupting effect of power. Rather, the decisions underlying these policies were forged within the context of the economic crises of 2001 and 2008.

The former crisis discredited the established parties and gave way to the election of the AKP, which proceeded to implement the very policies that the previous government aimed to pursue under the supervision of Kemal Derviş who had left his position as the Vice President of the World Bank to become the Minister of the Treasury. These structural adjustment policies did have the desired effect of stabilising the economy. Kuyucu argues that the resolution of this domestic crisis not only opened up the economy for the inflow of global financial capital but also created a new policy space in which further democratising reforms could be pursued with a view to full membership of the European Union. Given the dialectical nature of crises and their resolutions, however, this period of optimism also created the conditions in which real estate speculation and construction became key engines of economic growth. Thus an unstable balance was created between decentralisation, rational economic management, and rent-seeking urban transformation.

The contradiction between these three dynamics was resolved, according to Kuyucu, in favour of authoritarian centricism in the wake of the global financial crisis of 2008. This had very different knock-on effects than the 2001 one, cutting off the global financial flows that had fueled the investment boom. Just as importantly, the changing political climate in Europe meant that Turkey's membership aspirations were severely curtailed, resulting in the loss of a hugely important external incentive to persist with the difficult process of democratisation. Kuyucu shows that the authoritarian and centralising turn at this point can best be understood as an attempt by the AKP to shore up faltering economic growth and increasingly questioned the political basis of its legitimacy. It is within this context that the state, through its Mass Housing Projects Authority (TOKİ in its Turkish acronym) – which, endowed with the power to develop profit-oriented housing projects, expropriate land for real estate development, and coordinate and initiate urban gentrification – has also been deeply involved in private housing projects. This, given its size and influence, and the possibility of co-ordination with public works, has enabled the state to not just increase the housing stock but also actively shape the direction and nature of urban development.

As already mentioned, these dynamics also had a rural dimension, which Huri İslamoğlu tackles in Chapter 3 on the 'Politics of Agricultural Production in Turkey'. She begins by emphasising that the world turned upside down in the Turkish countryside in the 2000s with the introduction of market reforms in the framework of stabilisation packages of the IMF, WB and EU. These reforms entailed the removal of production-based subsidies, privatisation of credit, seed provisioning, as well as quotas in tobacco and sugar production in line with global market strategies of multi-national corporations – all leading to a major exodus of agricultural population into cities as well as reducing agriculture's share in total employment.[8] Yet this is only a part of the picture in which the AKP tried to boost economic growth and create employment for the newly displaced rural communities. The other part is that the exodus has now slowed down completely due to changes in urban governance and the accompanying commodification of land described in Chapters 1 and 2, making it increasingly hard for migrants to gain a foothold in urban areas.[9]

İslamoğlu shows that agricultural employment appears to be stable in the past ten years, indicating that leaving the countryside is no longer a viable option for the remaining rural population. This, in and of itself, could not be considered to be problematic (even though the entire modern history of Turkey is predicated upon expectations of a Rostowian rural–urban transition). What makes the predicament of rural communities tenuous, however, is that they are among the lowest income-groups, and agricultural employment for the young is either increasingly not available or financially untenable – forcing them to seek employment elsewhere in rural areas, often ending up with precarious conditions, for example in dangerous and poorly regulated mining work. Furthermore, Chapter 3 also argues that the encroachment of industry onto agricultural land continues, not only further squeezing out farm work as an option but also exacerbating environmental degradation. Ultimately, İslamoğlu argues that diminished in size and squeezed out economically, rural agricultural communities have seen their (already weak) influence on national politics eroded.

Thus, rather than being the 'masters' of society as Mustafa Kemal had declared in the early years of the Republic, rural communities nowadays factor into national development strategy mainly as problem cases, as surplus population that needs to be absorbed into the economy as cheap labour, lest they become a destabilising force. To the extent that their long-term interests are taken into account, this is mainly done through attempts at hegemony building through appeals to incipient return to national greatness. In other words, the sacrifices of today – be they cuts in subsidies, enclosure of commons or destruction of nature – are justified by appeals to their necessity in terms of their ability to bring Turkey closer to its long-overdue return to greatness, at first regional and ultimately global.

The involvement of the state in construction and urban development has, therefore, not been limited to housing development or even infrastructure building, where landmark projects have not only been means of injecting cash into the economy and quickly creating jobs in construction and associated sectors. Considerable financial and political capital has been invested into 'megaprojects' such as the third bridge in Istanbul (opened in September 2016), the Marmaray underwater metro tunnel connecting the two sides of the Bosphorus (opened in October 2013) and what is slated to become the largest airport in the world being constructed outside Istanbul (scheduled for completion in 2018). Erdoğan has taken personal credit for them and seems to take particular pleasure in announcing new 'crazy projects' such as the planned canal that will open a new shipping lane on the European side of

Istanbul by carving a 45-km waterway connecting the Black Sea and the Sea of Marmara.

In Chapter 4, 'The "Politics of Serving" and Neoliberal Developmentalism: The Megaprojects of the AKP as Tools of Hegemony Building', Hande Paker observes that the AKP has experienced yet another transformation (in addition to the one analysed by Kuyucu in Chapter 2). Whereas in its early days it distinguished itself through a critique of Kemalist modernisation, it has since become its chief proponent. Furthermore, the consolidation of its power has rested on its use of infrastructural power, materially as well as symbolically. She argues that the AKP has made extensive use of its discourse of 'politics of serving', which is meant to invoke a distinction of performance between its rule and that of previous (secular) governments that failed to meet the needs of (at least a large segment of) society. Paker also observes that the process of hegemony building in Turkey is more continuous than ruptured and the AKP's use of megaprojects is not unlike attempts from previous periods when the state sought to implement its vision of modernisation and achieve economic growth through infrastructure projects such as large hydroelectric dams. Yet, Paker also makes a crucial distinction by arguing that the manifestation of the AKP's infrastructural power is also characterised by novel dimensions as it is shaped by Turkey's integration into the neoliberal global economy as well as corporatisation of state services. Put differently, just as the AKP distinguished itself by 'better' implementing policies that rendered neoliberal ideology sovereign in the country, it has similarly excelled in forcefully implementing projects and practices that signalled the impending arrival of Turkey's own version of 'manifest destiny'.

Once again, it is important to emphasise that there exist strong continuities between the urban and the rural transformations taking place under the AKP. Of these, the road connecting the summer pastures of the Black Sea region that the government refers to as the 'Green Road' in an Orwellian doublespeak is another national prestige project that is premised on a dualist understanding of modernising development. Nevertheless, the truest symbol of rural transformation can be observed in the various energy generation projects. Energy was one of the latter sectors of the economy to come under the gaze of neoliberal policy making and was put firmly on its current growth trajectory with the 2005 law that deregulated the electricity market. As Sinan Erensü's

Chapter 5 on 'Turkey's Hydropower Renaissance: Nature, Neoliberalism and Development in the Cracks of Infrastructure' argues, of particular significance are the changes that enabled private producers to participate more extensively in energy generation projects hitherto undertaken solely by the state and to sell electricity to the national grid at guaranteed prices. Alone, this would have perhaps spurred a certain amount of growth in the marketplace but coupled with the watering down of environmental and forest protection codes and a forceful narrative built around the country's 'energy need', whose fulfilment was posed as a prerequisite for ensuring economic growth and stability, they resulted in an explosive growth driven by the private sector.

These projects have ranged from large-scale coal power plants to countless micro-hydro dam projects. While they have not displaced state-financed energy generation schemes completely, since prestige projects such as nuclear power plants continue alongside large-scale dams that have a long lead time in planning and construction, their scale cannot be understated. It is also worth emphasising that beyond their ostensible goal of meeting (projected) electricity shortfall, these energy generation projects at a certain level could also be seen as a continuation of the construction sector. As with many other contributions in this volume, Erensü also describes the neoliberal transformations taking place in Turkey in terms of a set of continuities of hegemonic intent that manifest themselves in distinctly novel practices. For instance, the rise of the 'suitcase' peddlers (*çantacı*) of micro-hydro initiatives at first forms a stark contrast to the megadam projects of previous decades. But Erensü also makes it clear that the emergence of such 'innovations' happened through the enabling conditions created by the state, which merely diversified its weapons put to use in the name of developmentalism. Chapter 5 also delineates the differences and similarities between energy generation projects and other (large-scale) infrastructure projects, both in terms of their analytical purchase and their ability to lend themselves to resistance movements. By reading the political potential of energy investments against their contestations through selected projects, the chapter discusses the fragility and the contradiction of politics of infrastructure and new geographies of energy as they blur the boundaries between the urban and the rural.

The most evident implication of the twin rise of construction and energy sectors has been the enclosure or destruction of rural and urban commons, displacement of communities as well as the erosion of their means of livelihood, modes of living, and the networks that sustain them.[10] Whether carefully organised and sustained such as the movement in Gerze against a coal power plant situated within fertile agricultural land and close to a scenic town (on the Black Sea coast)[11] or the Gezi Park uprising that swelled spontaneously upon the foundation laid by a small group of activists,[12] there have been countless acts, movements and organisations of resistance that challenged these energy and construction projects. One theme that emerges in the analyses provided in this volume concerns the motivations of the actors and activists in question. Do they reject the goals espoused in these projects, or are they mainly aiming to prevent their negative environmental, socio-economic and cultural impacts? Or are they rising up because of the way in which the AKP government has used its power – drawn both from state apparatus and its particularistic networks – to force through its vision of modernisation and to quash arising dissent? The book does not seek to provide a uniform explanation for the various cases it analyses nor does it claim to have uncovered the 'core' reason of resistance in any one of them. Rather, by confronting these cases that are emerging in increasing frequency, it documents the nature of state-society relationships under the AKP's rule and how these relationships can be discerned from contested meanings of justice, progress and sustainability.

Nevertheless, given the relative underdevelopment of environmental studies and allied disciplines such as anthropology, human geography and even sociology in Turkey, there exists a dearth of concrete data on how environmental values are formed, expressed and articulated within broader political positions. Ali Çarkoğlu's Chapter 6, 'Environmental Concerns in Turkey: A Comparative Perspective', thus reinforces the discussions of the book, especially in relation to environmental politics. He shows that the electoral success of the AKP in Turkey came not only with economic growth within a relatively stable politico-economic context but is also marked by the considerable deterioration of environmental sensitivities on the side of policy makers. Building on the observation that there exist limited public resistance and rejection to the destruction of the environment through a barrage of construction and energy infrastructure projects, Çarkoğlu interrogates the popular bases of the AKP's developmental policy and seeks to find out to what extent popular preferences are reflected onto the political arena in terms of environmental issues. By using data from the Comparative Manifestos Project (CMP) and the International Social Survey Program (ISSP), Chapter 6 shows how the political emphasis on environmental issues developed in election manifestos over the entire multi-party election period since 1950, especially in the past decade. Çarkoğlu notes that Turkey ranks very low in terms of public concern for the environment. To the extent that the electorate takes note of the issue, it is the support base of the social democratic Republican People's Party (CHP in its Turkish acronym) that leads the rest of the pack. That the AKP supporters lag behind CHP however cannot easily be reduced to a left–right dichotomy since the base of the pro-Kurdish and leftist Union and Democracy Party (BDP in its Turkish acronym) scores similar to that of the AKP. Ultimately, the chapter concludes that the theme of the environment 'is clearly not very salient and hence of little electoral importance' in Turkey. To the extent that the environment does get politicised and becomes a contested theme, it does so in issue-specific and in primarily rural settings.

By the 1990s, it seemed that one such issue would have been the topic of nuclear power. Yet this has not been the case, and Chapter 7 entitled 'The Radioactive Inertia: Deciphering Turkey's Anti-Nuclear Movement' by Bengi Akbulut, Fikret Adaman and Murat Arsel seeks to problematise the remarkable absence of meaningful social resistance against nuclear power projects in Turkey. The starting point of the chapter is the decision of the AKP government to construct two (possibly three) nuclear power plants. This ambition is significant not only because previous such initiatives ended up in failure. Furthermore, Turkey's massive potential for renewable energy on the one hand and location in an extremely earthquake-prone geographical location on the other would have been expected to dampen the AKP's appetite for nuclear power, especially in the wake of the Fukushima disaster. The chapter demonstrates the significance of a major anti-nuclear movement by putting the status quo in sharper relief against three considerations. First, both energy generation projects and 'mega' infrastructure projects have increasingly become politicised in recent years, attracting sustained social resistance at local and national levels. Second, there exists a relatively robust regional and transnational campaign, operated in neighbouring countries such as Cyprus, against their construction. Finally, there used to be a relatively dynamic anti-nuclear campaign that contributed to the abandonment of the previous push for constructing a plant at the turn of the millennium. The chapter interrogates this puzzle by placing the seemingly unpreventable construction of the Akkuyu and Sinop nuclear power plants (as well as a potential third one at İğneada) within, and attending to, the changing forms and manifestations of state power within the context of neoliberal development policy and the strategic calculations of environmental activists.

Part of the explanation as to why the AKP has insisted on nuclear power where other governments had ultimately given up can once again be explained as the AKP pursuing policies that form a continuity with past practices but in more efficacious ways, both in terms of bureaucratic management but also hegemony building. So it is possible to read nuclear power plants, and the twin booms of energy and construction, as political investments. They not only created a new class of wealthy elite but also tens of thousands of construction jobs. The AKP counted on the financial support of the former and electoral support of the latter. The partnering of speculative capital with precarious labour, while uneasy, delivered relatively affordable housing to newly-migrated residents (even if they themselves had been pushed away from the countryside) as well as those who had constructed their homes at the edges of the law. But the energy and construction sectors had to work for even bigger end goals. They were about more than creating safe, affordable housing and cheap, plentiful energy. The construction boom meant the 'cleansing' of urban centres, disciplining of 'problem' communities, and making Turkey more amenable to receive even more global financial flows. The meeting of global capital with plentiful energy flowing from the countryside, in turn, was to lay the groundwork for future industrial development and an even bigger boom in consumption.

The neoliberal modernisation paradigm that was consolidated under the rule of the AKP has presented the dream of ever intensifying economic growth as the solution to the first dimension of environmentalism. Any attempt to enunciate meanings of and relationship with the environment that detract from rapid accumulation has been written off as the work of misguided individuals at best and foreign agents at worst. Given the long history of how the state has built and maintained the modernisation paradigm, it is not surprising therefore that those individuals and communities that did not accept the

Faustian bargain of economic growth have been at the receiving end of heavy-handed state power taking the shape of the police baton, the tear gas canister or armoured vehicles.

This fast-paced, aggressive neoliberal developmentalist political project did of course create numerous social conflicts. As Chapter 8 on '"A Few Environmentalists"? Interrogating the "Political" in Gezi Park' by Murat Arsel, Fikret Adaman and Bengi Akbulut argues, the fight surrounding the eponymous park is one of the most striking and forceful social mobilisations witnessed in contemporary Turkey. However, the chapter states that contrary to the prevailing consensus in the scholarly literature, the Gezi Uprising does not come as a surprise if it is located within Turkey's post-1980 history of environmental conflicts. Engaging with the large body of literature that has emerged since May 2013, the chapter also problematises the dominant understanding of the meaning and significance of environmental politics in Turkey. The authors argue that to the extent that the Gezi Uprising has huge symbolic importance, its inability to advance a coherent, long-term political agenda is also notable. This failure is in many ways due to the absence of a viable critique of the idea of developmentalism – neoliberal or otherwise – which continues to dominate Turkey's public sphere.

Thus the main challenge facing those confronting the status quo in Turkey is to articulate and put into practice alternative ways of socio-economic organisation. Zeynep Kadirbeyoğlu and Nazlı Konya's chapter on 'Alternative Food Initiatives in Turkey' approaches this urgent task from the perspective of food, a theme whose potential to connect various political, economic, social and cultural processes is only beginning to be fully appreciated by critical social scientists. They observe that access to healthy and affordable food and the ability to make a decent living by producing food crops are important arenas of exclusion in today's globalised and corporatised food governance regime and that alternative food initiatives (AFIs) have been established worldwide in response to these challenges in order to re-conceptualise production, distribution and consumption processes. The authors focus on AFIs that have emerged in Turkey in order to imagine more inclusive and just food systems. The chapter, after reminding us that with the entrenchment of neoliberal policies, such as the cutback on agricultural subsidies and support mechanisms in the 1990s, mechanisms that lead to exclusion in food systems were intensified, suggests that there are two sides to the exclusionary practices within the food governance regime of the past three decades. On the one hand, these policies were combined with an increasing presence of agri-food corporations, which led to even more pressure on small peasant/family agriculture. On the other hand, consumers are excluded from access to healthy and affordable food as a result of processes such as unregulated use of pesticides and chemical fertilisers in agriculture and growth hormones in livestock and poultry. Given this state of affairs in the mainstream food regime, the chapter examines alternative food initiatives that respond to these challenges in Turkey. The ultimate aim of these AFIs is portrayed in the chapter as imagining an alternative social ordering and consequently attempting to bring about transformation through direct participation in creating a collective voice and alternative practices that are politicised and inclusive. The chapter traces these interrelated attempts – both in terms of the efforts of Çiftçi-Sen (Farmers Union Confederation) and those of consumers – to challenge the mainstream order and analyse their incremental gains.

Finally, the last chapter, 'Commons Against the Tide: The Project of Democratic Economy', by Bengi Akbulut sets out the basic framework for an alternative structure to neoliberal developmentalism and its severe social and ecological costs. By considering the Kurdish Freedom Movement's redefinition of its political project along the model of democratic autonomy with the onset of the 2000s, the chapter visits the debates on the concomitant construction of a communal and democratic economy along the principles of gender equality, ecology, democracy and egalitarianism. It situates the project of Democratic Economy and the emerging concrete experiences associated with it as an alternative to the dominant paradigm of neoliberal developmentalism. In doing so, the chapter utilises the conceptual analytic of the commons/commoning found in the works of Silvia Federici, George Caffentzis and Massimo De Angelis, among others, and locates the specific arenas of commoning practices within the democratic economy vision and the concrete steps taken to operationalise its foundational principles. The chapter ends with a discussion of the opportunities as well as the challenges lying ahead for the Democratic Economy project in institutionalising a solidaristic and participatory alternative.

As the book features an Epilogue by Erik Swyngedouw, Fikret Adaman, Bengi Akbulut and Murat Arsel make their concluding observations in the Conclusion entitled 'Neoliberal Modernisation Cast in Concrete'. The chapter begins by discussing the reasons behind the prominence of energy and construction projects under the AKP's rule. These require relatively little technical know-how, are germane to combining assets the state has in relative abundance (e.g. land) with readily available 'hot money', and generate employment for low-skilled workers. Among other reasons, the fruits of construction and energy projects – the world's biggest airport, thousands of miles of new roads, a nuclear power plant – also have a certain populist appeal. The conclusion also discusses the significance of the attempted *coup d'état* of 15 July 2016, noting that the infighting between Erdoğan's faction within the AKP and that of the presumed mastermind of the coup, Fethullah Gülen, had first become public over a corruption scandal concerning construction contracts. Before locating the Turkish experience within a broader, international setting by discussing the rise of neoliberal authoritarianism in such diverse contexts as Ecuador, Russia and Egypt, this chapter also positions the recent conflagration of the Kurdish conflict within the context of the themes discussed in this volume. The editors argue that the overwhelmingly violent response of the Turkish state is partly in response to the alternative development model articulated by Kurdish organisations in contradistinction to the AKP's neoliberal developmentalism.

It is within this context that the environment emerges as a critical arena of inquiry, one that has long been neglected in the study of Turkey, that unites the above-mentioned threads of transformation and dissent. While there have certainly been other periods in the history of the Turkish state where an equally radical alteration of the environment was witnessed, the contemporary period has been marked with the specific way the environment has been articulated into politics. Rapid economic growth is displacing peasants from their lands, replacing parks with shopping centres, pricing out communities from their traditional neighbourhoods, and exposing rural and urban populations to environmental risks. Apprehended from such perspectives, the 'environment' lends itself to a type of politics that has conservation at its heart.

However, the book also demonstrates by building on recent political ecology writing that the politicisation of the 'environment' goes deeper and broader than 'mere' conservation.[13] The onslaught of energy development and construction projects is not simply transforming the environment but the relationship between various communities and their environments. Put differently, environmental 'destruction' is not always the only or even the main concern. The arrival of neoliberal conceptions of what nature is, how it should be incorporated into economic processes and what 'work' it should do is changing commonly held values as well. The transformation of these values is not only eliminating certain livelihoods but also lifestyles. It is in this context that the 'environment' is also lending itself to calls for – as well as demonstrations of – alternative configurations of socio-environmental relationships, including practices of 'commoning', which signifies not just the defence of the commons but also their ongoing articulation in the face of neoliberal economic growth. As such, Turkey's still emerging environmental politics is as much a struggle over material processes and relationships of production as it is about the meaning attributed to them.

Notes

1. On the importance of energy and construction sectors under the AKP period, see Bengi Akbulut and Fikret Adaman, 'The unbearable appeal of modernisation: The fetish of growth', *Perspectives: Political Analysis and Commentary from Turkey* 5 (2014), pp. 14–17. Note that throughout this introduction and indeed the entire book, the term 'neoliberalism' will be used to describe an ideological vision that is based on the economisation of all human relations, which translates all social and political problems into economic ones and *ipso facto* believes that they are solvable via economic incentives. This conceptualisation accommodates a range of theoretical positions with diverse policy implications and does not limit itself to marketisation and private property. It includes those that can be identified as 'interventionist', i.e. those that have no problem in deploying state-apparatuses or other non-market devices to govern the social field and the behaviour of individuals. See Yahya M. Madra and Fikret Adaman, 'Neoliberal reason and its forms: De-politicisation through economisation', *Antipode* 46/3 (2014), pp. 691–716.
2. The contributions to this edited volume were already in advanced stages of completion at the time of the attempted *coup d'état* in Turkey on 15 July 2016. The Conclusion touches upon this event, discussing its relevance for the themes covered herein.
3. Sibel Bozdoğan and Reşat Kasaba, *Rethinking Modernity and National Identity in Turkey* (Washington, 1997).

4. Murat Arsel 'Reflexive developmentalism? Toward an environmental critique of modernisation', in F. Adaman and M. Arsel (eds), *Environmentalism in Turkey: Between Democracy and Development?* (Aldershot, 2005).
5. http://www.goldmansachs.com/our-thinking/archive/archive-pdfs/brics-book/brics-chap-13.pdf, accessed on 10 July 2016.
6. Türem, Chapter 1.
7. For a general discussion, see Fikret Adaman, Bengi Akbulut, Yahya Madra and Şevket Pamuk, 'Hitting the wall: Erdoğan's construction-based, finance-led growth regime', *The Middle East in London* 10/3 (2014), pp. 7–8.
8. Zülküf Aydın, 'Neo-Liberal transformation of Turkish agriculture', *Journal of Agrarian Change* 10/2 (2010), pp. 149–87.
9. For a discussion of the changes in urban governance in the late-1990s onwards with an emphasis on Istanbul, see Çağlar Keyder, 'Transformations in urban structure and the environment in Istanbul', in F. Adaman and M. Arsel (eds), *Environmentalism in Turkey: Between Democracy and Development?* (Aldershot, 2005).
10. Fikret Adaman and Murat Arsel, 'Globalisation, development, and environmental policies in Turkey', in T. Çetin and F. Yılmaz (eds), *Understanding the Process of Institutional Change in Turkey: A Political Economy Approach* (Aldershot, 2010); Fikret Adaman and Murat Arsel, 'Environment', in M. Heper and S. Sayarı (eds), *The Routledge Handbook of Modern Turkey* (London, 2013).
11. On the Gerze struggle, see Murat Arsel, Bengi Akbulut and Fikret Adaman, 'Environmentalism of the malcontent: Anatomy of an anti-coal power plant struggle in Turkey', *Journal of Peasant Studies* 42/2 (2015), pp. 371–95.
12. Mehmet Barış Kuymulu, 'Reclaiming the right to the city: Reflections on the urban uprisings in Turkey', *City* 17/3 (2013), pp. 274–8.
13. See, for example, Tom Perreault, Gavin Bridge and James McCarthy (eds), *The Routledge Handbook of Political Ecology* (London, 2015).

CHAPTER 1

THE STATE OF PROPERTY: FROM THE EMPIRE TO THE NEOLIBERAL REPUBLIC

Z. Umut Türem

Introduction

Recently an interesting piece of statistics was compiled and reported by the Anatolian News Agency (Anadolu Ajansı), a semi-official Turkish media outlet. Accordingly, in the five years leading up to the end of 2014, the size of immoveable property registered in the name of the Turkish State Treasury had increased by 20 per cent. The area/size of the immoveables in Turkey that are registered at the State Treasury had increased to almost 230 billion square metres. Moreover, according to the story, nearly half of Istanbul's land, 43.5 per cent to be more precise, is owned by the Treasury, either in the form of land/parcels of land, or in the form of buildings and the property that houses such buildings.[1]

That the state owns almost half of Istanbul, or a substantial part of Turkey's overall land, is certainly interesting but not striking, especially considering that this figure includes forests and mountains, uncultivable and uninhabitable land. Similarly, the land/property regime that was inherited from the Ottoman Empire rendered the Turkish Treasury a major owner of land, which again, makes the above figures not so surprising. What is striking, however, is the *increase* in ownership by the Treasury and that this increase came about in the last five years, during which the Turkish state appeared to be moving in the direction of full-scale neoliberalisation and privatisation.

Easy conclusions cannot be reached by these statistics, and I will touch upon the complexity of the question later, but here, I wish to use this increase in the size and amount of state property as a means to enter a broader discussion on the neoliberalisation of the ways the Turkish state relates to its land. This chapter is about the transformation of the modality the central Turkish state manages its (public) land. It constructs a sociological/historical framework to make sense of the 'state of property' in the neoliberal Turkey of today.

Among scholars who study urban transformations in Turkey, there appears to be a consensus that Turkey's state policy has shifted from a previous normal towards neoliberalism. Kuyucu and Ünsal write that 'since 2001, there has been a radical shift in the governance of urban land and housing markets in Turkey from a populist to a neoliberal mode'.[2] Kayasü and Yetişkul[3] offer a similar reading, with a slightly different periodisation: based on the former phase of the neoliberalism of the 1980s, that is a 'roll back neoliberalism', following Peck and Tickell,[4] 'the new government of the 2000s also followed to implement various forms of neoliberal governance in the face of the EU Accession Process'. This second phase, which would be the 'roll out neoliberalism', has not been successful, and indeed has been quite frail in many respects according to these authors. Lovering and Türkmen label the Turkish experience in the post-2000s as 'bulldozer neo-liberalism' and point to the heavy-handed role of the state in the construction of property markets.[5]

Agreeing with the consensus that there has been a neoliberal shift in how the state governs its land, this paper nevertheless employs a slightly wider historical lens to understand the ways in which neoliberalism articulates with the broad macro historical structures and trends in Turkey. This broadening of focus is needed because the Turkish state possesses large chunks of land inherited from its predecessor, the Ottoman Empire. Legally speaking, most land was owned by the central state in the Ottoman Empire and private property was the exception until relatively late in the Empire's lifespan. Despite the legal recognition of private property in the last phases of the Ottoman Empire, and later in the Turkish Republic, which inherited part of the administrative structure of the Empire, a certain modality of managing public lands continued until the neoliberal 1990s/2000s. In other words, the historico-institutional legacy of the Ottoman Empire conditioned the property regime in Turkey.

Until recently, the vacant public lands the Turkish state inherited from its predecessor, the Ottoman Empire, seemed to constitute a resource for popular redistribution: the land on the fringes of the valuable urban centres, Istanbul in particular, was appropriated by migrants from the countryside. The Turkish state turned a blind eye to such appropriation, even eased it through several mechanisms. This has acted on the one hand as a redistribution mechanism, benefiting those whose livelihoods were no longer sustained in the countryside due to macro-level trends such as the mechanisation in agriculture and the shift towards an industrial economic development model. On the other hand, easing the appropriation of public lands served to sustain the Turkish state's viability, even legitimacy,[6] particularly among the large urban masses whose poverty and dislocation could have posed a potential danger for the state. Distributing land in this manner not only provided a means to integrate internal migrants to the city, but also provided them with a valuable resource, urban land, thereby redistributing part of the national (and historical) wealth to them. This mode of relating to the land, and the use of it as a patrimonial resource, presents a line of continuity between the Ottoman Empire and the Turkish state.[7]

More recently, however, we are witnessing a state that jealously guards its (urban) land against 'intruders'. Not only are newcomers not welcome anymore, but the earlier migrants who managed to settle under the last phase of the old regime of (informal and formal) land distribution are being kicked out by various methods; by practices and ambiguities of urban transformation. It appears that state-owned lands are no longer up for grabs by the relatively less affluent. 'What we are witnessing', writes Kuyucu, 'is a major reorientation of public policy from tacit acceptance and encouragement of informal settlements as the dominant mechanism of low income housing provision to a policy of "clearing" such settlements'.[8]

In the pages that follow, I analyse this shift in how the Turkish state relates to its land. To be more concrete, I contrast the period that begins with multi-party democracy (1950) in Turkey and lasts until the early 1980s – which can roughly be called the developmentalist era, or the populist period regarding the property regime in land – with the neoliberal 2000s. In my analysis, I focus on whether or to what extent the deeply ingrained institutional, legal and political practices from the Ottoman times persist in these periods.

This chapter is an initial step towards thinking about the bearing of historical, institutional and political legacies on current state practices in Turkey. As such, situating practices of the Turkish state regarding land and property along a line of continuity with (late) Ottoman practices will make it possible to analyse the deep-seated changes that neoliberalism has been achieving in the Turkish context. While a shift from populism to neoliberalism is significant enough, this article probes whether there is an even broader transformation of statehood at work by looking at the connections between property and the state in Turkey.

In a nutshell, I start with the assumption that the neoliberal transition in the property regime in Turkey is not a wholesale, monolithic transformation, but involves moments of continuity and change. Within this broad framework, I make three related arguments: first, in the central state of Turkey, we see the continuation of a trend observed in the late Ottoman state as a way of garnering legitimacy: distributing land, among other resources. In 2016, public lands are similarly being mobilised as a resource for ensuring economic benefits, and by extension, generating legitimacy.

Second, despite this continuity, the distribution of land is increasingly mediated by the market and market mechanisms during the neoliberal period, in contrast to the post-World War II practices of the Turkish state. Moreover, market mediation is accompanied by the massive commodification of land as well. Third and finally, this neoliberal shift and the commodification and market mediation of land becomes possible, again in a seemingly contradictory manner, in the context of the increased material capabilities of the Turkish state. The *laissez faire* approach of the developmentalist period was partly conditioned by the relatively weak capacities of the Turkish state to enforce its gaze and control over its land. When the cadastral operations of the state were completed in the post-1990 period, the capacity of the Turkish state to 'see like a state'[9] was greatly enhanced. Similarly, the post-2000s saw a major concentration of power in the executive branch of government, leading to a record number of laws and regulations concerning urban renewal and construction. Such capacities and concentrations have facilitated the constitution of the market as a mechanism that allocates public resources, but this constitution and mediation through the market does not mean the absence of 'distribution'.

State and Property in the Ottoman Empire and Republican Turkey

'[F]ew concepts' write Gray and Gray 'are quite so fragile, elusive and so often misused as the idea of property. Frequently', they continue,

> the lay person (and even the lawyer) falls into the trap of supposing the term 'property' to connote the *thing* which is the object of 'ownership'. But the beginning of the truth about property is the realisation that property is not a *thing* but rather a *relationship* which one has with a thing.[10] (original emphases)

Realising the relational nature of property is important, yet it does little to further our understanding, for as İnce suggests, '[w]hile most people agree that property relations form the backbone of any social formation [. . .] there is considerable disagreement over *how* to define, interpret, and regulate them' (original emphasis).[11]

In the liberal understanding, which has constituted a globally hegemonic imaginary from the mid-nineteenth century onwards – with the exception, perhaps, of the interwar period – private property is essentially considered an individual's exclusive ownership and agenda-setting power over a 'thing', be it land, a household item, or at worst, other human beings in the form of slaves. The crucial point is that the individual is imagined as a fully formed sovereign entity with the ability to own a thing that stands outside of his or her own self.[12]

Needless to say, such a legalistic understanding of property is extremely narrow and in fact frequently works as an ideological mask that conceals the true nature and workings of property in society. As Cotterrell suggests, the designation of property as the legal relation between a person who owns and the thing he or she owns, and a strict separation between the two (the owner and the owned) is a 'truly remarkable ideological feat'.[13] 'The property form', Cotterrell continues, 'depends as a commonsense idea on our being able to conceptualise a person owning a thing', and by making sure that 'the attributes of power are seen as separate from the owner and attached to the assets which are owned'.[14] The property as a legal form, in other words, serves not only to erase social relations from property, but also exclude power from social relations.

Certainly nowhere, including the liberal West, has a complete merging/overlap of a legal understanding of property and social power been successfully achieved. It is impossible to hide the social power relations behind property in all its forms. From very early on, private property was the object of sociological and political critique as well. Marx was an early and influential critic. Under 'the misleadingly simple slogan "the abolition of private property"', Marx's objective was disentangling and 'transcending a social relation, "bourgeois property", which serves as the crucial nexus between the state [...] and the economy', and showing the system of domination that has been abstracted from what is essentially a social relation.[15]

Perspectives like these offer pathways for understanding property as a relational and social institution. While they suggest taking the 'legal fiction' of property seriously, they also suggest viewing such legal fictions in a critical light and analysing how actual property regimes co-exist with and in fact constitute the legal fiction. Similarly, these works suggest analysing legal fictions of property as discursive/ideological mechanisms that help constitute, stabilise and mask regimes of exploitation.

The land system and its management in the Ottoman Empire in the pre-modern era was based on the central state's ownership. 'All arable land belonged to the state as it had the right of absolute ownership (*rakabe*) over all land and the cultivators were tenants of the state. Thus, when public land changed hands, it was called "transfer", not "sale"'.[16] Certainly, as Aytekin emphasises, this was the 'legal fiction' that the system was based on, and the actual regime and politics of property in the Ottoman Empire were much more complex. The social relations of property were much richer and there were many actors – tax farmers, *malikane* (relatively large estate) owners, to name just two – between the central state and its subjects.

Still, in a major move, the Empire's legal fiction shifted towards recognising private property on land in the nineteenth century. The well-known 1858 Ottoman Land Code legally recognised private property on land and opened the way for the 'modernisation' of land management. While this change and the introduction of private property is usually considered part of the Empire's modernisation paradigm, Aytekin treats the emergence of this new code as an end result, as a dependent variable so to speak. Extending earlier analyses by prominent historian Ömer Lütfi Barkan,[17] Aytekin argues that while much work needs to be done on the topic, the legalisation of private property rights and the shifting property regime in the Empire resulted from emerging capitalist forms of production and the Ottoman Empire's uneven incorporation into the world capitalist system.

More nuanced treatments of the questions of land and property have been offered, in particular connecting these questions to that of political authority and its legitimacy. Keyder notes that 'the most revealing component of the systemic inertia conducing to the central [Ottoman] state's ascendancy over centrifugal tendencies was coded in the legal context'.[18] Accordingly, 'unlike its obvious pre-capitalist counterpart – feudalism in Europe – the Ottoman political and legal system never developed a category of alienable property rights'.[19] While certain notables (*ayans*), at times, developed sufficient strength to challenge the central state, 'the central bureaucracy maintained its self-avowed mission to uphold the status of an independent peasantry–both for reasons of fiscal expediency and because the alternative would have amounted to recognising rival nodes of authority.' This created an 'ideological contract [between the centre and the independent peasants] stipulating the exchange of order and justice emanating from the state against revenue from the direct producers [. . .]'.[20]

This type of contract would draw the contours of the system of legitimacy and political authority in the Ottoman Empire. By a series of mechanisms, the central state essentially retained the power to regulate and distribute land to independent peasants, making it possible for subsistence farming to continue. The state would protect such independent farmers by separating administrative practices related to peasants from juridical practices. The local tithe owners and tax collectors (administrative authorities) would be checked by the centrally appointed juridical personnel (*kadı*s), and this would generate a sense of justice for the independent peasants and hence a source of legitimacy.[21]

Even after the 1858 Land Code was passed and the legal fiction shifted, making it legally possible for land/property to accumulate in the hands of a few, we do not see a large-scale dispossession of peasants and accumulation in the hands of a few, as was the case with Egypt for instance, during the second half of the nineteenth century. There certainly was effort on the part of the rulers to navigate through the demands of an increasingly intrusive world market and covering the costs of modernisation efforts in the nineteenth century, both of which led to attempts to coerce and tax independent peasants more. Still, 'the state sought to protect the peasantry from the adverse effects of commercial development'.[22] Such protection, however much it contradicted with the recognition of private property, 'may in part explain the absence of peasant rebellions in Anatolia during the period of commercial expansion'.[23]

With its nineteenth-century modernisation efforts, the central Ottoman state's management of its land went through significant changes, in addition to the shifting legal fictions that allowed private property on land. İslamoğlu argues that nineteenth-century 'Ottoman land regulations and surveys recording land and agricultural resources introduced categories ordering property relations on land which were aimed at establishing the singular claim by the central bureaucratic state to tax revenues, to the exclusion of the claims of religious endowments and / or former tax farmers.'[24] The aspirations of the central state notwithstanding, these reforms led to what İslamoğlu calls 'concessional politics'. While the central state wanted to increase the legibility of the land and the population it ruled, as theorised by Scott,[25] these new regulations constituted sites of contestation and resistance, particularly by the old powerful and local actors the central state wanted to dispose of. This is the reason why, according to İslamoğlu, 'local actors [...] were incorporated into the new state environment through the formation of commissions or councils on all levels of provincial administration'.[26] Similarly, İslamoğlu argues that such concessional politics produced a new breed of bureaucratic personnel, who saw in standardisation and legal reforms a path for further empowerment within the Ottoman state.

These concessional politics, however, led to the (partial) curtailment of the aspirations of the central state. While the goal of legibility was supreme, the 'concessional politics of Ottoman administration [...] did not allow for a standardisation of the measurement of land and its division into individual parcels'.[27] The illegibility on the ground was mobilised by local actors to their own benefit, and prevented the full-scale development of the central Ottoman state. Therefore, even if/when individual ownership of land and property was recognised by law, the mechanisms of its realisation faced serious social and political obstacles.

Inspired by İslamoğlu's frame of analysis, I suggest that we can view/analyse the neoliberal transformation in a way similar to her observations of nineteenth-century transformations. Since my focus is on the central state and how it is managing its lands roughly from 1950 to this day, I need to fill certain voids particularly regarding the transition from the (mid-to-late) nineteenth-century Ottoman-Turkish state (that İslamoğlu writes about) to the Republic.

The construction of the modern state with aspirations for increased legibility continued and even strengthened in the twentieth century. While the Ottoman central state had already strengthened itself both in ideological and material terms during the Hamidian era,[28] the institutional rupture that was experienced from 1908 onwards – most notably with the promulgation of the Republic in 1923 – had sharpened the powers and capabilities of the central state. While it is certainly impossible to draw clear-cut boundaries between the state and society, the Turkey of the 1920s was a war-torn society deprived of its former social ties and networks, and certain state institutions – notably the army and parts of civilian bureaucracy – remained relatively intact during this transition. The elimination of the non-Muslim population that constituted the backbone of Ottoman society's budding bourgeoisie rendered the central state especially strong in the aftermath of the War of Independence.[29]

While such strength has never meant absolute power, let alone absolute authority, the 'statist capital' was particularly strong in the early Republican Turkish context. Theorising about the birth of the modern absolutist state, Pierre Bourdieu suggests that the 'genesis of the state' is a process in which the central state and bureaucracy obtains its power and rule over time by constructing itself as the final arbiter of conflicts in society and constructs state capital as a 'meta capital' that can be used to exchange any capital (be it social, cultural or economic) with another.[30] In this sense, while the Republican state has certainly faced difficulties in getting itself accepted as the legitimate authority, the concentration of coercive and ideological apparatuses in its body was highly effective in situating the central state as the meta field, with a significant impact on the other arenas of social life and social processes in general.[31]

The concessional politics that İslamoğlu points to in the context of the nineteenth century have certainly been visible in the early Republican setting. Morack, for instance, documents the contesting claims between the central government and local authorities in the process of distributing the abandoned properties of Greeks who left Anatolia in 1923 with the population exchange.[32] She suggests that these acts of distribution constituted sites of negotiation between the central state, local authorities and the people at large. Nevertheless, in such concessional politics, the central state appears to be the actor who shapes the terms and context of the negotiation, and the institution where people file their complaints. This presents a continuation with the understanding of the central state as the distributor of justice and basing part of its legitimacy on this very role. İslamoğlu's approach, indeed, allows for analysing institutional legacies and their power as sediments of historical evolution. So it is possible to suggest that from the mid-nineteenth century onwards, even when the contours of contestation changed, the central state and its administrative apparatuses emerged as sites for domination and modern governance. As such, in İslamoğlu's analysis too, the central state emerges as that field in Bourdieu, which every other field gravitates towards.

If the role of meting out justice constituted one leg of how the central state assumed the role of legitimate ruler in the early Republic, the other leg has to do with the actual (re)distribution of wealth to select groups in society as a way of preventing dissent and social crises. Here, unlike the agriculturally organised Ottoman state and society, where distribution took the form of allotment of subsistence farms to independent peasants, the late Ottoman and the early Republican states found new spoils to distribute. The lands and properties of the expelled non-Muslim population constituted one of the most important mechanisms of the creation of a 'national economy'.[33] Similarly, such wealth became a key ingredient in bringing together Muslim merchants and notables in various localities with the central state, initially run by the Union and Progress Party and later by the Republican People's Party during the single-party rule.[34] This constituted what Eric Zurcher calls the Young Turk coalition that formed the backbone of the political and economic system all the way until 1950.[35]

Coming back to the main axis of this chapter, the (attempts to) settle people, distribute land and the land reform in general during the single party era epitomised such distributional politics. Essentially two lines of state practice emerged: on the one hand, the central state's policies of settling people in designated areas – sometimes in the form of forced migration, at times in the form of settling migrants from outside Turkey in select locations – constituted the extreme example of such distributional politics. They were all made possible through legal and administrative measures such as laws that deal with Armenian property[36] or the 1934 *Iskan Kanunu* (the Settlement Law of 1934), or through outright coercion and violence as seen in the Dersim massacres of 1937–8. In moments like these, we see a conflation of the sovereign acts of the state with the more mundane/ordinary politics of property (distribution). These are the moments where efforts to take control and master territory – that is, sovereign efforts – were mixed and meshed with efforts to distribute land and legitimise political authority.[37]

On the other hand, more mundane efforts to distribute land, without implications for sovereignty constitute the second line in which distributional politics can be observed.[38] This kind of land reform had been on the agenda of the young republic at least since the mid-1930s[39] and was realised in 1945 by way of the *Çiftçiyi Topraklandırma Kanunu* (The Law to Provide Land to Peasants). Aware of its social and political 'distance' from the rural population that made up 75 per cent of the population, the party/state passed a law that aimed to distribute agricultural land to farmers who previously had little or no land. To date, the motives or the real causes behind the law are still being discussed.[40] Keyder and Pamuk see an essentially political motive in the law and argue that it essentially aimed to prevent the growing power of large land owners in the post-World War II years.[41] Karaömerlioğlu notes the significance of the intellectual and ideological environment in the making of the law, and suggests that the *köycülük* ('peasantism' – a form of peasant populism) trend, which in part shaped the minds of the Republican People's Party's ruling segments, played a role in the passage of the law.[42]

Particularly considering the political aspirations that Keyder and Pamuk mention, it can be said that the law repeated a pattern that was observed in the Ottoman state: using land as a resource to connect with independent and small producers and enhance the power of the central single party state.[43] While the authors rightly point to the fact that the law intended more to harm big land owners than to benefit small producers, combined with Karaömerlioğlu's point about the ideological roots of the law, their explanation still suggests that some form of land reform was one of the most important mechanisms of distribution in the arsenal of the modern Turkish state of the 1940s.

The Democratic Party continued the practice of land distribution in the post-1950 period, albeit changing certain measures of the law. The effect of the law, as Keyder shows, has been the entrenchment of petty commodity production in Turkish agriculture.[44] Lastly, in connection to the next section where I discuss urban land distribution more specifically, it needs to be mentioned that the way the state allocated land particularly in the 1950s was by legally recognising the right to property of the farmers who claimed land with their own initiative. In other words, as Keyder and Pamuk suggest, 'the way the law was applied in the 1950s was post hoc approval of an official distribution of title deeds for the once treasury-owned land to the villagers who had appropriated such land'.[45] The central state chose to ignore attempts to appropriate its lands.[46]

Urban Land as a Resource for (Re)distribution

The 1950s constitute a decade in which a significant wave of domestic migration from rural to urban areas occurred. By 1954, after briefly experimenting with it, the central state realised all too well that development through agriculture was not possible,[47] and began to head (back) to industrialisation for development. The import substitution industrialisation model was adopted. With the mechanisation of agriculture underway in the early 1950s, a significant number of people began moving from the countryside to the centres of the new industrialisation, where work opportunities were relatively abundant, however precarious. Istanbul and Ankara constituted such centres.

Part of what the state did to ease and enable industrialisation in this manner was to let those from the countryside take over land in urban areas. Newcomers to the city seized these areas and used the land for shelter. Constructions began to rise on these plots through the volunteer work by the domestic migrants. They erected makeshift buildings called *gecekondu*s, mostly in collective effort.[48] Squatter settlements that were formed of these *gecekondu*s became an integral part of urban sites.

'The government's response towards this mode of housing provision was twofold', according to Gülöksüz. Aware of 'the problem solving capacity [of these informal settlements] in the context of the general economy, where resources were scarce and cheap labour was required by the industrial sector', the central state turned a blind eye to the appropriation of land on the fringes of the emerging urban centres and 'successive governments tolerated these widespread activities by neglecting to implement the relevant legislation and periodically issuing amnesty laws'.[49]

In large part, migrants were able to appropriate land because the lands were public lands from the Ottoman Empire, registered in the name of the Treasury. The state was obviously free to dispose of its land to people it deemed fit. Even when the appropriated lands were (considered) private, however, enforcing the rights of the 'owner' was by no means easy.[50] This was partly because of the ambiguous state of property in these urban locations. It was not clear who owned what, as cadastral operations were not completed until after the 1990s, in addition to the complexities of titles, title deeds and inheritance problems dating back to Ottoman times.

Overall, by effectively providing migrants with a valuable resource, urban land, the state's blissful ignorance turned into a redistributive activity that would benefit people who were forced to move from their villages (due to the mechanisation in agriculture and opportunities to work in industry in urban centres). This, of course, was not just to distribute land for its own sake: workers who lived in their own homes and did not pay rent meant that the social cost of the reproduction of labour was minimised. This implicit state subsidy is partly what enabled newly emerging industrial enterprises to pay lower wages.

The essential tool that allowed the state to be blissfully ignorant and thus redistribute land was amnesty laws. Between 1948 and 1984, '10 laws that included amnesty clauses for *gecekondu*s were issued' and the 1984 Amnesty Law (no. 2981) was a particularly 'redistributive measure in the face of the sharp decline in wages caused by the structural adjustment programmes at the beginning of the 1980s'.[51]

Two points need to be highlighted further: first, with this redistributive agenda, the state did not necessarily operate on the basis of economic or efficiency concerns alone. While the appropriation/redistribution of land was possible in the 1950s partly due to the benefits it provided to the emerging economic system, this was not the only determining factor. Social and political factors similarly played significant roles in shaping the state's land management agenda. As for politics, the vote potential in the rapidly growing informal settlements made them the object of populist political interest. No political party could afford to remain isolated from these neighbourhoods, and hence the redistributive practices of the central state, which became apparent essentially in the amnesty laws, were complemented by relevant municipal services.[52]

On the social plane, *gecekondu*s and the ties/networks between migrants that formed on the basis of their places of origin generated mechanisms not only for welfare but also for a relatively smooth transition to urban life. From this perspective, *gecekondu*s should be seen as integral parts of modern and urban life in Turkey, not corrupt areas that infect cities.[53]

Second, the (re)distribution of land, and hence wealth, was not mediated by formal market mechanisms. On the contrary; the distribution/appropriation cycle essentially worked on the basis of family and community efforts and the non-market ties mentioned in the above paragraph. The redistributive agenda was not a fully conscious set of policies, but rather a series of separate yet connected actions that produced the distributive effects discussed above. The state took a passive stance here by turning a blind eye to the 'occupation' of its lands and not putting urban migrants through the legal system. Passing the amnesty laws were the most important acts/tools of this mode of governing urban/public lands and property.[54]

The Neoliberal Shift

The 2000s present a stark contrast to the passive stance of the state observed during the developmentalist/populist period. That passive stance was a continuation of earlier state practices, where vacant lands were considered to rightfully belong to the people who would make use of them. On top of this deeply historical layer of state(hood) practice, the early Republican years saw the building of yet another nationalist layer of meaning of land, one that was distant to a commercial understanding. While the legal fiction that was created with the 1926 Civil Code clearly recognised private property on land, these layers of historical state practices and meanings made possible an understanding and practice of land that differed greatly from before: as a common resource that the state could allow to be appropriated, and a tool that could be mobilised to produce or enhance the legitimacy of the state. Combined with the post-World War II state's limited means to provide welfare, land on the fringes of urban centres thus turned into a patrimonial resource that the state distributed as a way to garner legitimacy.

By the 2000s, however, public lands had been commodified at a significant scale; they were no longer seen as a patrimonial resource to be tapped into, but a commodity to be bought, sold and protected when necessary. As Türkün states, 'the cities began to transform from "Spaces of Hope" to "Spaces of Hopelessness" for newcomers, few of whom could expect to find the opportunities for integration, through settlement and employment that had been available to most of their predecessors'.[55] The central state, far from being willing to turn a blind eye to appropriations of its urban lands, was rather adamant about protecting them, in a highly centralised and top-down approach to urban transformation.[56] As mentioned above, Lovering and Türkmen call this new urban transformation practice 'bulldozer neo-liberalism'. Despite efforts to safeguard its lands and the fact that the modality of distribution changed, the central state maintains its position as the distributer of public lands in exchange for legitimacy. However, the distribution now has to pass through the market mechanism.

In order to succeed at guarding its land, the central state employs a variety of mechanisms. In addition to the increasing deeds of land and other immoveables in the name of the Treasury – as reflected in the news story in the introduction – there has been a striking increase in the use of various legal mechanisms or legal innovations to strengthen the central state, the executive branch in particular. Since the early neoliberalisation processes of the 1980s, a number of laws were passed, including the Local Government Reform Law (1984) or the Metropolitan Municipality Law, no. 3030 (1984) or amnesties for *gecekondu*s (1984 and beyond). Similarly, establishment of the Mass Housing Administration (TOKİ, as the Turkish acronym goes) through the Mass Housing Law of 1984 was a significant institutional creation that enabled the state to change its course of policy. From the 2000s onwards, however, this trend of legal and institutional innovation rose to new levels and TOKİ was effectively turned into a massive bureaucratic/capitalist machine.[57]

Laws, bylaws and regulations have been among the main tools in both developing a new urban land regime and further empowering the centre in managing its land. The difference between the developmentalist/ populist years and the neoliberal period of the post-2000s regarding the use of laws is that while laws in the former were employed in the form of amnesties and as such, *post hoc* rationalisations of land appropriations, laws in the latter are used as 'enabling mechanisms' that make a giant real estate agency such as TOKİ possible, for instance. As Kayasü and Yetişkul state, TOKİ has amassed significant powers through the laws that changed its statutes and the boundaries of its organisational responsibilities.[58] Unlike earlier laws that tended to be *post hoc* rationalisations, these more recent pieces of legislation focused on the prospective production of land as property and commodity.[59]

The state thus seemed to have shifted towards a neoliberal property regime in land. Even though TOKİ became much more powerful in the post-2000s, the roots of this market turn in property can be found in the late 1970s and the 1980s. The neoliberal shift that is apparent in the re-constitution of laws and institutions to produce and protect property markets, can also be seen in the increasing commodification of the squatter settlements and the public lands they occupy. The late 1970s witnessed the transformation of urban squatter lands from areas for shelter to properties from which rent can be obtained. The 1984 law that granted *gecekondu*s amnesty is quite important in showing the evolution of squatter settlements from residential areas that originated from the need to take shelter, to areas that have rent-generating properties. It not only provided amnesty for hitherto built *gecekondu*s, but also cleared the path to building multi-story buildings on squatted lands. As such, the law formalised an already emerging trend: that of the transformation of squatter areas into properties circulated within the market and used for rents.[60]

Highlighting the capitalist drives for profit and rent through land shaped the central state's attitude towards its lands. In this sense, the neoliberal turn in the property regime in Turkey is due to the state's attempts to synchronise itself with the turn to the market both inside and outside the country. The commodification of land also works to highlight the construction sector and its major players as beneficiaries of state support both directly and indirectly. Just like the Import Substitution Industrialisation (ISI) period, where the Turkish state selectively enriched certain groups through subsidies and lines of foreign exchange/credit, the neoliberal period similarly sees a state that uses – this time – land rent to help the growth of construction as a field/sector. As Kurtuluş et al. note, from 1983 onwards, the construction sector takes precedence over manufacturing in the five-year plans of the State Planning Organisation in terms of investment goals.[61]

In furthering this approach, the construction sector is designated by after 2002 governments as a strategically significant one to promote growth and development. While industrialisation based on manufacturing was once considered the key to development, construction has risen to match manufacturing; governments after 2002 heavily favoured this sector in order to secure economic growth. So while during the ISI period public lands were used to facilitate the working of an economic system by bringing down cost of labour, in the neoliberal period, the land itself became the commodity that would secure growth more directly.[62]

In this process of commodification and increasing value of urban land, shantytown dwellers who appropriated land on the fringes of valuable urban centres are pushed away to make room for massive construction projects. The state takes an active role in eliminating resistance by such people and clears spaces in cities for profit-seeking projects, mediated essentially by the Mass Housing Authority.

This constitutes a significant moment since the Turkish state appears to be breaking a historical trend; that is, using land as a resource to connect certain groups to itself through non-market mechanisms. While it is clear that there is still a distribution of resources, this is filtered through the market mechanism. Space is produced by the state in a capitalist framework to be handed over to capitalist profit-making, and distribution is carried out in conjunction with this capitalist machine. The land as such still constitutes an object of redistribution by the state, in this case from the urban 'intruders'/occupants to the middle class citizens who can (afford to) buy property that is constructed in this capitalist economy. The distribution is still significantly shaped by the state, but this time, it appears to be mediated and made possible through the market mechanism. This, I argue, signifies a change in statehood, and points to the difference of the neoliberal state from its previous version. Similarly, the state now sees through the market, and the distribution of wealth (and garnering of legitimacy) targets those who are visible and legible to a neoliberal economic logic.

All the while, however, the distributive angle seems to persist. Christened with new laws and regulations, TOKİ began acting as a giant real estate agency, promoting urban transformations and real estate development. The state used its own/public lands in some instances to construct mass housing projects. On many occasions, the Mass Housing Authority was given extensive powers to negotiate, buy and ultimately parcel out public lands or lands from private owners and turn them into massive housing units. So in a sense, an interesting reversal is at work: TOKİ, thus the state, no longer only employs its own possessions as a way of securing legitimacy, it now uses its muscle to turn even private lands into mechanisms for some form of (re)distribution, and hence legitimacy building. This, perhaps, is an indication of just how much urban space is produced in bureaucratic/capitalist circuits, much more so than the developmentalist period where the layers of regulation and state intervention were much thinner. Thus, commodification of land is not a simple production of land as private property. It involves a complex series of mechanisms and interventions by the state to produce land as such. It requires the central state to be able to 'see like a state' and render legible its land, only to 'act like a private market player' to secure profit and enrichment.

This seeming paradox that the state has to be even stronger for markets to exist, is in fact no anomaly. While neoliberalism can be and is generally defined as 'less state, more market' in common parlance, actual neoliberalism[63] cannot be possible without significant state intervention and the nurturing of the market.[64]

It is thus not much of a surprise that the neoliberal turn in the state's relation to its land came at a time when the tools of seeing like a state became more complete than ever in Turkey. While cadastral operations that aim to represent the land started in 1950, it was only in the 1990s that these operations were carried out with state-of-the-art technology in Turkey. Yaşayan, Erkan and Seylam claimed that Turkey's cadastral mapping was complete with a few exceptional problem cases, only in 2011.[65] As the state gained the capabilities to render its land more legible, this capability – combined with the already neoliberalising economy – was put to use in the emerging construction sector. The state also used this technological advance as a means to bolster an urban economy and transform itself to a state that runs on a different route to legitimacy than in the past.

The capabilities of the state in categorising and rationally ordering the land it governs helped construction grow as a sector and further enabled capitalist relations through governmental actions – such as the introduction of the mortgage system or the prioritisation of the construction sector for economic growth – to create an environment where the way the state relates to its land was significantly altered. The mortgage system was introduced in 2007 with the passing of Law no. 5582 and effectively confirmed the conceptualisation of home ownership as a saving and investment.[66]

The increased legibility of (public) lands and the increasing designation of land as property was thus coupled with the creation of subjects and households visible and legible to the market. In order to be able to take part in the process of receiving public land and its wealth, one now needs to be visible to the system of the market. While once it was possible to claim the land was based essentially on one's informal family and community networks, now such claims have to be made through market mechanisms, such as mortgage credits, bank loans or TOKİ credits.

As the relationship people and the state have with land shifted, the state itself also changed significantly. While the distributive angle certainly persisted, the Turkish state evolved into a neoliberal institution with a very strong centre, which uses its powers to distribute rents from land in a highly arbitrary and opaque manner. In other words, public lands are still used as a way to bolster certain segments of the economy and society. The process of selective distribution generates significant ambiguities, as Tuna Kuyucu[67] suggests. Ambiguity is used as a weapon against those whom the state considers intruders. This ambiguity, however, is quite selective and in fact, for those who can (afford to be) legible to the market and the state, and for those who can be part of the increasingly neoliberal landscape, legal ambiguity is less of a concern.

Conclusion

This chapter tried to situate the neoliberalisation of the Turkish state's approach to land within broader historical–institutional practices of the Turkish state. While I agree that there is a neoliberal shift, in this chapter I put forward that such a neoliberal shift is both more radical, and less of a rupture, than generally recognised. It is more radical in the sense that it points to a transformation of state practices since the Ottoman times. The distributional concerns of the central state are still significant; thus the transformation is less of a rupture. At the same time, however, the mediation of such distributional practices by the market, and the state's increasing approach to its land as property, as a commodity, points to a transformation of statehood. Thus the shift is even more radical than is generally recognised.

I will end by pointing to three potentially fruitful avenues for further research. First, the large number of legal cases in which the state's approach to property can be viewed await analysis. There are several legal lines that reflect the boundaries/thresholds of the state, which could be analysed. The cases that deal with forest lands (that have lost their forest status) and their sale is a case in point. Similarly, the opening and commodification of common pastures for various entrepreneurial activities and the legal conflicts that surround these decisions is another case in point. There is a mountain of cases regarding especially the former, and analysis of these administrative cases would give us a much clearer picture of the politics of commodification and property at work. In other words, an analysis of the actual law and the legal property regime would help clarify the politics behind the question of the politics of (re)distribution in a neoliberal age. There is, to this day, surprisingly little research on such legal cases.

Secondly and relatedly, there appears to be a growing body of literature focusing on the empirical politics of property in various parts of the world, ranging from land grabs in peripheral countries to takings of land for urban redevelopment projects in advanced capitalist countries. It would be extremely interesting to try and situate Turkey – based on empirical data – within this broader property regime. That the Turkish case fits in with the general neoliberalisation story is obvious; it is also clear, as I argued in this article, that the historical/institutional legacies of the Ottoman–Turkish state impacts the path of neoliberalisation in this country. Whether more nuanced yet encompassing categorisations can be created, and whether Turkey can be situated in these categories, would be an interesting and important project.

Lastly, such empirical politics of property are also enriched by analyses of meanings and consciousness attached to property, particularly in post-Soviet/Eastern Bloc countries. Such property consciousness, or legal consciousness of property, can be used as a way to explore and analyse the actual property regime in Turkey. A bottom up approach – so to speak – to property would highlight the extent to which neoliberal or market understandings of property have taken hold in Turkish society, and as such would provide a significant complementary angle to the kind of analysis presented in this chapter.

Notes

1. See http://www.memurlar.net/haber/508470/ (4 April 2015, accessed 30 March 2016).
2. Tuna Kuyucu and Özlem Ünsal, 'Urban transformation as state led property transfer: An analysis of two cases of urban renewal in Istanbul', *Urban Studies* 47/7 (2010), pp. 1479–99.
3. Serap Kayasü and Emine Yetiskul, 'Evolving legal and institutional frameworks of neoliberal policies in Turkey', *METU Journal for the Faculty of Architecture* 31/2 (2014), pp. 209–22.
4. Jamie Peck and Adam Tickell, 'Neoliberalising space', *Antipode* 34/3 (2002), pp. 380–404.
5. John Lovering and Hade Türkmen, 'Bulldozer neoliberalism in Istanbul: The state-led construction of property markets, and the displacement of the poor', *International Planning Studies* 16/1 (2011), pp. 73–96.
6. As a highly complex and contested concept, 'legitimacy' deserves further elaboration, which I provide in the following pages.
7. Keyder offers a highly informative and insightful discussion of such continuities and the Turkish state's postwar policy of land/property management. That discussion forms the starting point for the analysis in this paper. Çağlar Keyder, 'Enformel konut piyasasından küresel konut piyasasına [From Informal real estate market to the global one]', in Ç. Keyder (ed.), *İstanbul: Küresel ile yerel arasında [Istanbul: Between the global and the local]* (İstanbul, 2000).
8. Tuna Kuyucu, 'Law, property and ambiguity: The uses and abuses of legal ambiguity in remaking Istanbul's informal settlements', *International Journal of Urban and Regional Research* 38/2 (2014), pp. 609–27; p. 613.
9. 'Seeing like a state', as introduced by James Scott, refers to the powers of the modern state aiming at rendering legible and manageable lands under its control by way of modern mechanisms such as cadastral operations, aerial maps, etc. See James Scott, *Seeing Like a State: How Certain Schemes to Improve the Human Condition have Failed* (New Haven, 1998).
10. Kevin Gray and Susan Francis Gray, 'The idea of property in land', in S. Bright and J.K. Dewar (eds), *Land Law: Themes and Perspectives* (New York, 1998), p. 15.
11. Onur Ulaş İnce, 'Property', in M. Gibbons (ed.), *The Encyclopedia of Political Thought* (Chichester, West Sussex, UK; Malden, MA, USA, 2014), pp. 3008–17.

12. For a discussion and criticism of the liberal notions of individual (and group) identity and sovereignty, see Patchen Markell, *Bound by Recognition* (Princeton, NJ, 2003).
13. Roger Cotterrell, 'Power, property and the law of trusts: A partial agenda for critical legal scholarship' *Journal of Law and Society* 14/1 (1987), pp. 77–90; p. 83.
14. Ibid.
15. Brenna Bhandar and Alberto Toscano, 'Race, real estate and real abstraction', *Radical Philosophy* 194 (2015), pp. 8–16; p. 8.
16. Atilla Aytekin, 'Agrarian relations, property and law: An analysis of the 1858 land code in the Ottoman Empire', *Middle Eastern Studies* 45/6 (2009), pp. 935–51; p. 937.
17. For an early yet comprehensive and still authoritative study of the 'land question' in the Ottoman Empire and Turkey, see Ömer Lütfi Barkan, *Türkiye'de Toprak Meselesi, Toplu Eserler 1 {Land Issue in Turkey, Collected Works 1}* (İstanbul, 1980), pp. 291–375.
18. Çağlar Keyder, 'Introduction: Large scale commercial agriculture in the Ottoman Empire', in Ç. Keyder and F. Tabak (eds), *Landholding and Commercial Agriculture in the Middle East* (Albany, NY, 1991), p. 10.
19. Ibid.
20. Ibid.
21. Huri İslamoğlu-İnan, 'Peasants, commercialisation, and legitimation of state power in sixteenth-century Anatolia', in Ç. Keyder and F. Tabak (eds), *Landholding and Commercial Agriculture in the Middle East* (Albany, NY, 1991), p. 59.
22. Ibid., p. 61.
23. Ibid., p. 60.
24. Huricihan İslamoğlu, 'Towards a political economy of legal and administrative constitutions of individual property', in H. İslamoğlu (ed.), *Constituting Modernity: Private property in the East and in the West* (London, 2004), p. 26.
25. Scott, *Seeing Like a State.*
26. İslamoğlu, 'Towards a political economy', pp. 26–7.
27. Ibid., p. 27.
28. Selim Deringil, *The Well Protected Domains: Ideology and the legitimation of Power in the Ottoman Empire, 1876–1909* (London, 1998).
29. Çağlar Keyder, *State and Class in Turkey: A Study in Capitalist Development* (London, 1987).
30. Pierre Bourdieu, 'Rethinking the state: The genesis and structure of the bureaucratic field', in P. Bourdieu, *Practical Reason* (Stanford, 1998).
31. Erozan analyses, for instance, how the central state shaped the formation of the 'legal field' and how the latter was subservient to the former in the early Republican context. Boğaç Erozan, 'Producing Obedience: Law Professors and the Turkish State', unpublished PhD dissertation, University of Minnesota, 2005.

32. Elenor Morack, 'Refugees, locals and "the" state: Property compensation in the province of Izmir following the Greco-Turkish population exchange of 1923', *Journal of the Ottoman and Turkish Studies* 2/1 (2015), pp. 147–66.
33. Uğur Ümit Üngör and Mehmet Polatel, *Confiscation and Destruction: The Young Turk seizure of Armenian Property* (London, 2011); and Murat Koraltürk, *Erken Cumhuriyet Döneminde Ekonominin Türkleştirilmesi {Turkification of the Economy in the Early-Republic Era}* (İstanbul, 2011).
34. Uğur Ümit Üngör, *The Making of Modern Turkey: The Nation and State in Eastern Anatolia, 1913–1950* (Oxford, 2011); and Üngör and Polatel, *Confiscation and Destruction.*
35. Eric Jan Zurcher, *Young Turk Legacy and Nation Building: From the Ottoman Empire to Atatürk's Turkey* (London, 2014). On this point, Keyder argues that one of the underlying motives of the Republican 'independence war' was to get rid of the non-Muslim population in the country, and the fact that people could appropriate national/public land inevitably fed the Turkish nationalism that was highlighted by this underlying motive. In such an environment, 'an explicit commodification of land would mean the erosion of state's legitimacy'. See Keyder, 'Enformel konut piyasasından', p. 177.
36. Taner Akçam and Ümit Kurt, *The Spirit of the Laws: The Plunder of Wealth in the Ottoman Empire* (Princeton, 2015).
37. In fact, in 2016, we still see such conflation at work: on 30 January 2016, the Turkish prime minister of the time, Ahmet Davutoğlu, said that the government 'would build Sur {a district in the Diyarbakır province} in such a way that, just like Toledo {of Spain}, it will become a spot where everyone would want to visit for its architecture' (*Hürriyet Daily* – Akif Beki, 1 February 2016). This statement came after an intense military and police campaign – going on and off since September 2015 – left the whole district of Sur severely destroyed. The goal of these operations was to eradicate the urban Kurdish armed struggle brewing up in Sur and similarly in Kurdish-populated city centres. In an interesting – and, for many, disturbing – twist, the prime minister tied this security operation to urban renewal, claiming that Sur and other towns such as Silopi and Nusaybin – where similar operations had been carried out – needed urban renewal anyway (see Uygar Gültekin 'Sur'da yeni tehdit kentsel dönüşüm {A new challenge at Sur – urban transformation}', *Agos*, 24 December 2015). In the works, it seemed, was a creative destruction in which the state security forces did the destruction. That creative moment was to be realised by TOKİ, the Mass Housing Administration of Turkey, which recently turned into a massive bureaucratic–capitalist machine carrying out many of the urban renewal projects in Turkey. Indeed, the *Star Daily*, a keen supporter of the current AKP government, came out with a headline calling TOKİ to action more than a month before the Prime Minister's Toledo comment (see *Star Daily*, 22 December 2015, 'TOKİ Göreve {TOKİ should be in charge}'; see also 'Teröre TOKİ açılımı şart {TOKİ is a solution to terrorism}', http://haber.star.com.tr/guncel/toki-goreve/haber-1077767).

38. While both lines of state practice are highly important and intrinsically related, in this chapter, I problematise essentially the latter.
39. See Çağlar Keyder and Şevket Pamuk, '1945 Çiftçiyi Topraklandırma Kanunu üzerine tezler [Theses on the 1945 Law of Land Reform]' *Yapıt* 8 (1984), pp. 52–63; p. 53; and Asım Karaömerlioğlu, 'Köycülük ve toprak reformu: "Çiftçiyi topraklandırma kanunu"nun hikâyesi [Peasantism and Land Reform: A story of the 1945 Law of Land Reform]', in A. Karaömerlioğlu, *Orada Bir Köy Var Uzakta [There is a Village Up There, Far Away]* (İstanbul, 2006).
40. See Karaömerlioğlu, 'Köycülük'; and Ecehan Balta, '1945 Çiftçiyi topraklandırma kanunu: Reform mu karşı reform mu? [The 1945 Law of Land Reform: A reform or an anti-reform?]', *Praksis* 5 (2002), pp. 277–98.
41. Keyder and Pamuk, '1945'.
42. Karaömerlioğlu, 'Köycülük'.
43. Keyder and Pamuk, '1945'.
44. Çağlar Keyder, 'The genesis of petty commodity production in agriculture: The case of Turkey', in P. Stirling (ed.), *Culture and Economy: Changes in Turkish Villages* (Cambridgeshire, 1993), pp. 171–86.
45. Keyder and Pamuk, '1945', p. 61.
46. This can be seen as the continuation of an understanding that was prevalent in the Ottoman Empire. According to Keyder, 'Peasants could assert rights and privileges over the lands that belonged to the state. [A]s long as they paid the due taxes, peasants were considered to have the right to use and benefit from such lands, even though such possession did not amount to private ownership' Keyder, 'Enformel konut piyasasından', p. 172.
47. The development models of the Turkish state have gone through waves and changes since 1908, when the goal of creating a national economy became somewhat explicit. While industrialisation has always been on the agenda, there was a brief (and according to Korkut Boratav, exceptional) period between 1946 and 1954 where the state tried to generate a surplus for development through agriculture. This proved a failed strategy, however, and was mostly abandoned after 1954. See Korkut Boratav, *Türkiye İktisat Tarihi, 1908–2009 [The Economic History of Turkey, 1908–2009]*, 21. Edition (Ankara, 2015); and Şevket Pamuk, *Türkiye'nin 200 Yıllık İktisadi Tarihi [The Economic History of Turkey of 200 Years]* (İstanbul, 2014).
48. See Kemal Karpat, *The Gecekondu: Rural Migration and Urbanisation* (Cambridge, 1976).
49. Elvan Gülöksüz, 'Negotiation of property rights in urban land in Istanbul', in H. İslamoğlu (ed.), *Constituting Modernity*, p. 254.
50. Ibid.
51. Ibid.
52. Keyder, 'Enformel Konut Piyasasından'; and Keyder, *State and Class*.
53. Karpat, *The Gecekondu*.
54. This certainly does not mean that the central state had a hands-off approach to urban relocations. On the contrary, as the prime minister, Adnan Menderes in

the 1950s was very much involved with the creative destruction and planning of Istanbul. Similarly, for instance, in 1956 the Construction Zoning Law (no. 6875) was passed; or in 1958 the Ministry of Zoning and Settlement was created via Law no. 7116. These legal mechanisms were far less used and far less effective than the ones in the post-1980s period. Also, these new legal capacities did not significantly intervene in the workings of the land distribution/appropriation regime.

55. Asuman Türkün, 'Urban regeneration and hegemonic power relationships', *International Planning Studies* 16/1 (2011), pp. 61–72; p. 64.
56. Kayasü and Yetişkul, 'Evolving legal', p. 212.
57. For two meticulous studies of the legal and institutional changes regarding urban renewal, see Kayasü and Yetişkul, 'Evolving legal' and Hatice Kurtuluş, Semra Purkis and Adalet Alada, 'İstanbul'da yeni konut sunum biçimleri ve orta sınıfların sosyo-mekansal yeniden inşaası [The new forms of real estate supply and the socio-spatial reconstruction of middle-class people]', *TÜBİTAK Proje Raporu, no. 110K061* (June 2012).
58. These laws, in short, are Law no. 4966 in 2003; Law no. 5162 in 2004; 5273 in 2004; Law no. 5273 in 2004; Law no. 5609 in 2007; Law no. 5582 in 2007; Law no. 5793 in 2008. See Kayasü and Yetişkul, 'Evolving legal', p. 216.
59. In addition to the various laws and regulations that allowed TOKİ to become a massive, capitalist, bureaucratic land and property developer, two recent parliamentary acts have further enabled TOKİ and the state to claim, transform and ultimately commodify public lands: The 'Law on the Transformation of Areas under Risk of Natural Disaster' (no. 6306, 2012) and the 'Law on Supporting the Development of Forest Villagers, Valuation of Areas Taken out of the Forest Area Borders on Behalf of the Treasury and Vending Agricultural Lands Owned by the Treasury' (no. 6292, 2012). Along with significant easing of reciprocity requirements concerning land and property ownership in Turkey by non-nationals, these two laws have worked to enable the construction sector.
60. Kurtuluş et al., 'İstanbul'da yeni konut'.
61. Ibid.
62. In fact, the transformation of land from one of the infrastructural elements for capitalist accumulation in other sectors to a sector that can produce direct accumulation/added value itself is a pattern played out similarly in other industries. A case in point is telecommunications in Turkey, which until the 1990s was considered a sector that pretty much survived by state supports so that infrastructure could be provided for broader developmental activities/accumulation strategies. Following the 1990s, the sector itself became a site for direct profit-making and accumulation, and as such turned into a market in its own right. The state, in turn, used its powerful central position to distribute the profit potentiality in this sector so that new wealth (and wealthy groups) could be created.
63. Here Brenner, Peck and Theodore's definition of neoliberalisation is worth quoting at length because it provides a useful way to think about neoliberalism

and neoliberalisation. They 'conceptualize neoliberalisation as one among several tendencies of regulatory change that have been unleashed across the global capitalist system since the 1970s: it prioritises market-based, market-oriented, or market-disciplinary responses to regulatory problems; it strives to intensify commodification in all realms of social life; and it often mobilises speculative financial instruments to open up new arenas for capitalist profit-making'. Neil Brenner, Jamie Peck and Nik Theodore, 'After neoliberalisation?', *Globalisations* 7/3 (2010), pp. 327–45; pp. 329–30.

64. This point is made by authors as diverse as Michel Foucault, David Harvey and Loic Wacquant. See Michel Foucault, *The Birth of Biopolitics, Lectures at the College De France, 1978–1979* (New York, 2008); David Harvey, *A Brief History of Neoliberalism* (New York, 2005); and Loic Wacquant, 'Crafting the neoliberal state: Workfare, prisonfare and social insecurity', *Sociological Forum* 25/2 (2010), pp. 197–220.
65. Ahmet Yasayan, Hüseyin Erkan and Gökşin Seylam, 'Kadastro kavramı ve Türkiye kadastrosu [The concept of cadastre and the cadastre of Turkey]', paper presented at the Türkiye Mimarlar ve Mühendisler Odası, 13. Türkiye Harita Bilimsel ve Teknik Kurultayı (Ankara, 18–22 April 2011), p. 5.
66. Tunç and Yavaş show that the private savings rate in Turkey dropped substantially in the post-2000s and that the increase of mortgage loans is one of the most important reasons for it. This confirms the observation that real estate ownership is considered a type of saving and investment today. Cengiz Tunç and Abdullah Yavaş, 'Not all credit is created equal: Mortgage vs. non-mortgage debt and private saving rate in Turkey', *Central Bank Review* 16 (2016), pp. 25–32.
67. Kuyucu, 'Law, property, ambiguity'.

CHAPTER 2

TWO CRISES, TWO TRAJECTORIES: THE IMPACT OF THE 2001 AND 2008 ECONOMIC CRISES ON URBAN GOVERNANCE IN TURKEY

Tuna Kuyucu

Introduction

Since 2000, Turkey has gone through two major economic crises with momentous economic, political and social consequences. In this chapter I present a detailed analysis of the legal and institutional reforms in urban governance and the regulation of land/housing markets in the aftermath of the 2001 and 2008 crises, and argue that they served as 'critical junctures' for institutional change. The 2001 crisis was followed by wide-ranging reforms that not only significantly rationalised institutions of macroeconomic management, but also empowered local governments in decision-making processes, particularly in the implementation of large-scale renewal projects. The economic havoc and social upheaval brought by the crisis was the most important impetus behind these reforms, which had been introduced to revive the economy. External factors also played important roles in this moment of institutional rearrangement, such as the acceleration of Turkey's European Union (EU) membership process and the steady capital inflows into the country thanks to an expanding global economy. These post-crisis reforms, however, had their limits when it came to appropriating the rapidly rising urban rent in major cities. The institutional infrastructure created by the governing party (AKP) in housing production and land brokerage by the government's Housing Development Agency (TOKİ) openly contradicted the rational and decentrist reforms passed in the same period by the same political party.

'The mismatch between administrative decentralisation and the centralisation of land market regulations could be contained as long as the economy grew substantially, delivering adequate returns to all stakeholders involved in urban governance and the land/housing markets. The 2008 crisis, however, created an entirely different economic and political environment that made it impossible for the government to sustain such an urban policy. With the collapse of global financial markets and the subsequent slowing down of the Turkish economy, the AKP government overturned most macroeconomic and administrative reforms of the previous era and embarked on an authoritarian economic and political programme that dramatically re-centralised urban policy making as well as macroeconomic management. The virtual end of Turkey's EU membership prospects after 2008 also contributed to this policy shift by removing an important incentive for democratic reforms. This re-centralisation made it possible for the government to use controversial infrastructure and real estate projects to generate economic growth and employment during a period of low economic growth equilibrium. Furthermore, the government's increased control of urban land/housing markets enabled it to appropriate urban rent more directly, which has proven indispensable to the party in terms of financing the clientelistic networks that have been vital to its political survival.

This analysis of the relationship between economic crises and urban policy making contributes to the literature on (neoliberal) urban governance in three ways: first, the role of economic crises in shaping urban policy has not received the attention it deserves despite the major influence of economic shocks on institutional restructuring. The article adds to our existing empirical and theoretical knowledge on this crucial topic by developing an explanatory framework about why and how the two economic shocks that happened within a short time span in one country could produce such radically different policy outcomes. Second, by focusing on an emerging market economy with a highly centralised governing system, the article demonstrates that neoliberalisation does not necessarily lead to decentralisation and state devolution as it usually does in advanced capitalist contexts.[1] The Turkish case offers an interesting puzzle, where the highly centralised state undertook decentralising reforms after 2001, but quickly overturned them after 2008. An analysis of why this happened has the potential to enhance our understanding of the relationship between neoliberal dynamics and transformations in public administration. Finally, the analysis offered here demonstrates the value of comparative work in theory building and advancement in a field dominated by single case studies that are relatively limited in building theories.[2] This article shows the value of comparative analysis, a longitudinal comparison in this case, in constructing explanations rather than offering mere descriptions.

Economic Crises and Urban Governance: An Unexplored Link

Economic crises are arguably the most important drivers of policy shift in the governance of cities and their economies. By disrupting the existing mode of capital accumulation and its institutional apparatus, crises change the rules of the game and open the door to the possibility of sudden and wholesale institutional reorganisation that would not have been possible under conditions of relative stability. History presents us clear examples to support this claim: for example, suburbanisation in the United States is an outcome of the institutional responses to the Great Depression of 1929. The Federal Housing Administration, created in 1934 as part of Roosevelt's New Deal programmes, began a policy of insuring mortgages that turned suburban owner-occupied single-family homes into the norm among the US middle classes.[3] Another example comes from the mid-1970s when rising inflation and budget deficits in the US and Western European countries led to ambitious and aggressive neoliberal reforms in how their cities and urban economies were governed.[4] Differences in degree notwithstanding, all urban administrations in advanced capitalist states turned away from redistributive 'managerial policies' to embrace 'entrepreneurialism'[5] that consists of deindustrialisation, profit-driven urban regeneration, privatisation and gentrification in order to pull their economies out of systemic crisis.

Despite the transformative power economic crises have on urban governance, the literature that explores this link is still not yet fully developed. The results of a basic literature search we conducted in leading urban studies journals show that only 24 articles have been published on the subject, most of which are on the most recent financial crisis that began in 2007.[6] Equally striking is the fact that of these 24 articles, only seven focus on the impact of economic shocks on the cities in developing countries. This is puzzling given that many developing countries have gone through, at least in the last two decades, several economic crises with momentous consequences. As such, they present fertile ground on which the complex causal links between crises and urban governance can be comparatively explored. Given the dearth of comparative work in urban studies[7] and the problems this creates for theory building, it is unfortunate that this opportunity has not been seized. Furthermore, cities in developing countries experience much higher degrees of demographic, economic and social transformations compared to advanced capitalist settings, increasing the need to understand their underlying causes.[8] Since economic crises are prime movers of policy shift, one must (i) empirically explore *how* urban policy changes with economic crises and (ii) build theoretical explanations as to *why* such changes take place. This is the primary purpose of this chapter.

Economic crises are 'critical junctures'[9] where the dissolution of a given set of institutions presents a variety of new institutional paths likely to be followed. Their outcomes are never predetermined and contingent on a variety of internal and external structural factors as well as transformative events. Moreover, moments of crisis disrupt actors' existing incentives and present alternative blueprints for action. Old alliances and networks are likely to dissolve and new ones form, consisting of a range of new or old actors. It is even possible, as the Turkish case shows, for the same actors and networks to embark on radically different paths of action in a short span of time. As such, looking at how new institutional forms and assemblages emerge in the aftermath of crises require an 'eventful analysis'[10] that simultaneously assigns causal roles both to underlying structural factors as well as highly contingent events.

Focusing on Turkey is ideal to develop such an analysis, for a large number of crises have been experienced since neoliberal reforms were initiated in the 1980s, resulting in different policy outcomes. Since 1994, the country has experienced four major economic crises (1994, 1997, 2001 and 2008). While the first two did not lead to significant policy changes with respect to urban governance, the latter two certainly did. Why this was the case presents an interesting contrast, with the potential to yield solid theoretical insights. However, this article does not pursue that *problématique*, limiting itself to explaining different policy responses to the 2001 and 2008 crises. Whereas the 2001 economic crash led to wide-ranging reforms that institutionalised a more rational, rule-bound and transparent economic governance system compared to the past,[11] the 2008 crisis gave way to the dismantling of these reforms. In the domain of public administration, while the first crisis led to ambitious decentralisation attempts to strengthen municipal governments, the latter overturned them and gave way to unprecedented levels of centralisation, particularly in the implementation of large-scale renewal, transportation and infrastructure projects.[12] That the same government – i.e. the AKP – followed such different trajectories in less than a decade presents an opportunity to build an explanatory framework for this interesting puzzle.

I argue that the answer mostly lies in the radically different states of the global economy when the two crises occurred as well as the dramatically different incentives for the Turkish government to abide by international and multilateral agreements – i.e. the IMF and World Bank programme of 2001 and EU membership reforms. The 2001 crisis took place in a global economic environment of growth and abundance of liquidity, offering Turkey the possibility of quick recovery via foreign capital inflows. In order to pull the economy out of crisis, the AKP government closely followed the structural adjustment programme of the IMF and World Bank, accepted in 2001. This programme formed the institutional backbone of post-crisis economic and administrative reorganisation. Moreover, the aftermath of the 2001 crisis was one of serious opportunities for Turkey's EU membership, which provided added incentive to the government to enact democratising reforms in many areas, including urban governance. Rapid economic recovery and high rates of economic growth – until 2008 – also fuelled a real estate speculation frenzy and construction boom, with the government taking centre stage. In other words, despite the wide-ranging macroeconomic and administrative reforms that rationalised economic management and democratised public administration, high urban rents motivated the government to use its power to appropriate a large share of this rent, thereby creating a contradictory institutional and administrative structure.[13]

Unlike the 2001 crisis caused mostly by domestic factors, the 2008 crisis was global in origin and scale. What started as a collapse in markets for mortgage-backed securities in the US turned out to be the greatest economic recession the world has experienced since 1929. Turkey's success after 2001 – i.e. greater integration into the global economy via foreign capital inflows – ironically became the source of its economic fragility after 2008. Because Turkey relied so much on foreign capital inflows to sustain economic growth, global contraction and capital outflow from the country signalled tough economic times. Given this environment, the government moved away from the structural reforms of the previous period and embarked on an authoritarian and centrist economic and political agenda.[14] Direct appropriation of urban rents and maintaining growth through megaprojects such as a third bridge over the Bosphorus Strait and a third airport in Istanbul, turned into political and economic lifelines for the government whose power and legitimacy were increasingly questioned and challenged. Adding to this authoritarian swing was the strong opposition of France and Germany to Turkey's EU application since 2007, which brought an end to EU-driven democratic reforms in the country. When the EU stumbled into its own economic and political turmoil after 2008, Turkey's EU bid virtually ended. Due to these twin-factors – i.e. the global economic crisis and the end of Turkey's EU prospects – the AKP's move towards relentless centrism and authoritarian rule gained momentum. In short, the economic crises and the global political–economic conjuncture that followed were largely responsible for the major institutional reforms witnessed in Turkey from 2001 onwards.

My argument parts with two commonly held views regarding the twists and turns of the AKP administration, and offers a theoretically and empirically more accurate perspective. The first of these views, commonly held among Kemalist circles in Turkey, argues that the AKP had always been an authoritarian Islamist party with the grand mission of Islamising Turkey's political and social life. The democratic reforms in the first part of its rule were pragmatic steps to garner enough support from within the country and without, and to pacify its main opponents such as the armed forces, so that it could reach its ideological mission. The turning point, according to this view, is the 2010 Constitutional Referendum, which the party won by a landslide. Afterwards, the argument goes, the party went back to its root ideology, which is

Islamism, and has been advancing its mission ever since. International dynamics, such as the Great Recession or the turmoil in the EU, are seen only as minor contributing factors to the AKP's grand plan and unchanging ideology. The second view, which can be summarised as 'power corrupts', holds that as the AKP elite gained more power through successive electoral victories and greater respect in foreign policy circles, they became poisoned by their success and abandoned principles of democratic rule such as power sharing, deliberation, and checks and balances. The fact that strong institutions to protect political pluralism and power sharing never took off in Turkey helped them easily dismantle any existing institutions and establish an authoritarian one-party rule.

While appealing to common sense, both views contain flaws that limit their utility for solid academic analysis. First, neither can account for the timing of the AKP's turn to authoritarianism, which began in 2009 when the party was at its weakest in terms of public support. In the local elections that year, the total vote of AKP candidates fell to around 38 per cent, a major drop from the 47 per cent attained in the 2007 general elections. This weakens the 'power corrupts' argument. The party's extraordinary success in the 2010 referendum certainly played a major role in accelerating the slide towards authoritarian rule, but cannot be seen as its cause. The economic crash of 2008 constitutes a more important event in the AKP's policy turns, especially in urban governance, as I will discuss below. Second, the 'AKP had a grand mission, it just hid it' argument is a perfect demonstration of an essentialist argument that pays absolutely no heed to the very complex institutional, economic and social dynamics in how history unfolds. It also entirely overlooks how transformative events can change the course of history. Consequently, while this essentialist argument might appeal to an ideological position, it offers little in the way of a strong analytic argument. Third, arguing that political actors become more authoritarian as they gain greater electoral power, especially in countries without strong democratic institutions, is simply stating the obvious. It offers nothing in the way of a serious analysis regarding internal or external factors – structural or contingent – responsible for the legal and institutional changes that took place since the AKP came to power.

The multi-causal framework developed in this chapter, which puts the emphasis on the 2008 economic crisis, overcomes all these three problems simultaneously. First, it provides a more accurate account of the timing of the AKP's political U-turn. Second, it avoids falling into the 'essentialist' trap based on hidden intentions and non-falsifiable truth-claims. Finally, it is anything but 'obvious'. What it does, as will become clear in the rest of the chapter, is to build a complex argument that assigns causal roles to both underlying structural factors and unforeseen events in explaining institutional change. Furthermore, it empirically demonstrates that externally generated factors – i.e. the global economic recession and major policy changes – played a more important causal role in transforming politics in Turkey, particularly in urban governance and the land/housing markets.

Decentralisation and Democratisation after the 2001 Crisis

The Crisis, Recovery and the Period of High Growth

The 2001 economic crisis is a turning point in recent Turkish history. What began as a political confrontation between the prime minister and the president during a National Security Council Meeting on 19 February 2001, quickly turned into worst economic crisis ever experienced in Turkey.[15] The underlying factors of the crisis were long in the making. Throughout the 1990s, the country was governed by a series of weak coalition governments that relied on deficit spending to finance populist policies and low-intensity warfare with Kurdish separatists. In such an environment, rampant inflation and very high interest rates became the norm. The minimally regulated private banking system created further instabilities with periodic bank failures throughout the decade.[16] Also important were the corrupt public banks whose operations defied all sound economic practice.[17] The final blow to the economy was the 1999 earthquake in the city of İzmit, an industrial powerhouse, which killed at least 17,000 people and brought economic devastation. The ill-designed stand-by agreement with the IMF in 2000 to decrease budget deficits and reform the banking system aggravated economic weaknesses and in November 2000, the first major shock took place.[18] Only three months later, the crash of February 2001 ensued, tarnishing the Turkish economy.

In the immediate aftermath of the crisis, the then Vice President of the World Bank, Kemal Derviş, was invited to Turkey as the Treasury Minister to stabilise the downward spiralling economy. Known as the 'Derviş Program', his policies essentially continued the IMF programme that aimed to control public finances, reform the banking sector, increase privatisation revenues, curb inflation and interest rates, enhance competitiveness and create independent regulatory agencies. Thanks to the strict implementation of these reforms, the economic meltdown came to an end and stable growth followed. The devastating crisis, in a sense, put an end to populist inflationary policies and irrational economic management in Turkey.

The crisis did not only cause a break with past economic policy; it also ended 13 years of weak coalition governments. In the 2002 elections a newly formed religious-conservative party, the AKP, won by a landslide to everyone's surprise and formed a single-party government.[19] Based largely on the anti-inflationary Derviş Program, the AKP's macroeconomic policies from 2002 to 2008 were highly successful. Growth reached an impressive 6 per cent per annum; inflation and interest rates dropped to single digits; public debt was greatly reduced and net foreign direct investments reached US$ 70 billion[20] (see Table 2.1).

Table 2.1 Key Macroeconomic Figures (2002–15)

Year	GDP Growth Rate	GDP per Capita (USD)	FDI (million USD)	Value of REITs (million TLs)	Total Household Debt (per cent of GDP)	Inflation Rate
2002	6.2	3,492	1,082	339	1.9	29.8
2003	5.3	4,565	1,702	543	2.9	18.4
2004	9.4	5,775	2,785	1,446	4.7	9.3
2005	8.4	7,036	10,031	2,489	7	7.7
2006	6.9	7,597	20,185	2,082	8.9	9.6
2007	4.7	9,247	22,047	3,190	11	8.4
2008	0.7	10,444	19,851	3,046	12	10.1
2009	−4.8	8,561	8,585	2,854	13.3	6.8
2010	9.2	10,003	9,099	11,062	15.3	6.4
2011	8.8	10,428	16,176	20,769	16.7	10.5
2012	2.1	10,459	13,282	24,087	18.1	6.2
2013	4.2	10,822	12,457	37,573	20.3	7.4
2014	2.9	10,395	12,539	41,400	19.5	8.2
2015	4	9,261	16,800			8.8

Source: Capital Markets Board of Turkey (CMB), the Turkish Statistical Institute (TURKSTAT) and the Central Bank of The Republic of Turkey (CBRT).

The nature of the growth was also more solid compared with previous periods. Private investments and total factor productivity significantly rose while poverty and inequality levels dropped considerably.[21] Thanks to major increases in public healthcare and education expenditures, the gap in these areas between Turkey and OECD countries substantially decreased.[22] This economic environment secured the AKP's hegemonic political position. In the 2007 general elections, the party received 46.7 per cent of the votes, a significant increase from the 34 per cent it received in 2002.

Its impressive economic performance notwithstanding, the AKP's macroeconomic management also created two serious problems: rapid increase of the current account deficit and mounting private debt (see Table 2.1). Thanks to an overvalued Turkish Lira, imports rose faster than exports while the saving rate decreased, leading to dangerously high account deficit levels.[23] This deficit was financed by vast short-term capital inflows – so-called 'hot money'. Furthermore, the AKP's economic policies also caused a consumption surge that was fuelled by debt. Between 2002 and 2008, total outstanding household debt rose from 2 per cent to 12 per cent of the GDP, and the ratio of household debt to assets shot up from 5 per cent to 29 per cent. Furthermore, while public finances came under control, the private sector debt increased substantially, making firms particularly vulnerable to shocks in foreign exchange rates.[24]

Partial Decentralisation and Democratisation in Urban Governance

This rapid economic growth was accompanied by important reforms in urban governance implemented mostly to fulfil EU requirements and constituted important steps towards decentralisation. In 2005, the Turkish Parliament passed two crucial legislations concerning public administration – the Municipality Law (Law no. 5393) and the Metropolitan Municipality Law (Law no. 5216) – that significantly strengthened local governments. Because Turkey is a highly centralised country, local governments have always been under the tutelage of the centre. In fact, the main piece of legislation regulating local governments dates back to 1930 (Law no. 1580), a period of authoritarian state building. Even though this outdated law was reformed several times, its centralist spirit remained intact.[25] The 1982

Constitution, passed under a military junta government, also left minimal room for local autonomy. The Metropolitan Municipality Law, passed in 1984 under a civilian administration, kept the centre's tutelage over localities but strengthened the operational and financial capacity of metropolitan bodies.[26]

With the new laws, 'local autonomy' was, for the first time, laid as the foundation of local governments despite the fact that the Constitution had no such clause.[27] Both laws also designated local administrations as the 'sole authorities' in using the rights given to them by law. This was a major step in curtailing the influence of the central government via provincial authorities over municipalities. Another decentralist measure was the limiting of central government's unchecked power in rejecting local policies. According to the new laws, the centre could *only* take local decisions to court, a major move away from the old system where it could singlehandedly reject local decisions. The more rational criteria introduced by the new Metropolitan Municipality Law, through which municipalities could acquire Metropolitan status and enjoy enhanced financial and administrative powers, constituted a further step in curtailing the centre's excessive power. Before this law, such criteria were loosely defined, leaving the process open to political manipulation and gerrymandering. The new law introduced a minimum population threshold (750,000) residing within a 10 km radius of a municipality for it to acquire a metropolitan status, thereby shielding this process from political manipulation from the centre.[28] The changes in the area of municipal finance also strengthened local governments by raising the level of revenue municipalities receive from the centre. However, the laws did not give autonomy to localities in raising local taxes, thus maintaining their financial dependence on the centre.

The new laws also improved the channels of participation of inhabitants of a particular locale in decision making. For example, the Municipality Law changed the criteria of urban citizenship (*hemşehrilik*) from 'one's place of birth' to 'one's place of residence', thus turning all residents of a district into potential participants in governance.[29] Furthermore, by opening City Council meetings to public attendance, the new laws greatly increased the level of transparency in rule making. Finally, the creation of a new institution – *Kent Konseyi* – whereby NGOs, interest groups and individuals would meet regularly to form agendas that a City Council is obliged to discuss, constituted a major step towards participatory governance.

These democratic reforms must be seen in the larger context of Turkey's post-crisis rationalisation of public administration as well as its EU membership process. With respect to the former, key institutional reforms were realised following the crisis such as the creation of independent regulatory agencies in the telecommunications, energy, tobacco and alcohol markets and the banking sector.[30] The Central Bank gained independence in 2001 for the first time, putting an end to reckless populist lending practices.[31] Public finance and debt were also put under strict controls with laws passed in 2002–3. The new Public Procurement Law (2002) reduced corruption and enhanced competitiveness in the distribution of public contracts. Until 2009, the AKP abided by these more rational institutional regulations. Acemoğlu and Üçer[32] argue that the high growth experienced until 2008 was a direct consequence of this rational institutional framework.

The acceleration of Turkey's EU membership process after the AKP took office played an equally important role in passing the decentralist reforms in urban governance. Even though Turkey signed the European Charter of Local Self Government in 1985 and applied to become an EU member state in 1987, it always placed important reservations on increasing the autonomy of local governments, which drew strong criticism from the EU. However, in 2005, the aforementioned reforms led to formal accession negotiations with the EU for the first time. The 'carrot' of EU membership, in other words, was a strong driving force behind the reforms that transformed political and economic dynamics in the country.

The Real Estate Boom and the Centre's Growing Power

Reforming public administration was not the AKP government's only ambitious agenda. Immediately after taking office, the new government passed an Emergency Action Plan, identifying urgent reforms needed to lift the country out of crisis. One area of reform was the real estate sector that contracted by 17 per cent during the crisis. Problems were multiple. Rampant informality in the land/housing markets badly distorted markets and cost the government huge sums due to tax evasion. Equally important was the country's low-quality housing stock, posing grave safety threats given that most settlements are on active fault lines. In a sense, the 1999 earthquake was a bitter wake-up call. Yet another problem was the institutionally weak and vulnerable housing finance system. Outstanding mortgage credits made up less than 1 per cent of the GDP in 2001. Public housing finance via TOKİ had also collapsed by 2001, due to corruption in state-owned banks as well as the economic crisis. The final challenge to overcome was the legal and administrative obstacles in the way of implementing regeneration/renewal projects in derelict, risky and unfashionable parts of cities.

The AKP's response to these problems was comprehensive. Yet unlike the reform measures in public administration, reforms in the land/housing markets mostly strengthened central state institutions *vis-à-vis* municipalities. The first thing the AKP did was to take TOKİ, a credit-dispensing mechanism, and remake it into the most powerful contractor and land broker in the country.[33] In the span of only a few years TOKİ gained the authority to sell all state-owned plots, save for military sites. In addition, it was authorised to build for-profit and not-for-profit housing on this land, either directly or via partnerships with private contractors. It also had the power to change the zoning of these plots single-handedly, thereby bypassing municipalities. In the words of Atiyas, TOKİ is 'a policy maker, a regulator, and a service provider'.[34] By 2008, TOKİ had built close to 350,000 housing units, 15 per cent of which was 'for-profit' and the rest for lower-middle and lower-class citizens. In addition, it has built numerous mosques, schools, dormitories, hospitals and even stadiums. TOKİ also has a unique legal status: even though it operates under the Prime Ministry, it is not technically a 'public institution' as it is excluded from the general budget. It raises revenue by selling land and housing and through revenue-sharing deals with private developers. Furthermore, it owns the country's largest real-estate investment trust, which implements large projects around the country. Finally, TOKİ contracts are exempt from the Public Procurement Law, which opens the door to large-scale corruption.[35]

As part of its reform agenda, the AKP also constructed the first legal/institutional framework for urban renewal. Prior to 2002, neither the centre nor municipalities could undertake renewal projects due to financial limitations and the lack of a legal framework. The 2005 Municipality Law and the law titled 'Law for the Reuse of Timeworn Historical and Cultural Property with Restoration and Protection' (no. 5366), also passed in 2005, laid the framework for renewal projects in obsolete and risky areas as well as in 'conservation' areas faced with losing their historical and/or cultural significance. Both laws initially gave the authority to designate 'transformation zones' to local governments. Project implementation, however, has been carried out entirely by TOKİ or by private contractors; municipal authorities have had minimal roles after deciding on the site. Even this power was taken away from them in 2010, as I will discuss below. In most projects implemented since 2005, TOKİ has been the primary implementing actor. TOKİ draws up the new plans for these areas, builds the new buildings and houses the displaced populations. Existing research on renewal projects shows that project terms and details are mostly imposed on residents, who are kept out of decision making processes.[36] Furthermore, a substantial portion of the directly impacted populations are inadequately compensated, leading to worsening of their economic and social conditions. Moreover, projects are more likely to be implemented in areas with more rent-generating potential rather than those with more pressing needs.[37]

The AKP's land/housing market reforms were not limited to government agencies. In order to integrate financial markets with real estate, the government passed what is known as the 'Mortgage Law' in 2007 (Law no. 5582), which resolved many of the legal/administrative complications of using housing finance. Before the AKP came to power, outstanding mortgage credits made up 0.08 per cent of the GDP; this figure had climbed to 3.7 per cent by the end of 2008, which is a considerable increase. The falling interest and inflation rates and the inflow of foreign capital into Turkey also played important roles in the credit surge. The AKP's macroeconomic policies and the laws it passed definitely contributed to the financialisation in the Turkish economy in general and in the real estate sector in particular.

The reforms in real estate and urban governance during this high growth period have been highly transformative by all accounts. As evidenced by the unprecedented number of permits given for new constructions, the real estate market soared. While 160,000 permits were given in 2002, this number had shot up to 330,000 by 2004 and a staggering 600,000 by 2006. Between 2002 and 2007, the share of construction-related activities in the GDP increased from around 5 per cent to 6.5 per cent. The number of publicly traded real estate investment trusts (REITs) in the same period increased from nine to 14 and their net asset value almost quadrupled from 1.1 billion TL to 4.3 billion TL. The number of shopping malls rose from 66 to 214 and 'branded housing complexes' that come with multiple integrated functions became commonplace in big cities. According to a 2013 study, in Istanbul alone there are 852 branded projects with a total of 400,000 residential units, constituting 8 per cent of Istanbul's housing stock.[38] All these developments took place in a confusing political environment in which partial decentralisation existed simultaneously with undeniable centralisation. This contradiction was resolved in the aftermath of the 2008 global economic crisis by relentless centralisation.

The Centre Strikes Back: Re-centralisation after the 2008 Crisis

The Crisis, Short-lived Recovery and the Slide into Low Growth Equilibrium

When financial meltdown began in the US in 2007, the Turkish economy had already slowed down from its peak of 9.4 per cent growth in 2004 to 4.7 per cent in 2007. The impact of the global crisis of 2008, however, was severe. In 2008, growth plummeted to 0.7 per cent and to negative 4.8 per cent in 2009. The exceptionally high growth rates during the following two years created optimism among politicians who were quick to announce that the crisis hit Turkey only 'tangentially', but the volatility of this recovery soon became apparent as growth steeply declined in 2012 and has remained very low ever since (see Table 2.1). Average growth between 2008 and 2015 was only 3 per cent per annum, half the rate of the prior period. GDP per capita, which rapidly rose from around US$ 3,000 to US$ 10,000 between 2002 and 2008, remained stagnant at that level after 2008. Given its weak performance, the country that was once hailed as a 'miracle' by foreign analysts is now treated as one of the riskiest economies in the world. So what went wrong?

There are three main reasons why Turkey is presently among the most fragile economies: a very high current account deficit, the drastic slowdown in the EU zone and the turmoil in the Middle East and North Africa (MENA) following the Arab Spring uprisings. To begin with, while the AKP's policies during the high growth period from 2002 to 2008 brought budget deficits under control, they led to massive increases in the private sector debt as well as in the current account deficit, as discussed above. This serious structural problem was not addressed when the crisis hit. On the contrary, the AKP administration decided to fuel growth by relying even more aggressively on foreign debt during 2010 and 2011, when global financial markets were flooded by capital as a result of the FED's quantitative easing policy.[39] Turkey's total foreign debt jumped from 38 per cent to 50 per cent of the GDP from 2008 to 2014. The structure of this debt to finance the account deficit also changed: while the private sector's more volatile short-term debt constituted 25 per cent of the total private sector debt in 2008, by 2014 it had increased to 40 per cent.[40] In short, Turkey's excessive reliance on foreign capital inflows made it highly vulnerable to external shocks. In the face of this bleak economic situation, the AKP administration put enormous pressure on the Central Bank to refrain from raising interest rates, despite increasing inflation and a 25 per cent drop in the value of the Turkish currency against the dollar. Since then, real interest rates have remained close to zero.

The second and third reasons why Turkey was badly affected by the global recession are related to the composition of Turkey's main export partners. Prior to 2008, exports to EU countries experienced a drastic increase from US$ 16 billion in 2000 to US$ 60 billion in 2007, constituting 56 per cent of Turkey's total exports in 2007.[41] When the EU was hit by the economic recession, Turkish losses were big. By 2013, the share of exports to the EU zone in total exports had dropped to 41.5 per cent. To compensate for their losses, exporters turned to markets in the Middle East and North Africa (MENA).[42] When mass uprisings throughout the Arab world reached their peak in 2011, however, Turkey once again lost significant export markets.

In addition to keeping interest rates low, the AKP government responded to the crisis also with fiscal stimulus.[43] The contribution of government spending to GDP growth rose substantially from 10 per cent in the period prior to the crisis to 25 per cent in the latter period. Meanwhile, private investments slowed down, as well as the country's total factor productivity. The domestic savings rate dropped from 17 per cent to 15 per cent.[44] The main engines of economic growth after 2008 became government spending and domestic consumption rather than private investments or productivity increases. Between 2008 and 2014, domestic credit provided by the financial sector jumped from

55 per cent to 88 per cent of the GDP and total household debt from 12 per cent to 19 per cent of the GDP – clear indications of an economy driven by debt and consumption.[45] It is in this negative economic context that we must approach the AKP's relentless recentralisation moves, particularly in the domains of urban governance and urban regeneration, which form the basis of the AKP's post-crisis capital accumulation strategy.

The Recentralisation of Urban Governance and Urban Regeneration Policies

The first move to centralise urban policy making came in the wake of the 2009 local elections, when the then Prime Minister Erdoğan announced plans to build a third bridge over the northern tip of the Bosphorus Strait. This came as a shock to everyone, including the Istanbul Metropolitan Municipality (IMM), as the Istanbul Master Plan accepted in 2009 was staunchly against a third bridge in that location due to potential environmental damage, as well as its likely effect on further population growth. This Master Plan was prepared by a large team of experts employed by Istanbul Metropolitan Planning (IMP), a subsidiary firm of the IMM, and was the first Master Plan developed for the city since 1984. The violation of the plan by the head of the central government in the year it was accepted signalled a different orientation to urban policy making compared to the period until 2008. In protest, the entire team that worked on the plan resigned from their posts. This, though, had no effect as the announcement of the third bridge was followed by two more megaprojects that had no place in the plan: a third airport, to be built on the Black Sea coast, and a canal project that would connect the Black Sea with Marmara Sea on the western edges of the city. Both projects were also announced to the public by the PM rather than Istanbul's mayor. Currently, the third bridge has been completed at an estimated cost of US$ 1.5 billion. The third airport project, at a staggering cost of US$ 20 billion, is being implemented despite numerous lawsuits against it. The 'Crazy Project', as the canal project came to be known in Turkey after the PM referred to it as such, has yet to begin. According to estimates, it will cost around US$ 40 billion.[46]

The next move towards centralisation came in 2010, when the government changed the 2005 Municipality Law and transferred the authority to designate 'transformation zones' from districts to metropolitan municipalities (Law no. 5998).[47] Even though it is still local administrations that are legally charged with this critical authority, this move should be considered a centralisation attempt at the local level for two reasons: first, the new law disempowers lower-level local administrations and gives further power to higher-level bodies. Second, the two most important cities for transformation projects, Istanbul and Ankara, are AKP strongholds at the metropolitan level. Therefore, by making metropolitan administrations the sole decision makers in urban renewal, the AKP government in effect centralised this power, at least for the most important cities, and effectively pushed district-level administrations out of decision making.

The attempted policy to disempower district municipalities and concentrate power at the metropolitan level was concluded in 2012 when a new Metropolitan Municipality Law (Law no. 6360) was passed only seven years after the last one. By lifting the restrictions that the 2005 law had in place in forming new metropolitan bodies, the new law increased the number of metropolitan municipalities from 16 to 31.[48] Of the 15 new municipalities, eight are governed by the AKP. Furthermore, the new law expanded metropolitan jurisdiction to cover the entire provincial unit, thereby eliminating 552 provincial municipalities (*belde belediyesi*) and 16,000 villages that used to be governed by separate bodies. As a result, the share of Turkey's urban population increased from 77 per cent to 91 per cent.[49] More importantly, the new law authorised municipalities to alter the zoning and planning regulations of the former rural areas, thereby opening the door to massive rent-generation opportunities.[50] The law also further stripped lower-level district municipalities of crucial powers they used to hold such as preparing development plans in their jurisdiction. They now are mostly responsible for the delivery of basic municipal services such as garbage collection and street lighting.[51] Finally, the new law created a new agency responsible for monitoring and coordinating investments at the municipal level (*Yatırım İzleme ve Koordinasyon Daire Başkanlığı*), which is directly affiliated with the Ministry of the Interior and thus further evidence of the administrative tutelage of the centre over local governments.

A more definite move in the way of centralising urban policy making was the creation of a new ministry, the Ministry of Urban Development and Environment, in 2011. That the same Ministry became responsible for making decisions on urban development and environmental protection has made it possible to bypass obstacles that large urban projects face due to their negative environmental impacts. Furthermore, the Ministry also has strong zoning and planning authority, and thus can sidestep municipal plans, particularly with respect to projects in renewal areas. The construction of the twin towers in the Izmir port area is a case in point. Even though the Izmir Metropolitan Municipality strongly opposed the project, the Ministry passed the necessary planning/zoning revisions to make it happen.[52] Similarly, at all stages of the implementation of the large-scale renewal project in the Fikirtepe neighbourhood, which is under Kadıköy Municipality's jurisdiction in Istanbul, the municipality has been entirely barred from decision making. The Ministry declared the neighbourhood a transformation area, and the project is being executed by a partnership between TOKİ and private developers. Working in close cooperation with TOKİ, the Ministry has become a very powerful central governmental agency that overcomes any obstacles that might hinder rapid urban (re)development.[53]

Following the creation of the new Ministry, the AKP government took another bold step towards centralisation in 2012 – what came to be known as the Disaster Law (Law no. 6306). The stated goal behind it is to speed up the process of urban renewal in cities under the risk of natural disasters, most important of which are earthquakes. With the law, the Ministry became the only authority to determine 'risky areas' to be renewed.[54] Even though the intention of the law is to prepare cities for potential natural disasters, implementation so far has proven otherwise.[55] The law also allows for individual buildings to be demolished and rebuilt once they receive an official 'risk report' and/or two-thirds of property owners give consent. This has been frequently used by property owners and contractors in high-rent areas, such as the Kadıköy district, where rebuilding significantly increases property values. So far, the Disaster Law has mostly been used for rent-generation purposes rather than target riskier areas.

The government has been utilising three additional mechanisms to centralise urban policy making. The first is the excessive use of executive decisions in the areas of urban (re)development, including eminent domain decisions, since 2008. While only 5 per cent of cabinet decisions in 2009 concerned these areas, this figure jumped to 17 per cent in 2010, 41 per cent in 2012 and a staggering 48 per cent in 2014.

Between 2010 and 2014, the expropriation decisions of the cabinet increased from 19 to 265.[56] These accounts vividly show how the central government became more involved in decision-making processes regarding urban (re)development at the expense of lower-level administrative bodies. The second mechanism is the repeated revisions of the Public Procurement Law that was enacted in 2002. By 2013, the law had been changed 35 times, mostly by adding exceptions, thus making it possible for politically connected firms to win public bids and enable controversial projects to be realised.[57] The final mechanism that strengthened the centre was that of weakening the independence of regulatory institutions created in the aftermath of the 2001 crisis. With two executive decrees in 2011, respective ministries were authorised to 'inspect' the activities of regulatory agencies, thus putting them under political pressure and tutelage.[58]

The overall impact of these policies on real estate markets has been significant. Construction became a crucial sector in fuelling economic growth in the context of a slowing economy, as can be evidenced by the 1 percentage point increase in the share of construction in the GDP from 5 per cent to 6 per cent. More importantly, construction projects undertaken by the public sector account for most of this increase. While the private construction sector has also started recovering from the major collapse of 2008, this has been at a much slower rate compared to the public sector.[59] As mentioned earlier, the government is currently implementing several megaprojects, including a new airport and a new bridge in Istanbul as well as hundreds of thousands of TOKİ housing units.[60] The upsurge in construction can also be seen through the rise in total number of building permits given, from around 290,000 to 468,000 between the pre-2008 and post-2008 periods. Between the two periods, total outstanding mortgages rose from 3.7 per cent to 7.1 per cent of the GDP. Perhaps most striking is the dramatic increase in the total market value of real estate investment trusts (REIT), from 3 billion to 41 billion TL.[61] Relative to small construction companies, REITs undertake much larger projects, such as shopping malls and branded housing complexes, which have considerable impact on the social, economic and spatial geography of cities. Reflecting the government's excessive presence and power in real estate is Emlak GYO, a subsidiary firm of TOKİ, which is by far the largest of all REITs being traded on the Istanbul Stock Exchange.[62]

In addition to these quantitative increases, excessive centralisation has also contributed to the scale and prevalence of corruption in real estate markets. This became apparent when public prosecutors ordered the arrest of four ministers and many other public personnel in December 2013 for alleged involvement in massive corruption.[63] One of them was the Minister of Urban Development and Environment who allegedly used his powers to illegally strike lucrative construction deals with politically connected firms that have been financing the AKP's political machinery. The scale of this corruption in construction is massive. When forced by the PM to resign from office, the Minister publicly announced that all his actions during his ministerial term had been directly ordered by the PM. When the corruption probe reached the PM's own son, thus indirectly the PM, thousands of prosecutors and police officers were forced to resign, several were jailed for plotting a coup against the government and many oppositional journalists were arrested. The corruption charges and the government's draconian response were yet another major milestone in the AKP's turn to authoritarianism after the brutal repression of the Gezi Park protests in the summer of 2013. Ever since the unfolding of these two crucial events, Turkey has been in a state of political turmoil and chaos.

Conclusion

What conclusions can be drawn from this analysis of how economic crises affected urban governance in Turkey? Major economic shocks are crucial turning points for institutional restructuring. The institutional reorganisation after such events is comparable only to the impact of wars and *coups d'état*. Because economic crises disrupt existing regimes of capital accumulation, they force economic actors and decision makers to search for new institutional fixes to overcome the structural problems of the previous mode of accumulation and lead the economy on a steady path of growth. The new institutional configuration, however, cannot be predicted from the outset because too many internal and external variables are at work in shaping the final institutional outcomes. Some of these intervening variables are the internal power struggles among the political and economic elites, how open an economy is to outside influence, the state of the global economy, and the kind and strength of international/multilateral organisations a state is a member of and the agreements it has signed.

The Turkish case is telling in this regard. While the two economic shocks in 2001 and 2008 were followed by wide-ranging institutional reconfiguration, the nature of the respective reforms has been radically different. In the aftermath of the 2001 crisis, the political and economic elites acted in unison to reform the country's macroeconomic system and its administrative structure, to make them more rational, rule-bound and democratic. Several new institutions were created to this end, including independent regulatory agencies. Existing institutions (for example, the Central Bank) and laws, such as laws on urban governance, public administration and public procurements also underwent significant reforms to make them more aligned with these overarching goals. The reform measures began before the AKP took office and the new party, brought to power largely due to the crisis, closely followed the core ethos of these reforms until 2008.

It was the specific domestic and global circumstances that turned the post-2001 era into one of rationalisation in economic management and democratisation in the administrative system. The 2001 crisis was largely the result of unbridled populism in the country that was prevalent throughout the 1980s and 1990s. The crisis, in a sense, brought populism to its economic and political limits. The political elites who were in power when the shock occurred had no other option but to accept major institutional reforms devised by the IMF and World Bank. When the AKP won the elections in 2002, the success of these reforms was evident to the party elite who campaigned on a platform of breaking from the past. Furthermore, even though the new party won the elections with a wide margin, it still had to form alliances with multiple actors in order to strengthen its position. This increased the likelihood that the party initially agreed to continue the reform programme accepted before it took office and advance its own goals afterwards.

That the global economy was on an unprecedented upward swing between 2000 and 2007 provided further impetus to the new political elite to stick to the macroeconomic policies that turned Turkey into a very attractive market for foreign investors. As confidence in the economy and foreign investments soared, interest and inflation rates sharply dropped, enabling the AKP to finance many of the ambitious infrastructure and social programmes that formed the backbone of the party's political success. In other words, as solid economic performance translated into political success, the party elite had no incentives to seek other institutional arrangements. Furthermore, the economic and political reforms accelerated Turkey's EU membership process, which created added incentive for Turkey's leaders to pass further democratic reforms in order to fulfil EU membership criteria. In this unique environment, the AKP took some very bold steps to curb the central government's power over local governments, and significantly rationalised and democratised urban governance in the country.

However, these positive steps were contradicted by the new institutional framework to regulate land and housing markets, which enhanced the central government's capacity to appropriate a larger share of rapidly increasing urban rents. This open contradiction between steps towards decentralisation and economic rationalisation and centralising moves in rent appropriation could be sustained as long as the economy performed well enough to deliver returns to all stakeholders – a kind of *neopopulist consensus*. As long as the AKP's domination of the market did not translate into losses for actors in the private sector such as construction and others, consensus could be maintained without friction. However, the sudden economic slowdown that started in 2008 as a result of the severe recession in the global economy turned things around and made it increasingly difficult to sustain this tenuous balance.

The AKP's reaction to the new low growth equilibrium has been the fierce recentralisation of the country's economic management as well as its administrative systems. Recentralisation allowed two things simultaneously: overcoming legal and administrative obstacles that were in the way of creating economic growth and employment through major public infrastructure projects *and* generating and appropriating urban rent more directly, which is a vital financial source for the party to sustain its hegemonic hold on society. The continued slowdown of the Turkish economy after two years of exceptional growth in 2010 and 2011 has been accompanied by sustained increases in the dose of centralisation and authoritarianism, evident in the new laws and institutions created since then such as the Ministry of Urban Development and Environment and the Disaster Law. As the contribution of private sector investments to GDP growth faltered, the main sources of generating economic growth became government investments and domestic consumption. The former could only be maintained through extraordinary measures that allowed the government to bypass all legal and bureaucratic obstacles to its plans, while the latter depended on a steady expansion of credit use – i.e. financialisation. Thus, the AKP's new economic regime depends largely on an authoritarian and undemocratic form of Keynesianism sustained through infrastructure and real estate as well as direct political intervention into monetary policy to keep interest rates low. It is highly questionable how sustainable such a strategy is, given the escalation of political and economic risks that the country faces.

The heightened centralisation and authoritarianism of the party since 2009 also created a major backlash among certain segments of the population, the peak of which was the Gezi Park protests in May and June of 2013. The sudden mobilisation of hundreds of thousands of people against the planned demolition of a park in the middle of Istanbul to make way for a shopping mall was actually preceded by several similar protests against the AKP's authoritarian interventions into urban space; including the renovation of the Emek Movie Theatre, renewal projects in the neighbourhoods of Tarlabaşı and Fener-Balat and the reorganisation of Taksim Square, the legality and legitimacy of which was disputed by activists. The project in Gezi Park, which openly went against court orders against building a mall, was the last drop, or the tipping point that instigated the largest public protest movement in the country's history. That it was another controversial urban intervention was not a coincidence, given the centrality of such rent-generating projects for the party's political survival. The protest wave, however, did not achieve its goal of curtailing the unchecked power of the AKP and its leader, Tayyip Erdoğan. After the brutal suppression of the protests, the AKP faced further challenges such as the corruption probe in December 2013 and the major electoral losses in the general elections of June 2015. Yet after each of these challenges, the party and its uncompromising leader tightened their grip on power by openly using violence and scare tactics to pacify opponents. Since the repeat-elections of November 2015 that resulted in a clear AKP victory, the country has been rapidly moving towards the institutionalisation of a one-party regime with Tayyip Erdoğan at centre stage, ruling the country from his illegally built new presidential palace in the heart of Ankara.[64]

As this narrative shows, the AKP's route to authoritarianism was neither preordained nor inevitable. It had several twists and turns and was overdetermined by a multiplicity of factors, the most important of which, I argue, was the economic crisis of 2008. Another significant contributing factor was the strong objection of the German and French leaders to Turkey's EU membership prospects, which began as early as 2007. Given how strong an incentive EU membership was in passing democratising reforms, this rather miscalculated move by two of the strongest EU members contributed immensely to the AKP's move away from democracy, especially after 2008. As Turkey's EU prospects dwindled, so did the Turkish population's support for membership, which dropped from 71 per cent to 42 per cent between 2004 and 2010.[65] Being a party that relies heavily on public opinion polls in policy making, AKP strategists certainly took notice of this changed public opinion and used it to garner support for their new, anti-democratic direction. Absent the EU 'carrot', there remained virtually no incentives for the central government to share power with local administrations. As I discussed above, all the new laws and institutions introduced after 2008 diminished the power of local governing bodies *vis-à-vis* the central administration, including the new Metropolitan Municipality Law, which seemingly strengthened metropolitan units but in practice became a tool of gerrymandering as well as eliminating district level decision making. Given that most key metropolitan areas are governed by the AKP, the law actually strengthened the party's grip on urban policy making in cities like Istanbul and Ankara, thereby making it easier to generate and appropriate urban rent.

The final contributing factor to the AKP's authoritarian turn after 2008 is the successful pacification and/or elimination of the party's opponents both from within and without. For example, when the Turkish Armed Forces threatened the party via a public memorandum for its anti-secular activities, the party's response was to imprison most high-ranking officers known to oppose the party through the controversial Ergenekon and Balyoz trials in 2007 and 2010. Dissenting voices from within the party ranks – such as Abdullatif Şener, one of the founding members of the party – have all been forced out of politics. In a similar vein, main opposition parties have experienced immense internal turmoil and infighting.[66] Finally, mass public demonstrations against the party's rule in 2007, the so-called *Cumhuriyet Mitingleri*, failed to create any substantial change and ironically made the AKP even more intolerant of opposition. Once all internal and external opponents were pacified, the AKP leadership had the green light to monopolise power and decision making in the country. That this coincided with a period of major economic crisis and international political isolation paved the ground for the uncontrolled authoritarianism since 2013.

To conclude, it is safe to argue that monocausal arguments regarding radical political and economic transformations are not only theoretically and empirically flawed, but also politically debilitating. The AKP's authoritarianism cannot be explained by some essential quality of its core ideology or its leadership. Neither can it be linked only to the increased power of its leaders who basically became intoxicated by it. The same party, after all, undertook the most ambitious democratisation campaign in the country between 2002 and 2008. In this same period, it also significantly rationalised economic management and put a (temporary) end to unsustainable populist economic policies. What drove the party leaders off this track was the drastically changed external economic and political conditions that forced them to find a new direction and develop new policies to sustain their grip on power. The irony is that this 'new direction' is rather old in a country with a bitter history of political authoritarianism, centrist rule and irrational economic populism.

Notes

1. Sylvia I. Bergh, 'Introduction: Researching the effects of neoliberal reforms on local governance in the Southern Mediterranean', *Mediterranean Politics* 17/3 (2012), pp. 303–21; and Pranab Bardhan and Dilip Mookherjee, 'The rise of local governments: An overview', in P. Bardhan and D. Mookherjee (eds), *Decentralisation and Local Governance in Developing Countries* (Cambridge, MA, 2006).
2. Tuna Kuyucu and Didem Danış, 'Similar processes, divergent outcomes: A comparative analysis of urban redevelopment projects in three Turkish cities', *Urban Affairs Review* 51/3 (2015), pp. 381–413.
3. Rosalyn Fraad Baxandall and Elizabeth Ewen, *Picture Windows: How the Suburbs Happened* (New York, 2000); and Kenneth T. Jackson, *Crabgrass Frontier: The Suburbanisation of the United States* (Oxford, 1985).
4. Jason Hackworth, *The Neoliberal City: Governance, Ideology and Development in American Urbanism* (Ithaca, 2007); and Neil Brenner and Nik Theodore, 'Cities and the geographies of "actually existing neoliberalism"', *Antipode* 34/3 (2002), pp. 349–79.

5. David Harvey, 'From managerialism to entrepreneurialism: The transformation in urban governance in late capitalism', *Geografiska Annaler* B 71 (1989), pp. 3–17.
6. This is the result of a comprehensive article search me and Berkcan Deniz, my research assistant, conducted in 13 leading journals in urban studies. We consulted the website of each journal and ran a search for articles containing the keywords 'urban governance', 'urban policy', 'urban politics', 'economic crisis' and 'crisis' in different combinations. The journals we searched are: *International Journal of Urban and Regional Research*; *Urban Studies*; *Urban Geography*; *Urban Affairs Review*; *Annals of the Association of American Geographers*; *Antipode; Environment and Planning A, B, C, D*; *Cities; Local Economy*; *Habitat*; *World Development*; *Development and Change*; *Local Economy*; and *Review of Radical Political Economics*. We also searched for these keywords in the *Summons* database. A total of 40 separate articles turned out in the overall search, 38 of which were articles and two were reports. Of the 38 articles, only 24 were directly related to the topic under study.
7. Kuyucu and Danış, 'Similar processes'; and Jon Pierre, 'Comparative urban governance: Uncovering complex causalities', *Urban Affairs Review* 40/4 (2005), pp. 446–62.
8. UN Habitat (2014) World Urbanisation Prospects: The 2014 Revision. New York: United Nations. https://esa.un.org/unpd/wup/Publications/Files/WUP2014-Highlights.pdf, accessed on 22 June 2016.
9. James Mahoney, 'Path dependence in historical sociology', *Theory and Society* 29/4 (2000), pp. 507–48.
10. William H. Sewell, *Logics of History: Social Theory and Social Transformation* (Chicago, 2005).
11. Daron Acemoğlu and Murat Üçer, 'The ups and downs of Turkish growth: 2002–2015', *NBER Working Paper* no. 21608 (2015); and İzak Atiyas, 'Economic institutions and institutional change in Turkey during the neoliberal era', *New Perspectives in Turkey* 14/Fall (2012), pp. 45–69.
12. Ulaş Bayraktar, 'Decentralisation, poly-centralisation and re-centralisation of Turkish politics: A matrix of central-local relationships', in K. Göymen and O. Sazak (eds), *Centralisation/Decentralisation Debate Revisited* (Istanbul, 2014); and Ayten Alkan, 'New metropolitan regime of Turkey: Authoritarian urbanisation via local government restructuring', *Lex Localis* 13/3 (2015), pp. 849–77.
13. Seda Demiralp, Selva Demiralp and İnci Gümüş, 'The State of Property Development in Turkey: Facts and Comparisons', *New Perspectives on Turkey* (forthcoming); Acemoğlu and Üçer, 'The ups and downs'; Bayraktar, 'Decentralisation'; and Atiyas, 'Economic institutions'.
14. While I limit my analysis in this article to economic management and urban governance, authoritarianism in other domains of public life has been rising steadily and rapidly since 2009. Particularly following the Gezi Park uprisings in 2013, the AKP government restricted a wider range of civil and

political rights, put immense pressure on newspapers to follow the government's line, imprisoned many opposition journalists and seized oppositional newspapers and other corporations. Since the election of the party's unquestioned leader, Recep Tayyip Erdoğan, to presidency, the party has been aggressively campaigning to change Turkey's political system from parliamentarism to a 'Turkish style' presidential system, which basically means a system with an overpowered president and limited checks and balances to curb his powers.

15. On the third day of the crisis, the value of the Istanbul Stock Exchange Index dropped by 30 per cent and overnight repo rates skyrocketed to 7,500 per cent. The Turkish Lira also lost a third of its value against the dollar. During 2001, the Turkish GDP shrank by 5.7 per cent. Yılmaz Akyüz and Korkut Boratav, 'The making of the Turkish financial crisis', *World Development* 31/9 (2003), pp. 1549–66.
16. C. Emre Alper and Ziya Öniş, 'The Turkish banking system and the IMF in the age of capital account liberalisation', *New Perspectives on Turkey* 30/Spring (2004), pp. 25–55.
17. Atiyas, 'Economic institutions'.
18. Akyüz and Boratav, 'The making'.
19. None of the three previous coalition partners, however, could pass the 10 per cent vote threshold to enter parliament.
20. The county's public sector debt dropped from 75 per cent of the GDP in 2001 to 35 per cent within five years. In the same period, US$ 40 billion was raised through privatisation, far exceeding the US$ 8 billion between 1984 and 2002.
21. According to data compiled by Acemoğlu and Üçer, 'The ups and downs', half of the growth in per capita GDP stemmed from total factor productivity increases, and private investments increased from 12 per cent of the GDP in 2001 to 22 per cent in 2007. Between 2003 and 2008, the Gini coefficient fell from 42 per cent to 38 per cent.
22. Between 2002 and 2008, healthcare expenditures rose from 11 per cent to 17 per cent of the GDP, while those in education rose from 10 per cent to 14 per cent.
23. Between 2002 and 2008, total imports increased from 24 per cent to 32 per cent of the GDP. The current account deficit was at 6.1 per cent of GDP in 2006 and 5.7 per cent in 2008.
24. The total external debt of private sector rose from 43 billion TL to 189 billion TL, while domestic credits to the private sector jumped from 22 billion TL to 157 billion TL. https://www.hazine.gov.tr/tr-TR/Istatistik-Sunum-Sayfasi?mid=120&cid=12, accessed on 28 December 2015.
25. Vahide F. Urhan, 'Türkiye'de yerel yönetimlerin yeniden yapılandırılması', *Sayıştay Dergisi* 70 (2008), pp. 85–102; and Arif Erençin, 'Belediye görevleri üzerine bir inceleme', *Çağdaş Yerel Yönetimler* 15/1 (2006), pp. 17–29.

26. Çağlar Keyder and Ayşe Öncü, 'Globalisation of a third world metropolis: Istanbul in the 1980s', *Review* 17/3 (1994), pp. 383–421.
27. Abdullah Çelik, 'Yerel özerklik açısından 5393 sayılı Belediye Kanunu'nun genel bir değerlendirilmesi', (2013), pp. 17–28.
28. Alkan, 'New metropolitan'; and Şenol Adıgüzel, '6360 sayılı yasanın Türkiye'nin yerel yönetim dizgesi üzerine etkileri: Eleştirel bir değerlendirme', *Toplum ve Demokrasi* 6/13–14 (2012), pp. 153–76.
29. Urhan, 'Türkiye'de yerel'.
30. Atiyas, 'Economic institutions'.
31. Acemoğlu and Üçer, 'The ups and downs'.
32. Ibid.
33. Tuna Kuyucu, 'Law, property and ambiguity: The uses and abuses of legal ambiguity in remaking Istanbul's informal settlements', *International Journal of Urban and Regional Studies* 38/2 (2014), pp. 609–27; Dilek Özdemir, 'The role of the public sector in the provision of housing supply in Turkey: 1950–2009', *International Journal of Urban and Regional Research* 35/6 (2011), pp. 1099–1117; Osman Balaban 'The negative effects of construction boom on urban planning and environment in Turkey: Unraveling the role of the public sector', *Habitat International* 36 (2011), pp. 26–35; and Tuna Kuyucu and Özlem Ünsal, '"Urban transformation", as state-led property transfer: An analysis of two cases of urban renewal in Istanbul', *Urban Studies* 47/7 (2010), pp. 1479–99.
34. Atiyas, 'Economic institutions'.
35. Ibid.
36. Emine Yetiskul, Sevgi Kayasu and Suna Yaşar Özdemir, 'Local responses to urban redevelopment projects: The case of Beyoğlu, Istanbul', *Habitat International* 51 (2015), pp. 159–67; Bahar Sakızlıoğlu, 'Inserting temporality into the analysis of displacement: Living under the threat of displacement', *Tijdschrift voor economische en sociale geografie* 105/2 (2014), pp. 206–20; and Kuyucu and Ünsal, '"Urban transformation"'.
37. Kuyucu, 'Law, property'.
38. EVA Gayrımenkul, *2014 Markalı Konut Araştırması* (2014).
39. By 2011 the current account deficit had increased to a staggering 9.7 per cent of the GDP. It declined to 5.7 per cent in 2014 only because growth stalled.
40. https://www.hazine.gov.tr/tr-TR/Istatistik-Sunum-Sayfasi?mid=120&-cid=12, accessed 30 December 2015.
41. http://www.kalkinma.gov.tr/Lists/Yaynlar/Attachments/672/AB%20Krizinin%20Sektörel%20İhracata%20Etkisi.pdf, accessed on 30 December 2015.
42. Between 2003 and 2013, share of exports to MENA countries almost doubled from 13 to 25 per cent of all exports. http://www.tcmb.gov.tr/wps/wcm/connect/1c9fa052-7373-4738-8bc6-696af565d970/EN1305.pdf?MOD=AJPERES&CACHEID=1c9fa052-7373-4738-8bc6-696af565d970, accessed on 30 December 2015.
43. Acemoğlu and Üçer, 'The ups and downs'.
44. Ibid.

45. http://data.worldbank.org/indicator/FS.AST.DOMS.GD.ZS, accessed on 30 December 2015. The value of total outstanding credits rose from 301 billion TL to 1.4 trillion TL in the same period; http://evds.tcmb.gov.tr/, accessed on 30 December 2015.
46. http://www.wsj.com/articles/SB1000142405274870418760457628851O9 64898824, accessed on 22 June 2016.
47. The results of the 2009 local elections in certain districts in Istanbul, such as Maltepe and Sarıyer, where the ruling AKP candidates lost and were replaced by mayors from the main opposition party (CHP) were instrumental in passing this revision. The outgoing AKP mayors had announced several transformation projects in these districts, which received strong criticism and opposition from the public. The first thing that the new CHP mayors in both districts did was to cancel these projects. In response, the AKP central government transferred the authority from district to metropolitan municipalities.
48. According to this new law, the only criterion to attain metropolitan status is to have a population above 750,000 within the entire provincial boundaries, as opposed to the municipal boundaries that were specified in the last law. See Alkan, 'New metropolitan'; and Adıgüzel, '6360 sayılı'.
49. Adıgüzel, '6360 sayılı'.
50. Alkan, 'New metropolitan'.
51. The Haydarpaşa Port Project is a good example of disempowering district municipalities. Even though most of the project area lies within the jurisdiction of Kadıköy municipality, the municipality has absolutely no power over the preparation of the plans for this crucial project. All decisions have been taken at the Metropolitan Municipality level. In response, Kadıköy municipality filed several lawsuits against the project, which have so far stalled its implementation.
52. http://www.egedesonsoz.com/haber/Yerel-irade-Folkart-icin-imar-baypasina-direnecek/879617, accessed on 10 December 2015.
53. That the former head of TOKİ has been appointed as the first Minister of Urban Development and Environment is also telling. A contractor by training, he has no education in environmental matters and was severely criticised during his term at TOKİ. He was forced to resign from his post in 2013 due to allegations of his involvement in large-scale corruption, particularly related to distributing building rights to politically connected firms.
54. In the original version of the law, legal channels available to property owners who opposed Ministerial decisions were blocked. This particular clause was dropped in 2014 when the Constitutional Court deemed it unconstitutional, but the rest of the law remains.
55. Miray Özkan Eren and Özlem Özçevik, 'Institutionalisation of disaster risk discourse in reproducing urban space in Istanbul', *ITU A/Z* 12/1 (2015), pp. 221–41; and Yeşeren Eliçin, 'Neoliberal transformation of the Turkish city through the urban transformation Act', *Habitat International* 41 (2014), pp. 150–5.

56. T.C. Resmi Gazete, *Gelişmiş Arama: Bakanlar Kurulu Kararları*, http://www.resmigazete.gov.tr/default.aspx#, accessed on 13 December 2015.
57. Acemoğlu and Üçer, 'The ups and downs'; and Ayşe Buğra and Osman Savaşkan, 'Politics and class: The Turkish business environment in the neoliberal age', *New Perspectives on Turkey* 46 (2012), pp. 27–63.
58. Işık Özel, 'The politics of de-delegation: Regulatory (in)dependence in Turkey', *Regulation & Governance* 6/1 (2012), pp. 119–29.
59. Demiralp et al., 'The state of property'.
60. The share of for-profit housing built by TOKİ also increased after 2008.
61. http://www.spk.gov.tr/apps/aylikbulten/index.aspx?submenuheader=0, accessed on 20 December 2015.
62. There are currently 31 REITs registered in the Istanbul Stock Exchange Market. The total market value of Emlak GYO is a little over 9 billion TLs. The second largest REIT, Torunlar GYO, has a market value of 1.5 billion TLs.
63. Hendrik Muller, 'Turkey's December 17 process: A timeline of the graft Investigation and the government's response', *Central Asia-Caucasus Institute, Silk Road Studies Program* (2014), http://www.isdp.eu/images/stories/isdp-main-pdf/2014-muller-turkeys-december-17-process-a-timeline.pdf, accessed on 28 Mar 2016.
64. http://www.dw.com/en/erdogans-palace-declared-illegal-by-turkish-court/a-18477337, accessed on 26 September 2016.
65. http://ec.europa.eu/public_opinion/archives/eb/eb74/eb74_tr_tr_nat.pdf, accessed on 1 June 2016.
66. This was not merely due to 'traditional' internal power struggles, but at least in the case of the Republican People Party (CHP), also because its leader was discredited after an illegally obtained tape of his extramarital affair was released to the public. It is rumoured that there exist other similar tapes that can be used against other political figures.

CHAPTER 3

THE POLITICS OF AGRICULTURAL PRODUCTION IN TURKEY[1]

Huri İslamoğlu

Changes in 'the Rules of the Game' in Turkish Agriculture

This chapter addresses the specific trajectory that the global market transformation in Turkish agriculture has followed since the mid-2000s, when 'the rules of the game' radically changed in terms of who produced which crops, how much and for which markets, and who was to have access to credits and state subsidies. These changes marked the moment of the 'great global transformation' in the Turkish countryside, which spelt the simultaneous end of the peasant household economy and the birth pangs of a new economy of small entrepreneurial farmers. The new order favoured ownership of sizeable plots of land and contractual relations. Its introduction to Turkish agriculture has been a tormented process where land ownership is fragmented and not clearly defined, and where producers lack an institutional infrastructure – e.g. producer organisations, storage access, resources or capital accumulation – that will provide them leverage in contractual relations with powerful buyers and suppliers of inputs and credits in open markets.

The chapter will focus on how these changes affected the lives of producers of different crops, who were thrust into a market environment where they lost any say over production, determination of prices of their products and inputs, and found themselves at the mercy of private buyers and suppliers.

Conceptually, the chapter looks beyond state/economy and state/market binaries that dominated analyses of global market development, and focuses on institutions and rules (legislation, statutes, regulations) that were instrumental in organising different markets (for credits and inputs as well as products) and establishing the status of producers and the land in terms of its use and ownership. It highlights the political character of the rules by pointing to their specific contexts and their responsiveness to power relations in the global market economy.

By doing so, the chapter questions the universality and objectivity ascribed to market rules by the global governance bodies that introduced these rules in Turkey and elsewhere from the 1980s onwards – including the International Monetary Fund (IMF), the World Bank (WB), the World Trade Organisation (WTO) and the European Union (EU). These rules claimed immunity both from politics and from multiple societal interests that had previously occasioned state interventions in the economy in terms of price supports and protectionist trade policies. Once such interventions ceased to exist, it was expected that individuals would be free to engage in market transactions to pursue gains, which would promote growth. Instead, the chapter focuses on the relations between different actors in the market economy and addresses the politics of that economy as it examines the different rules and institutions that organise markets. To this end, the chapter asks the following questions: Who made the rules or had the power to influence the making of the rules or institutions that shaped different markets? Who governed markets and was responsible for implementing the rules, how and for whom? In this context, rules and rule-making are highly political domains; they are domains of power relations. Those who have the power to influence the making of markets, largely determine who gains and who loses in the market environment.[2]

In the present global market order, rules more often than not favoured propertied 'individuals' – including transnational corporations – at the expense of small farmers and powerless workers.[3] However, the underlying politics of inequity in the rules of governance was concealed (and justified) by claims of universality and objectivity that rooted these rules in the natural laws of the market. Rule-making and power devolved on expert bodies that claimed technical objectivity and scientific legitimacy for their practices, described by one expert as that of reading signals from natural markets.[4] More concretely, expert bodies addressed particular domains of economic activity; in agriculture, they assumed the form of expert boards (e.g. the Sugar and Tobacco Board in Turkey) responsible for determining production levels, product certification and standardisation and trade regulation. What differentiated these expert boards from earlier bureaucratic regulators was their freedom from democratic accountability, or more accurately, their lack of accountability to a broad-spectrum of interests in the national economy or society.[5] In practice, especially in the US there were close ties between transnational corporations and the members of expert bodies, who were generally drawn from corporate environments. In countries with strong state involvement in the economy – such as Turkey – members of expert bodies came from the bureaucracy and had consequences we will discuss later.

Meanwhile, although initially circumscribed by the politics of large propertied concerns, the political character of rules and institutions allowed for contingency, or the possibility of other actors to articulate their demands politically under changing conditions. The articulation of such demands led to revisions in market rules and even to institutional innovations that provided openings for less powerful actors in the market order. These institutional departures also accounted for the diversity of transformation patterns in different regional contexts, which points to the multiple political mediations of allegedly universal market rules.[6] The trajectory of market development in Turkish agriculture that is outlined here sheds light on this diversity.

Moreover, the 2007–9 financial crisis in the developed world and its consequences in developing economies revealed the fault lines in the market order, its unsustainable discrepancies in distribution of income and wealth in favour of the few[7] and unemployment at a huge scale. It led to a serious questioning of market rules and how markets are governed.[8] Simply put, these rules responded to neither the conditions nor the demands of large segments of the population, such as peasants, small farmers, workers and the middle classes. Hence, in the post-crisis era there is increasing pressure to make the rules more responsive to groups that were excluded or aggrieved; at issue is a call for a politics of the market that speaks to the concerns not only of the few but a broad spectrum interests. In consequence, the power of governance has been devolving towards central governments – or more accurately, to executive power often represented by strong leaders that rely on a popular base – with claims of adjusting global market rules to respond to specific conditions and concerns in different world regions.[9] At issue is an attempt to impart agency and therefore political accountability to governance. In that sense 'new sovereign governments' can be seen as a reaction to governance by expert bodies, which lacked broad-based political accountability and sought to justify their decisions in quantified and technical representations of 'the economy' in the abstract, while these decisions served limited large propertied interests that were often transnational in character.

Yet these 'new sovereign governments' should not be confused with earlier developmental states in the context of national economies with their distributionist priorities, which were essential to the functioning of those economies. First and foremost, 'new sovereign governments' are rooted in concerns of the present market order; given the pattern of interdependencies and the integrated character of the global economy, they represent responses to its governing crisis by claiming a measure of authority not only in the government of national economies but of global markets as well.[10] Accordingly, the distributionist policies of new sovereign governments are not a defining or a structural feature, but often represent transient or stopgap measures to address immediate grievances.

Another important point is to consider 'new sovereign governments' as actors in the global market environment; as investors, for instance (as in the case of Chinese state-owned enterprises (SOEs), or promoters of small and medium-sized enterprises (SMEs) including contractors in the construction sector). This chapter will address how market rules that were initially introduced to the Turkish agricultural sector by global governance organisations are increasingly mediated through interventions by a re-structured, invigorated central government, especially since 2008. While these interventions sought to remedy some of the dire consequences of various reforms by extending grants and services to producers, they should not to be seen as the revival of earlier developmental states and policies that aimed to sustain the peasantry, who were both responsible for food production in the national economy and also constituted the body of consumers targeted by national industries. The present centralised state simply seeks to create an entrepreneurial farming sector and fashion agriculture into an investment domain for Turkey's SMEs and foreign interests.

Finally, it is important not to equate recently created political spaces in market economies with the creation of democratic spaces, which assumes that the government takes the interests of groups other than powerful market actors into account (for instance small farmers, workers), and enables their participation in the governing process. This appears to be a weak link in the recent developments, since little progress has been made, for instance, in the establishment of producer's unions in Turkey.

Vagaries of the Great Transformation in Turkish Agriculture

The observations and insights related to the global market transformation in Turkish agriculture that are provided in this chapter derive from field research conducted between 2006 and 2008, which aimed to capture how the actual lives of farmers who produced different crops were affected by the changes in 'the rules of the game' in agriculture.[11] At the time the research was carried out, the agricultural sector was in a state of disarray, in the midst of dramatic changes that had been underway since the 1990s and accelerated in the 2000s. Stabilisation packages that the IMF and WB introduced in the aftermath of Turkey's financial meltdown in 2001 set out to cut down state expenditures, end state intervention in the economy and make way for the country's global market integration. In agriculture, the Agricultural Reform Implementation Project (ARIP) introduced by the World Bank and IMF between 2001 and 2008 was instrumental in eliminating institutions that represented state intervention, including the removal of price subsidies in products and inputs and the privatisation of state marketing and credit cooperatives. Since these institutions had formed the mainstay of peasant household production, many producers failed to survive ARIP and left agriculture for urban centres. Earlier in the 1990s, the effects of WTO membership – including export restrictions and quotas in tobacco and sugar beet production – and the EU's Customs Union were largely mediated and circumvented by a 'protectionist interregnum'[12] that followed the radical liberalisation of the economy in the 1980s after the military *coup d'état* of 1980.

Turkish agriculture's integration to the global market economy gained new momentum in 2005, when negotiations for Turkey's accession to the EU began and the government decided to carry out reforms along the lines of the EU's Common Agricultural Policy (CAP). Unlike ARIP, which had focused on eliminating institutional obstacles that stood in the way of market activity, these reforms introduced a new institutional groundwork for a market economy in agriculture. They focused on developing entrepreneurial farmers whose livelihood and income largely depended on their ability to manage assets, their productivity or ability to produce efficiently by minimising costs and adaptability to changing market conditions.[13] The main categories and concepts of the new market order in Turkish agriculture were summed up in the Agricultural Law (no. 5488) of 2006. At issue was the competitiveness of farmer entrepreneurs in global markets; gone were the days when the main concern of household producers was how much they produced, with state cooperatives buying their produce at subsidised prices and providing them with cheap inputs and credits.[14] Entrepreneurial farming that required asset management also presupposed a non-ambiguous definition of property rights especially with respect to land, a farmer's most important asset. Here, property rights refer to the delimitations on assets that individuals control or over which they have the power to decide whether or not to mobilise according to their competitive or profit maximisation concerns.[15] Market reforms made ownership of cultivated lands central to the definition of being a farmer, by making the title of ownership to cultivated plots a prerequisite for farmer registration. As such, ownership became a precondition for 'economic citizenship' in agriculture and determined farmers' ability to access credit, commodity and input markets. In the context of Turkish agriculture, where land ownership is fragmented and the boundaries of property ill-defined due to historical–societal reasons,[16] the priority attributed to individual ownership of plots proved to be problematic. In the era of market reforms, this became a primary cause for differentiation among farmers, threatening to exclude large numbers of holdings from the new market order.

The CAP's model for entrepreneurial farming primarily addressed large agribusiness enterprises that are often transnational in character. Mega agribusinesses in the EU were mostly located in the north-west – in the Netherlands, France and Germany – and the CAP represented a highly complex web of negotiations among the agribusiness enterprises and western European governments.[17] These enterprises received more than two-thirds of EU agricultural subsidies, corresponding to a sizeable portion of the EU budget, while small farmers in southern Europe received the rest of the subsidies ultimately with an eye to phasing them out.[18] This scheme assumed a blurring between urban/rural, industrial/agricultural distinctions with agricultural land increasingly allocated for use in the service sector (tourism, recreation and housing, including weekend cottages) or for industry.

The Turkish agricultural sector, made up mostly of small farmers (over 50 per cent), did not lend itself to the establishment of agribusinesses and large holdings (over 500 decares) did not prevail. Instead, contract farming by small farmers has been the favoured form of organising agricultural production, especially in cash crops (corn, sugar beets and tobacco), where merchants who bought the farmers' produce often act as intermediaries for foreign or domestic retail companies or industries. This development is in line with those in the new member states in eastern and central Europe that have a significant number of small farmers, who were conveniently left out of EU subsidy schemes in EU accession agreements as per the EU's agribusiness bias.[19] In the Turkish case, the Agricultural Law of 2006 (that embodies the main categories and principles of the CAP) emphatically pointed to the role of the Ministry of Food, Agriculture and Livestock in promoting the development and generalisation of contractual relations in agriculture. It meant shifting the responsibility for the global market integration of agriculture to the national government.

One major consequence of the market reforms in Turkish agriculture has been the acceleration of massive population movements out of agriculture[20] with agriculture's share in total employment declining from 37.6 per cent in 1999 to 23.2 per cent in 2008 and the share of agriculture in total GDP declining from 17.5 per cent to 9.2 per cent during the same period. Furthermore, large numbers of farmers that have holdings under 100 decares (accounting for half of the total number of enterprises) remain susceptible to elimination while all segments of the farming population experienced a decline in income (figuring significantly in the rather high Gini coefficient or income discrepancy rates for Turkey).[21]

From the mid-2000s onwards, however, the rural exodus lost momentum if not came to an end. An overwhelming majority of the farmers who remained in the countryside and covered by our research did not view moving to cities as a viable alternative and were desperately seeking for ways to survive in the new market economy and provide their children with an education so that they would not be dependent on agriculture for their livelihood.

Yet the dispossession of producers' lands was not widespread – due to sales to pay debts or out of necessity – despite the fact that one could speak of general impoverishment or a decline in standards of living.[22] Farmers who made the choice to remain in the countryside often belonged to the rural middle class who had some means or were younger farmers who were hopeful of gains in the market environment. The latter were heartened by increased commodity prices worldwide after 2007.

Nonetheless, a dramatic consequence of the market reforms for farmers who remained in the countryside has been increased differentiation among them in terms of income and wealth. First and foremost, making it necessary to have titles of ownership – which constituted the very core of the market reforms – was largely responsible for the differentiation between the propertied and the non-propertied, between those with access to large and small properties (often under 50 to 100 decares). It became necessary for farmers to hold a title of ownership for the lands they cultivated in order to register as farmers, which then became a precondition for membership in privatised cooperatives (suppliers of inputs and credits, as well as buyers of farmers' products), access to bank credits and eligibility for income support (abolished in 2008) as well as other income transfers.[23] Meanwhile, landowners with larger plots had access to more credits and more leverage *vis-à-vis* buyers of their produce in terms of when and whom they sold to, as well as *vis-à-vis* the suppliers of inputs. Clearly, those with holdings less than 100 decares were at a disadvantage. I will discuss the advantages and disadvantages of producers of different crops with small and large holdings in terms of their interactions with cooperatives, banks and vertically integrated enterprises both as buyers of their produce and as suppliers of inputs including credits. A central issue facing farmers in the present market environment in Turkey has been indebtedness. While indebtedness was especially acute prior to

2007, when world commodity prices were low, it continues to be a scourge for smaller farmers whose ability to access bank credits is limited given the limited collateral they are able to provide. Similarly, small farmers are often cut off from credit cooperatives: even when they possess the titles of their small plots and are eligible for cooperative membership, they often have problems in paying back loans, and cooperatives expect payment of back loans before they extend new loans. Consequently, small farmers often have to resort to usurers or buyers (e.g. processors in cotton production) who provide high-interest loans, which are then deducted from prices at harvest, leaving farmers with very little income.[24]

Lastly, the new market order spelt a loss of (democratic) political leverage for the rural population. Beginning in the 1950s until 2002, peasant household production had been a lynchpin of national economic policy under liberal right governments. Peasant production was supported through price subsidies and tariffs on imports, government policy ensured sustainable income levels to peasant households who provided food and raw materials for the national economy and were also consumers of goods produced by national industries. In turn, peasants enjoyed a great deal of political leverage, providing a reliable vote bank for liberal right political parties which saw to it that peasants maintained their privileged status.

Under the new market order, however, agricultural producers are largely excluded from the political domain; they practically have no say in decisions related to production or their livelihood. In the mid-2000s, various legislation that introduced the institutions, categories and terminology in line with the EU's CAP was passed in parliament, often without any substantial debate or consideration of how the new measures might impact producers. Moreover, urban public opinion and the media were so elated with the prospect of EU membership, the plight of farmers and problems in the agricultural sector mostly went unnoticed.[25]

From the farmers' perspective, there were serious issues about their representation in parliament under the present Political Party Law, according to which regional representatives are appointed by the party leadership and have to be neither from the regions they represent nor acquainted with issues specific to that region. Farmers also understood that the governance of agriculture – especially when it involved big players – often eluded the elected representatives. Hence, producers had little recourse but to look to governmental decisions, voting in general or local elections for the political party they gauged to be more knowledgeable in dealing with market-related issues, have more leverage in securing export markets for their goods and offer them cheap imported inputs or grants, be it in the form of cheap credits or direct payments.

Since 2008, the newly reorganised Ministry of Food, Agriculture and Livestock has turned to addressing problems in the agricultural sector, with an eye to improving production conditions and providing farmers leeway by transferring funds in the form of grants not conditional on land ownership or farm registration. These transfers have been particularly crucial in supporting animal husbandry – an activity that had practically disappeared after the market reforms had been introduced and farmers finding themselves in difficult straits, with no other options but sell all their livestock.[26]

However, for a large majority of the farmers in Turkish agriculture, survival presupposes radical changes in institutions or in the rules of the game that would give farmers access to credit, input and product markets on favourable terms and change ownership patterns or access to land, the primary resource in agriculture. These changes would imply shifts in the politics of the market environment, which presently favours major commercial buyers who supply farmers that have little clout, with credits, inputs and access to markets for their crops. Power relations between producers and buyers as well as suppliers of inputs largely determine the prices at which farmers sell their goods, the interest they pay for credit and the price of inputs. Farmers had already been on the losing end of these relations, and their situation had worsened with the widening gap between world market prices and input prices prior to 2007. Institutionally, power relations in the Turkish countryside follow the general trend in world agriculture, and focus on contract farming and property rights on land.

Recently, certain institutional changes (or changes in rules) point to a shift in the government's attitude toward agriculture that had previously been marked by almost total abandonment of the sector to CAP regulations – often adopted from poorly translated texts – and implemented in a cursory, *ad hoc* manner. That changed: there is increased attentiveness to production trends and land use and to providing farmers with access to markets; agriculture is being viewed as a possible domain for investment and a venue for export production. It remains to be seen how the 'revised' rules will affect power relations in the agricultural sector, which have so far worked to the disadvantage of small farmers who either owned no land or held titles to small plots. In this context, recent revisions to the Contract Farming Regulations are rather disappointing; the legislation actually does very little to impart leverage to farmers *vis-à-vis* buyers, except for pointing to the fact that the newly reorganised Ministry of Food, Agriculture and Livestock is in charge. This also brings to light the role of producers' unions, and the role they might play for producers to have any leverage in bringing about changes in agriculture. While these organisations are among those introduced by the Agricultural Law and are paid lip service to in the Contract Farming Regulations, they have yet to take root in the Turkish agricultural sector. Meanwhile, the 2014 Soil Protection and Land Use Law represents a serious step by the government in terms of attempting to revise former market rules, in the direction of addressing power relations in agriculture and making an effort to alter the distribution of landowners and non-landowners in agriculture. Again, how this measure will impact the lives of producers of different crops, who will win and who will lose, remains to be seen.

The shift in the government's approach also coincided with developments in the global economy. First, there has been a visible rise in world agricultural prices from about 2007 onwards and an emerging trend for niche markets in agricultural products, in particular, an increased demand for organic goods, mostly for fruits and vegetables. In Turkey, the opening of Russian markets has been a boon to farmers and became a main contributor to Turkey's exports and foreign currency reserves. At the same time, global unemployment has been on the rise, as a result of which production by small farms alongside large agribusiness enterprises was promoted in global economic policy circles as a way to provide rural employment and halt rural-to-urban migration.[27] Finally, following the 2007–9 crisis in developed economies, governments in emerging economies began to assume more responsibility for governing the world economy.[28] What this means or will mean from the perspective of agricultural producers, will largely depend on their political access – be it through their political organisations or by putting pressure on governments to change political institutions which would provide them with more say in the making of agricultural policy.

The remainder of this article will focus on two fundamental institutions: the rules of contract farming that govern all transactions between farmers, their buyers, and suppliers of their inputs, and the title of ownership in agriculture that forms the basis for farmer registration and makes participation in agricultural activity incumbent on the amount of land owned. The next two sections include detailed discussions on contract farming, its rules and its practice in the context of different crops and on recent attempts to change land holding or ownership patterns in Turkish agriculture. These institutions have been responsible for the plight of farmers in rural Turkey as agriculture opens to global markets, and will largely shape their fate in the future.

The Rules and Politics of Contract Farming

In the global market economy, contract farming is the predominant means for producers to integrate into the market; especially the producers of industrial crops such as corn, tobacco, cotton, canola and fruit, and vegetables, as well as organic goods.[29] Contractual farming is the bottom rung in the commodity chain that brings produce from the field to the table. Contractual relations did previously exist in Turkish agriculture, but between producers and state cooperatives and factories that bought producers' crops and supplied inputs.[30] Since the 2000s, however, written commercial contracts became an essential feature of agricultural economy, regulating relationships among private or market actors; most importantly and very often, between contract farmers and vertically integrated companies that operate through merchants or agents.

Regulations for contract farming were issued in 2008 following the enactment of the Agricultural Law of 2006, which introduced CAP categories to Turkish agriculture. First, the fact that the rules to regulate contract farming were embodied in a regulation rather than a law meant they were not formulated through the legislative process and subjected to political scrutiny; instead, their formulation was the responsibility of the regulator, a role ascribed to the Ministry of Food Agriculture and Livestock in 2014.[31] Consequently, the regulator enjoyed a certain latitude in making changes to the regulations without having to go through an often lengthy legislative process. Second, because farming contracts were not featured in a law, they did not belong to any legal category of contracts; they were 'unnamed contracts', which also gave the regulator the freedom to pick and choose features from different types of contracts.[32] In addition, unlike regular sales contracts, farming contracts dealt with future sales before the harvest or before the good came into existence, and thus were addressed in Article 19 of the Law of Obligations. Article 19 concerned the 'freedom of transactions' and stated that transacting parties were free to determine the terms of the contract, albeit within limits defined by the law. Once again, the law allowed for some flexibility that provided space for negotiation, but in practice, this benefitted the party with leverage, and in Turkish agriculture – where farmer organisations such as producer's unions, prescribed by the Agricultural Law, were not developed – that leverage largely rested with buyers.

The Contract Farming Regulation of 2008[33] and its revised version in 2014 defined farming contract as one between producers and buyers, based on their mutual interests. Yet both versions seemed to tilt the balance of advantage in favour of buyers. Producers assumed the financial risks of production, for instance, and were liable for delivering crops on time as well as for any damages to the crop due to diseases (2008 Regulations, Article 5, Clause 4b), while any liabilities caused by natural disasters became subject to negotiation between producers and sellers.

Both the 2008 and 2014 Regulations emphasised that contracts be written, unlike the oral contracts of the pre-reform era. Written contracts are generally favoured by buyers of industrial crops; in the case of exported canola, for instance, contracts are very detailed and allow buyer companies to have strict control over the production process. Similarly, comprehensive and detailed contracts are also the norm in the production of organic fruits and vegetables when major retail companies (foreign or domestic) are involved or when production is geared to export markets; to Russia, for instance.[34]

With the privatisation of credit and input cooperatives in Turkish agriculture, contract farming became a last resort for small farmers who either had no land or had titles to very small plots. These farmers were often barred from joining privatised cooperatives that required their members were registered farmers and could not access credits from private banks, which required collateral in real property, often in the form of both cultivable fields and urban property. Following the withdrawal of state funds, privatised cooperatives strove to sustain themselves by contributions from their members, and to that end, demanded on-time delivery of the produce the farmer had committed to sell and set aside a share as membership contribution. They also demanded on-time payment of debts; failing to pay one year meant that the farmer was not eligible for credit payments the following year. Finally, the fact that small farmers were excluded from membership to privatised cooperatives with strict requirements meant that they faced the prospect of having to sell their produce at harvest at lower prices, because cooperatives provided storage for any surplus crop that exceeded the amount the farmer had initially committed to sell to the cooperative.

In contrast, merchant buyers in contract farming arrangements were far more lax in their demands from producers than were the cooperatives. The 2008 Regulations had made being registered as a farmer a necessary condition to enter into a contractual relationship (Article 5(2)). This stipulation was often violated by both producers and buyers, and thus was changed in the 2014 version of the Regulations so that possession of a rent contract was sufficient to enter a contractual relation. The 2014 Regulations included further changes to make contract farming more inclusive of poorer farmers; for instance, making it optional for producers to insure their crops (a cost item that was an obligation in the 2008 version). In addition, broadening the scope of the contract to include rental contracts made contract farming an attractive alternative for larger producers who grew most of their crops on rented lands.[35]

From the perspective of poor contract farmers, buyers in contractual relationships were unlike privatised cooperatives in that they neither extracted a part of the produce as membership fees nor punished the sellers by withholding credit payments the following year if they defaulted on their debts (incurred for purchase of inputs, seeds, etc.). Buyers or merchants simply deducted all liabilities incurred by the producers from the final price of the crop.[36] Moreover, buyers and merchants did not provide storage facilities for producers, as a result of which prices offered to farmers immediately after the harvest were lower than what they could get for their produce if they waited and sold their goods later in the season when prices rose. Consequently, exclusion from cooperative membership and contractual relations with commercial actors in open markets were factors that contributed to the differentiation among farmers, especially between those who held titles to large plots and small farmers who had limited or no access to land titles. I will return to this point below, in relation to a discussion of a tendency towards the proletarisation of contract farmers.

The differentiation among agricultural producers also had to do with the nature of contracts, with the specific nature of the contractual relationship between producers and buyers for different crops. The study of individual contracts shows that the amount of leverage producers had was an important variable in determining whether contract farmers became victims of the contract farming system and transformed into waged slaves, or managed to maintain the status of independent farmers.

In the case of tobacco production in Turkey, for instance – another export crop – with production dwindling to a fraction of what it had been prior to passage of the Tobacco Law (2001)[37] and the introduction of the market reforms, written contracts only stated the type of tobacco to be cultivated (with the buyer supplying the seed)[38] and the amount to be delivered by the producer; signed by the producer, the contract specified neither the price nor how it would be calculated (as per the Regulations). In addition, there was no indication of who the buyer would be (who were, for the most part, merchants buying for large foreign companies) or a delivery date, since it was assumed that farmers would be desperate to sell their perishable goods immediately after the harvest at whatever price the merchant offered because they no longer enjoyed a guaranteed buyer in the form of the State Monopoly (Tekel) that had also provided them with storage opportunities.

In contrast, detailed written contracts prevailed in the case of sunflower seeds, a crop produced for both domestic and foreign markets (especially in Adana). Unlike tobacco producers who cultivated very small plots of land – most of which were rented – producers of sunflower seeds held titles to relatively large plots and thus joined cooperatives (Trakya Birlik, for instance). This enabled them to choose between merchants and cooperatives as buyers and provided them leverage in the buyers' market. A similar argument can be made for farmers who grew corn for the corn starch industry with buyers such as the transnational giant Cargill and its corn starch factory in Adapazari, and the privatised cooperative Pankobirlik that served both corn and beet producers, the produce of which was subject to quotas and producers encouraged to shift to corn production.[39] Industrial corn production is encouraged through government grants whereby producers expand their plots with new purchases of land.

Finally, in the case of cotton – an industrial crop where producers were caught in the grip of cotton processors – most contracts were oral contracts, often based on long-standing relationships between producers and processers who bought the cotton crop. The relationship between them was generally a patriarchal one, where processors supplied the seeds for producers and bought their crop at the time of harvest, not giving them a chance to sell later in the season when prices would be higher.

Furthermore, prior to 2007, cotton farmers had to contend with low prices in world markets. This resulted in a crisis of debt; many cotton farmers were barely able to pay off their bank debts after the harvest, and had little choice but to resort to usurers to purchase fertilisers and pesticides for the following year.[40]

Contract Farming: The Route to Proletarisation?

In the present global economy, contract farming assumes, above all, an environment of vertically integrated enterprises where contract farmers are the price-takers who assume the financial risks while buyers or the integrated enterprises dictate the character of the production process including the type and extent of inputs used, with contracts that offer producers little protection and can be terminated with only a few days' notice.[41] At issue here is the matter of reducing farmers to the status of low-wage employees: their proletarisation. Put differently, the primary question here is whether contract producers are independent farmers or employees.

One finding of our research in the Turkish countryside between 2006 and 2008 was that farmers were not categorically opposed to contract farming. At a time when the state withdrew its price supports and cooperatives from agriculture and privatisation was underway, contract farming provided them with markets for their produce, supplied them with inputs (seeds, fertilisers) and even credit, albeit often on unfavourable terms. This was especially true for small farmers, who comprised around 50 per cent of all producers who possessed titles to very small plots[42] and were eligible to register as farmers – and therefore to join a cooperative – but lacked the means to meet the stiff requirements of privatised cooperatives with regards to debt payment and membership fees. Clearly, the new system favoured farmers who not only held titles to their plots, but had relatively large plots that could serve as collateral to counter financial risks they were expected to take in the production process. Hence, it is not surprising that farmers were asked for titles of their flats in the city as well as for land titles when they tried to secure credit from private banks.

This is why farmers rejected the underlying politics of contract farming in a particular context of global economic development, and not contract farming itself. So, what had been the global context before and how did it change from 2007 onwards?

The Agricultural Reform Implementation Project (ARIP) of the World Bank and the IMF that was in effect in Turkey between 2001 and 2008 spoke to that context; to 'the rules of the larger game of global markets'. Dramatic reductions in agriculture's share in total employment followed ARIP applications, discussed earlier. Beginning in 2005 when the Turkish government started accession negotiations with the EU, agricultural policies adopted the guidelines of the EU's Common Agricultural Policy (CAP). The 2006 Agricultural Law, fashioned in the EU context, became the primary vehicle for introducing the institutional categories of the global economy. As mentioned earlier, the CAP and its institutions emerged out of the political struggles that pointed to the dominant positions of major corporate interests in agriculture and operated in a system of contract farming that consisted of vertically integrated enterprises (in industry as well as retail trade) and contract farmers. It also assumed the elimination of large numbers of peasant producers; those who remained in agriculture were engaged in contract farming and organised in producer's unions, rooted in a long history of farmers' unions in France and elsewhere. Meanwhile, in the EU, historical struggles and the 'recent retiring of smaller farmers' resulted in patterns of land tenure characterised by individually owned plots with a certain viability in the market environment.[43] Hence, there has been a tendency towards creating a 'professional' class of farmers or producers that operate in commodity chains with mega transnational commercial and manufacturing companies, fashion production and products according to their technical specifications for global certification and presuppose a flow of technical knowledge from expert governance boards to farmers. All the while, however, there was a steady stream of EU subsidies to farmers and agribusinesses.

According to Turkish farmers, the agricultural policy in the 2000s – fashioned after the CAP – was simply alien; it took neither their needs nor their conditions into account; it belonged to the EU.[44] Moreover, the government itself did not seem very invested in it, as indicated by the rather haphazard implementation of the passed legislation. First, there was the almost total disempowerment of producers and the rising political discontent; simply put, once state subsidies were removed and cooperatives were privatised, producers were abandoned to the mercy of the markets – and mechanisms that would enable farmers to survive in the market environment were unavailable. There were neither producers' unions for which there was no historical precedent nor any institutional channels through which 'market knowledge' could be transmitted to those who either produced or aspired to produce for global markets. In this regard, although provincial agricultural agencies (*İl ve İlçe Tarım Birlikleri*) had apparently been established with significant EU funding, their work seemed limited to providing research funds to local universities, and their services did not seem to reach farmers in any significant way (as evidenced through our extensive field visits). In addition, direct income supports benefitted not the majority of farmers but those who owned large pieces of land. Moreover, yearly cash-payments made to producers of industrial crops were only helpful if producers were doing well and not much help to those who were in dire straits due to low world prices, as had been the case with cotton producers prior to 2007.

From the perspective of contract farming, it appears that before world agricultural prices increased in 2007 and 2008, the tendency to transform farmers into employees, if not 'coerced cash crop labourers', was already underway.

Problems in the governance of agriculture further reinforced such concerns. That governance was initially entrusted to boards (such as the Sugar and Tobacco Boards) responsible for setting prices of individual crops and controlling production amounts; boards also had a say in the nature of the contracts and the parties involved.[45] Put simply, they were responsible for organising the production processes of different crops and ensuring that these processes met the requirements of buyers in the global economy; most notably the big players like Cargill in sugar beet and corn production and certain major tobacco companies.[46]

By the mid-2000s, governance boards had proven to be useless if not entirely inefficient and irrelevant; the central government began to take charge of agricultural policy – as indicated by the formation of the Ministry of Food, Agriculture and Livestock in place of the Ministry of Agriculture and Village Affairs. The new ministry clearly did not view agriculture from the perspective of villages or village households and their activities; instead, policy focused on individual producers and production, land productivity related to land use (e.g. fragmentation) and competitiveness in domestic and global markets with an eye to ensuring food production and safety. As a result, while policy did not shift away from the CAP's market development perspective, market governance increasingly shifted towards the centre and away from the so-called technical boards that had little political accountability.

The shift in agricultural governance toward the central government was in line with the global debate and questioning of the governance of markets in advanced western economies, especially the EU, in the aftermath of the 2007–9 crisis. In the EU, central to this debate had been the democratic deficit of governance institutions, their unresponsiveness in the face of rising unemployment especially in southern European countries and their intransigence in enforcing austerity programmes which meant severe cuts in public services, including public education and health. At the same time, China was experiencing a slow-down in growth largely due to the crisis in major export markets in advanced countries, and the focus of economic policy turned inwards to emphasise domestic investments, accompanied by the centralisation of the governance of the market economy under Xi Jinping.

What were the implications of the shift to the centre in governance of the market economy in terms of agricultural policy? In closing, I will explore these implications in relation to contract farming and land ownership, both institutions pivotal to the market economy in agriculture.

Contract Farming: Possibilities for the Making of Independent Farmer Entrepreneurs?

The shift in agricultural policy away from the complacency that characterised the period when ARIP and the CAP institutional model were implemented came about through the convergence of a number of factors. In addition to the questioning of global governance institutions following the financial crisis of 2007–9, increases in world agricultural prices from 2007 onwards was a game changer. The latter was celebrated in the World Bank's 2008 Development Report and pointed to the central role small farmer entrepreneurs play in agriculture. In Turkish agriculture, the rising world commodity prices and opening of job opportunities in agriculture occasioned a return to agriculture that began in 2007 and continued for the next four years.[47]

On the policy side, The Ministry of Food, Agriculture and Livestock paid close attention to production trends during this period, including the introduction of a production map for different regions in Turkey (2009), followed by channelling a plethora of grants to producers of different goods – most significantly livestock.[48]

A crucial policy thrust was the valorisation of land, making it an attractive investment vehicle and stimulating the market for farmland. Our field work in 2006–8 indicated that given limited investments in irrigation, land was generally cheap, which accounted for high levels of land leases. On the demand side, the land market was limited because farmers whose lands were 50 decares or less – making up nearly half of all holdings – had low levels of income. Conversely, land purchases increased as the size of holdings increased, most significantly for holdings between 101 and 500 decares, with owners of holdings over 500 decares purchasing and leasing land equally. In ascendant crops such as corn, where producers were ensured a place in the commodity chain (headed by Cargill) and cash payments by the government made production attractive, land purchases were high for holdings between 101 and 500 decares. Another factor which made land purchases attractive for corn producers was that corn production required better quality land, which was expensive and made leasing land a poor option.[49]

From the perspective of contract farming, one might say that policy could respond in one of two available options: it could weigh on the side of commodity chains and tilt in the direction of enslaving producers and turning them into mere 'employees' with limited claims; the 2014 version of the Contract Farming Regulations seemed to point in this direction. Yet the Soil Protection and Land Use Law of 2014[50] sounded another tune; it appeared to be a step in the direction of empowering contract farmers as a class of 'owners' that had leverage *vis-à-vis* the vertically integrated enterprises.

Most significantly, the Land Law addressed land fragmentation, which largely accounts for the predominance of holdings that are 50 decares or less in Turkish agriculture, where average plot size is 5.9 hectares compared to 52.1 hectares in France, 45.7 in Germany, 53.8 in Great Britain. Through this law, the Ministry assumed responsibility for establishing the minimum size of holdings in different regions by taking land productivity, climate characteristics and irrigation availability into account. The law then proceeded to affect changes in the Inheritance Law, to make it possible to concentrate shares in the hands of a single heir. Similarly, forming limited liability companies by multiple shareholders is another way to concentrate ownership, which the Law offers to prevent land fragmentation.

Indeed, the Law addresses a central issue in agricultural production in the global economy; namely that size matters not so much for economies of scale, but for imparting farmers the ability to effectively engage in the market environment by providing them leverage *vis-à-vis* buyers, be it vertically integrated enterprises or cooperatives. After the market reforms in Turkish agriculture until 2014, titles of ownership – a requirement for farmer registration – became a precondition for contract farmers to engage in the market environment, including access to cooperatives and bank credits, literally throwing those without titles to land to the sharks in that environment. Notwithstanding the discrepancies in official figures provided by TUIK (the Turkish Statistical Institute), findings of our fieldwork indicated that about 46 per cent of producers held the titles to the plots they cultivated.

While a greater percentage of producers who cultivated small plots (between 0-to-50 and 50-to-100 decares) had titles to their plots, 70 per cent and 48 per cent, respectively, a smaller percentage who cultivated larger plots (between 100-to-500 decares and over 500 decares) had titles to their plots, 30 per cent and 29 per cent, respectively. Yet because producers who owned large holdings – over 100 decares – cultivated more land, they were at a greater advantage in terms of access to cooperatives, banks and direct income supports.[51] Here, producers who cultivated lands 100 decares and less appear to have been the least advantaged under the current system – and they made up some 56 per cent of the producers. They seem to be a target of land fragmentation addressed by the Law.[52]

However, the matter of whether the law and other measures will be sufficient to include this group in the category of independent contractors in the present context of market relations in Turkish agriculture, remains to be seen.

One point that needs to be remembered is that 44 per cent of farmers cultivate holdings over 100 decares, and they are the ones most actively engaged in the market environment, as indicated by their high levels of borrowing from credit cooperatives and banks.[53] This group of farmers also leased land the most, further pointing to the intensity of their activities. They were mainly involved in growing wheat, sunflower seeds and recently corn, and candidates to become powerful independent farmers or engage as contract farmers with vertically integrated enterprises, national or local. The question remains whether governance measures from a strong centre that aim to empower smaller farmers via institutional interventions – such as the Land Law – will succeed in including them in the enchanted sphere enjoyed by independent farmers/entrepreneurs and contractors.

Notes

1. This chapter was written during my fellowship at the Institute for Advanced Studies at Tsinghua University in Beijing, China. I am grateful to Professor Wang Hui, the Director, for inviting me to the Institute and to him and Professor Zhuyian Cui for the intellectual stimulation, and for their warm friendship and hospitality during my stay at the Institute. My deepest gratitude and thanks goes to all my friends at the Institute, to Zhang Jing, Yipei Shen, Liu Jing, Win Xin and Xian Xin for the warm welcome they extended to me and for being a true family to me. Huanna Deng was involved in the initial phases of the writing of this article, which owes a great deal to her meticulous reading and editing.
2. Robert Reich, a Berkeley economist and former Secretary of Labor in the Clinton Administration, argued in a recent book called *Saving Capitalism: For the Many, not the Few* (New York, 2015) that in the present global market environment, the power that transnational corporations and financial institutions exert in the making of market rules largely accounts for unsustainable income and wealth discrepancies, resulting in wealth and income to be concentrated in a very few hands – the popular figure is 1 per cent – while the rest struggles to cope with unemployment, dislocation and poverty.
3. As developments that followed the American occupation of Iraq indicated, often at the expense of societies concerned. Ugo Mattei and Laura Nader, *Plunder: When the Rule of Law is Illegal* (Oxford, 2008).

4. Robert Rubin, one-time Treasury Secretary who was subsequently employed by Goldman & Sachs, when questioned about the responsibility of financial experts in charge of the regulation of financial markets in the 2007–9 crisis, said that the experts were simply reading signals from markets. *Inside Job* (2010), documentary film.
5. Fritz Scharf, *Governing in Europe: Effective and Democratic?* (Oxford, 1999).
6. Conception of rules as domains of power relations should not suggest that social reality is an exact reflection of these relations and the resulting domination of one group over others. These power relations and domination undergo multiple mediations through politics and social reality is ultimately a product of such mediations. As a result no given domination is total, invariably providing possibilities for political openings for different groups to explore.
7. Thomas Piketty, *Capital in the Twenty-First Century* (Cambridge, MA, 2014).
8. Reich, *Saving Capitalism*.
9. Recent discussions at the Chinese National People's Congress represented painstaking efforts to reconcile the concerns of Chinese capital holders – including state-owned enterprises (SOEs) and private businesses in the global economy, and their global investments – with the concerns of workers and peasants in the domestic economy who are facing unemployment and low incomes.
10. Huri İslamoğlu, 'New politics of governing global capitalism: Sovereign governments and living law', *Society and Economy* 38/4 (2016), pp. 497–512.
11. The field study, funded by the Scientific and Technological Research Council of Turkey (TUBITAK), focused on a detailed study of seven crops – cotton, wheat, corn, sugar beet, grapes, tobacco and sun flower seeds – and was based on in-depth interviews with farmers (100 farmers per crop), merchants, administrators in privatised credit and marketing cooperatives, bank officials in charge of extending credits to farmers, members of expert or regulatory boards (for example, Sugar and Tobacco Boards) and officials at the Ministry of Food, Agriculture and Animal Husbandry. The results of the research are summed up in a 650-page report that can be accessed at TUBITAK's website Huricihan İslamoğlu, Alp Yücel Kaya, Elvan Gülöksüz, Derya Nizam, Ayse Çavdar, Ulaş Karakoç and Göksun Yazıcı, *Türkiye'de Tarımda Dönüşüm ve Küresel Piyasalarla Bütünleşme Süreçleri {Agricultural Transformation in Turkey and the Integration Process with Global Markets}*, No. 106K137, 2008. Hereafter: *Report*.
12. A large number of farmers interviewed for the project referred to this 'interregnum' period as the 'Golden Age in Agriculture', when a liberal right government came to power thanks to its electoral base among the peasantry (at a time when peasant households corresponded to nearly half of total employment) and showered agriculture with subsidies and cheap credits (*Report*, pp. 1–93).
13. On a concept of New Agriculture that highlights the significance of contract farming and 'contract entrepreneurs', see Jeffrey Lawrence D'Silva, Bahaman

Aby Samah, Jegak Uli and Hayrol Azril Mohamed Shaffril, 'Towards developing a framework on acceptance of sustainable agriculture among contract farming entrepreneurs', *African Journal of Business Management* 5/20 (2011), pp. 8110–16.

14. In the conception of the new market economy, production played second fiddle to trade, producers were invisible lest such visibility – be it in the form of demands for better prices for products, for better pay, etc. – hindered the free flow of commodities globally. In the new institutionalist perspective that dominated the thinking about global market transformation, any organised intervention on the part of labourers or producers for betterment of work conditions or better pay constituted transaction costs that had negative effects on exchange and therefore on profits, and was to be shunned. D.N. Douglas North, *Institutions, Institutional Change and Economic Performance* (Cambridge, 1990). Full automation or fully exploitable labour would be the ideal solution for production schemes in free market environments.
15. Armen A. Alchian and Harold Demsetz, 'The property right paradigm', *Journal of Economic History* 33 (1973), pp. 16–27.
16. Huri İslamoğlu, 'Property as Contested Domain: A re-evaluation of the Land Code of 1858', in R. Owen (ed.), *New Perspectives in Property and Land in the Middle East* (Cambridge, MA, 2000). When individual land ownership was introduced in the nineteenth century (under the 1858 Land Code), Ottoman jurists who drafted the Code saw to it that certain restraints were placed on land alienability, lest unrestrained alienability lead to peasant dispossession and rural unrest. In France, the introduction of individual or private land ownership had resulted in such unsettling consequences, which the Ottoman government sought to avoid.
17. It was largely inspired by the advent of American notions of economies of scale in the post-World War II era, related to the production of food and raw materials and food security that rested on the mass production of cheap food. Vaughan Higgins and Geoffrey Lawrence, *Agricultural Governance: Globalisation and New Politics of Regulation* (London, 2005).
18. Marjoleine Hennis, *Globalisation and European Integration: Changing Role of Farmers in the Common Agricultural Policy* (Boulder, CO, 2005).
19. Contract farming in Romania involves farmers committing to supplying agricultural products of a certain type, at a specific time and price, and in specific quantities to a known buyer according to advance contracts. D'Silva et al., 'Towards developing'.
20. The rural-to-urban migration trend in Turkey dates back to the 1960s and 1970s and was largely set in motion by the mechanisation of agriculture and the opening of job opportunities in urban areas as a result of industrialisation. One might say that in the context of the market reforms, this trend has been accelerating from the early 2000s onwards.
21. Feride İnan, 'Civil G20 Turkey Report', originally in *Civil 20 Proposals for Strong Sustainable, Balanced and Inclusive Growth* (Moscow, 2013); and Fikret Şenses,

Küreselleşmenin Öteki Yüzü Yoksulluk: Kavramlar, nedenler, politikalar ve temel eğilimler {The Other Side of Globalisation is Poverty: Concepts, Reasons, Policies and the Main Tendencies} (İstanbul, 2006).

22. Land prices and the demand for land was low except for regions where sunflower seeds and corn were grown; in these regions, the land market was very lively.
23. A title of ownership was also a precondition for accessing income subsidies (subsequently abolished in 2006) that benefitted owners with titles to large plots, either as producers themselves or as landlords renting out their land. Large landowners often submitted fake documents attesting to income acquired from sales of produce in order to collect income subsidies. This practice was widespread in the Adıyaman region in Eastern Anatolia.
24. For cotton farmers compelled to borrow from usurers in Söke, Aydın, see note 39.
25. For the urban elite, membership represented admission to the civilized world, despite the fact that the EU was a market project that demanded sacrifices from large parts of the population, including farmers who bore the brunt of the reforms. So distanced from the farmer's world was the media that when I was interviewed for the TUBITAK project, the journalist who conducted the interview could not help but express his surprise that I devoted time to agriculture; had agriculture not disappeared? Another asked if I had peasant ancestors to be so interested in them. Only after the Soma disaster in 2014, which was closely related to impoverishment that resulted from the crisis in agriculture brought about by market reforms and compelled young men to take up work in the mines under the worst conditions, did the issue gain public interest once more.
26. For the difficulties in raising livestock by producers of all crops studied in the *Report*, pp. 70–5.
27. *World Development Report 2008: Agriculture and Development* (Washington DC, 2007).
28. For a discussion on the new sovereign governments in emerging economies in the aftermath of the 2007–9 crisis in developed economies, and the view that the crisis was essentially due to problems in the governance of the global economy – where governing expert bodies had little public accountability and only answered to transnational corporations, and thus were largely responsible for the unsustainable income levels and wealth disparities revealed by the crisis – see İslamoğlu, 'New Sovereign Governments'.
29. There is an upward trend in contract farming, especially in the production of tomatoes and peas in western Anatolia, with the share of contract farming in market transactions at 75 per cent compared to 25 per cent of spot buying. Sait Engindeniz, 'Economic analysis of processing tomato growing: The case study of Torbali, West Turkey', *Spanish Journal of Agricultural Research* 5/1 (2007), pp. 7–15; and Erkan Rehber, 'Vertical integration in the food industry and contract farming: The case of Turkey', *Outlook on Agriculture* 33/2 (2004), pp. 85–91.

30. For instance, contracts were important in regulating transactions between sugar beet producers and state sugar factories; between producers of sunflower seeds and state cooperatives. Oral contacts were also common in commercial transactions among individuals. At issue here is the making explicit of contractual relations and their exclusively commercial character.
31. This, coupled with the existing system of party politics that made it possible to appoint representatives from non-farm areas to farm areas, gave farmers little chance to be heard by the central government other than voting for the ruling party that the Ministry was attached to and hoping that the Minister had good intentions on regarding conditions of contract farms.
32. I am grateful to Mustafa Kadıoğlu for an excellent legal analysis of farming contracts compared to other types of contracts and for an insightful reading of the Contract Farming Regulations. Mustafa Kadıoğlu, 'Tarımsal üretim sözleşmeleri: İsimsiz sözleşmeler [Contract Farming: Unnamed Contracts]', presentation for Law and Economics Program at Istanbul Bilgi University, Istanbul, Spring Term, 2008.
33. 2008 represented a fully developed form of the earlier 2006 Regulations as prescribed by the Agricultural Law of the same year.
34. Zerrin Kenanoğlu, 'Production and marketing of organic raisin in Turkey', in A. Nikolaidis, G. Baourakis, E. Işıklı and M. Yercan (eds), *The Market for Organic Products in the Mediterranean Region* (Chania, 2003).
35. Rental activity among producers who had over 100 decares of land may also indicate the intensity of engagement in economic activity; producers in this category indeed showed high levels of renting land as a way of expanding production.
36. Often, cooperatives set the prices to which merchants had to conform.
37. Huricihan İslamoğlu, 'Yeni düzenlemeler ve ekonomi politik: IMF kaynaklı kurumsal reformlar ve tütün yasası [Political Economy of New Regulations: Tobacco Law and IMF-based Market Reform Package]', *Birikim Dergisi* 158 (2002), pp. 20–7.
38. The type of tobacco grown by fewer and fewer farmers in Tokat, Bafra and Akhisar was of a variety of oriental tobacco called '*Yunan*'. On production of 'Oriental Tobacco' in Turkey, S. Güler Gümüş 'Economic analysis of Oriental Tobacco in Turkey', *Bulgarian Journal of Agricultural Science* 14/5 (2008), pp. 470–5; on contract farming in tobacco production, O. Murat Koctürk and A. Nuray Cebeci, 'Contracting tobacco growing in Turkey', *Journal of Agriculture and Rural Development in the Tropics and Sub-Tropics* 106/2 (2005), pp. 167–76.
39. While Pankobirlik was formerly a cooperative for sugar beet producers where sugar beet production was subject to quotas, efforts led by Cargill to replace beet-based sugar with corn-based sugar caused Pankobirlik to extend its activities to include corn production. *Report*, pp. 249–68; 365–86.
40. The tragedy of cotton producers in Söke, Aydın. *Report*, pp. 311–64. The usurers in Söke were often Kurds who were settled in the region following

the war against the Kurdish PKK in 1990s and had accumulated cash through their engagement in entertainment business in tourist sites in Kuşadası and Didim. This practice largely accounted for the strong anti-Kurdish sentiment we have observed throughout Söke during our field-work.

41. Glenn A. Hegar, Jr. 'Adhesion contracts, debt, low returns and frustration – Can America's independent contract farmer overcome the odds?' *Hamline Law Review* 22 (1998–9), pp. 213–57.
42. Seventy per cent of the farmers who cultivated lands between 0 to 50 decares had titles of land. The larger the plot, the more important land titles and rent relations become. Smaller holdings are leased less and larger ones are leased more.
43. In contrast, in Anatolia where the land to labour ratio is high, renting allowed more flexibility in volatile economic environments and was favoured over acquiring large plots.
44. In many of the villages we visited, farmers who were asked what they thought about policies in agriculture simply said 'it was not theirs but belonged to the EU'. For instance, in a village in Akhisar, Manisa, farmers also blamed the government for not being their government but that of the EU. With jobs in agriculture dwindling in the region after the sharp decline in tobacco cultivation, these farmers were hard-pressed to find employment for their children and blamed the government for giving away jobs at a nearby NATO installation to Kurds under pressure from the EU. One destination for the unemployed in the formerly tobacco-producing areas of Akhisar has been the Soma mines, privately run with little concern for security and with little government supervision, resulting in the 2014 disaster that killed hundreds of miners.
45. On the regulatory board for tobacco production, Ebru Kayaalp, 'Torn in translation: An ethnographic study of regulatory decision-making in Turkey', *Regulation & Governance* 6 (2012), pp. 225–41.
46. The failure of this top-down control is evidenced in shortages in sugar beet supply in local factories – for example, in Adapazarı.
47. Seyfettin Gürsel and Zümrüt İmamoğlu, 'Why is agricultural employment increasing in Turkey?', *Bahçeşehir University Center for Economic and Social Research (Betam)*.
48. *Report*.
49. Ibid., p. 52.
50. 'Toprak Koruma ve Arazi Kullanımı Yasası' [Soil Protection and Land Use Law], numbered 6537, was published in *Resmi Gazete* (Official Gazette), No. 29001.
51. *Report*, p. 24. In addition, the largest producers with over 500 decares of land leased the most land as well. Of the smallest producers, who cultivated plots smaller than 50 decares, those who did not hold titles were less than 10 per cent, while farmers who cultivated lands between 50 and 100 decares had titles only for about 20 per cent of the land they cultivated.

52. *Report*, p. 52. Land purchases are limited, but only show an increase among those who hold between 100 and 500 decares; owners of holdings greater than 500 decares prefer to lease lands.
53. Interestingly enough, owners of holdings of 500 decares and over seem to conduct their financial transactions exclusively with banks, suggesting that their investments are not limited to agriculture alone. That banks also ask for urban real estate properties as collateral underlines an expectation that owners of larger agricultural lands will have urban connections.

CHAPTER 4

THE 'POLITICS OF SERVING' AND NEOLIBERAL DEVELOPMENTALISM: THE MEGAPROJECTS OF THE AKP AS TOOLS OF HEGEMONY BUILDING

Hande Paker

Introduction

State-society relations have been highly strained in Turkey recently, amidst the backlash against liberal freedoms and rights, the end of the peace process carried out with the Kurds and debates over regime change in an extremely polarised setting. This chapter revisits state-society relations during the Justice and Development Party (*Adalet ve Kalkınma Partisi* – AKP) government in power since 2002, in a context where the future of democracy seems to be at stake. Political polarisation and the imposition of top-down state policies have crystallised especially in relation to ecological issues. Priorities concerning energy and neoliberal economic growth have led to unprecedented ecological demise as the state embarked on or assigned construction investments to the private sector energy in the form of hydroelectric, thermal and nuclear power plants as well as urban renewal and mining projects, and megaprojects.

They have also generated contention, as people in Turkey lost their homes, livelihoods, 'way of life', ecological diversity, archaeological heritage and environmental commons. In this context, the chapter focuses on megaprojects, which have been paraded by the government as infrastructural services, and argues that they have become tools of hegemony building that marginalise contestations over them. It investigates how the construction of megaprojects is linked to state power. These megaprojects are used to generate consent through a powerful developmentalist discourse, building on the four axes analysed below. Yet they also generate discontent and exclusion, reinforcing a polarised political context in Turkey and weakening the state's capacity to govern.

Skocpol defines state capacity as the ability of the state to implement goals.[1] State capacity, in turn, is linked to the state's infrastructural power. The capacity to build projects such as megaprojects has been considered an indication of infrastructural power. Infrastructural power refers to the institutional capacity of a state to coordinate (as well as control) a wider net of social relations and logistically implement decisions.[2] Infrastructural power is understood as interactional, where society's capacity to check the state also increases by strengthening representation and democratic control. In the case of Turkey, however, I argue that the state uses infrastructural power to build its authoritarian power, which reinforces undemocratic and exclusionary dynamics between state and society. Far from integrating various groups in society, the state elite uses infrastructural power to cater to its political base.[3] It creates consent but it is not absolute: it also generates discontent, exclusion and displacement, a process epitomised by the megaprojects. This discontent is expressed in many ecological and urban conflicts in relation to energy and construction projects. However, mobilisation and participation in these struggles is limited, which points to the success of the AKP's hegemony building on the one hand, while on the other, the fact that the hegemonic developmentalist discourse is contested signals the AKP's incapacity to integrate different social groups.

Additionally, these infrastructural projects are part of a neoliberal growth agenda pursued by the state. It has been shown that neoliberalisation requires substantial state intervention, and as such, cannot be analysed in isolation from state power. The link between state capacity and neoliberalisation has already been made in the case of megaprojects.[4] The megaprojects have in fact become tools of hegemony building in the Gramscian sense in Turkey.

Gramsci explained state-society relations through an analysis of both consent and coercion. Hegemony cultivates consent, and as such, differs from the mere exercise of state power. A Gramscian framework can unpack the power relations that emerge from state intervention in natural as well as urban space.[5] An analysis of how megaprojects are integrated into the political stance of the AKP makes it possible to understand how infrastructural services by the state in Turkey help build legitimacy and widespread consent while simultaneously generating discontent and exclusion.

That is why the construction of megaprojects is not simply an exercise of state capacity in conversation with social actors, as the infrastructural power framework implies. An infrastructural state power framework envisions a mutual increase of control between state and society. As the state increases its capacities of surveillance and logistical intervention, society can also find ways of restraining the state through channels of representation and democratic participation. However, in the case of Turkey, the megaprojects become tools for the state to actively build hegemony. The state uses its infrastructural power to frame its policies (e.g. investment in megaprojects) as services for the people, but this kind of 'politics of service' is used to block any criticism of the governing elite. This framing reinforces the powerful discourse of developmentalism in Turkey. Yet resistance to the megaprojects shows us that coercion is used to inhibit resistance to hegemonic control by the state as much as consent.

The Third Bridge, the Third Airport and Canal Istanbul

The rule of the AKP has been marked by the endorsement of numerous megaprojects in a variety of locations; but the third bridge, the third airport and the canal planned for Istanbul are the most prominent examples of these infrastructural projects due to their size, the prestige they are expected to bring and their being located in Istanbul – a city which has a distinct place in the Turkish economy as the motor of growth. These three projects are often packaged together and are the pride of the government. They are also highly controversial. This section describes these megaprojects and their controversial aspects.

The third bridge across the Bosphorus was the first of these projects to undergo construction, and has very recently been completed. The bridge and its connecting routes cut across the Northern Forests of Istanbul. The Northern Forests are crucial because they are considered to be among the 100 environmental hotspots in Europe that need urgent protection.[6] They are also the last remaining forests in Istanbul and thus an important source of clean air and water. The project threatens this ecosystem along with the sustainability of Istanbul. This is why it has long been in the midst of controversies. Two-and-a-half million trees have been cut down for the project and it is expected that the area will be open to further urban settlement, as was the case with the second bridge. The damage to the Northern Forests will soon reach a colossal scale, because the area was chosen as the site of the third airport as well.

The third airport construction spans an area of approximately 7,500 hectares in the Northern Forests, which comprises of woods, forestland, lakes, ponds, brooks as well as villages. When completed, it will be one of the biggest airports in the world, projected to bring in 150 million passengers annually. This number is contingent on the level of economic growth to be achieved in the 2013–19, 2020–30, 2031–50 periods (5, 4 and 2 per cent, respectively).[7] The size of the area allocated to the project raises questions as well, for while it can be shown through comparative calculations that the area needed for an airport with a 150-million passenger capacity is about 3,500 hectares, the actual project area is 7,400 hectares.[8] The unaccounted difference lends support to the opposition argument that the project was motivated by a desire to pave the way for further construction and integration into the global neoliberal economy, rather than meeting the needs created by increased air travel through Istanbul. In fact, the designer of the airport, the architectural consortium Nordic Architecture, has revealed that the plan is to build an 'airport city with hotels, shopping and commercial units, and food and beverage areas'.[9] Partner firms in the consortium that have undertaken the construction of the airport and environmental impact assessment (EIA) reports have confirmed the project as an 'airport city'.[10] The construction of an airport city increases the area allocated to the project and has an exponential adverse impact on the ecosystem, considering the fact that it is being built right in the middle of the Northern Forests. In fact, this impact is expected to be so great that natural thresholds will be exceeded, the population limit of 16 million will be surpassed by at least four million and Istanbul will no longer be sustainable as a result of climate change (due to blocked northern winds), increased pollution and degraded water basins.[11] The EIA reports also confirm the ecological damage that will be caused by the airport construction, thereby acknowledging the area as an ecosystem with forestlands, ponds and lakes, as well as 70 different wildlife species.[12]

Canal Istanbul completes the triad of the biggest megaprojects in Turkey. This is a megaproject whose construction has not yet started, hence much less is known about it. Canal Istanbul involves opening a 'waterway' that is parallel to the Bosphorus. Not being a part of the Urban Development Law, it did not even have legal status until it was defined as an artificially made waterway in a law passed recently, on 26 April 2016.[13] It has been announced (in a rather semi-official manner) that the canal will be 43 kilometres long, 400 metres wide and 25 metres deep. A city is going to be built around the canal as well as six bridges over it.[14] Similar to the third bridge and the third airport, a project of this size is likely to irreversibly change and eventually adversely affect the marine ecosystem, and increase urban sprawl.[15]

Not surprisingly, civil society actors, most notably the Northern Forests Defence (*Kuzey Ormanları Savunması* – KOS) – but also national environmental organisations such as the Turkish Foundation for Combating Soil Erosion, for Reforestation, and the Protection of Natural Habitats (*Türkiye Erozyonla Mücadele, Ağaçlandırma ve Doğal Varlıkları Koruma Vakfı*–TEMA) and WWF-Turkey – have raised the alarm about these megaprojects, pointing to the massive ecological destruction they will inflict. Organisations have been advocating against the megaprojects with different but related objections, including location choice, project size (in terms of both the area allocated and its financial cost), flight security in the case of the airport (quality of the fields, risk of landslide, migration routes of birds), the fact that they are not merely transportation projects but rather aimed at building an urban complex guaranteed to increase urban sprawl, the availability of alternatives (such as expanding the capacity of existing airports), procedural and legal irregularities and the devastation of ecosystems. The government has relentlessly fed arguments of growth, development and expected enhancement of Turkey's international position to marginalise these concerns.

The 'Politics of Serving', Environmentalism and the New Developmentalism

In this chapter, it is argued that the megaprojects described above are exemplary tools of the hegemony building process in Turkey. As such, it is suggested that the reading of the megaprojects that is offered here can unpack the various mechanisms of hegemony building. This hegemony is characterised by a strongly developmentalist discourse, the neoliberal organisation of state power and a large degree of arbitrariness employed by the state, made possible by circumvention and amendment of existing laws and regulations. Megaprojects embody all of the aspects of this hegemony building process.

A constituent element of the hegemony building process is the developmentalism discourse[16] that was shaped by four main pillars under the AKP rule: the primacy of development/economic growth, the emphasis on grandeur, the politics of serving and claims of environmentalism. The primacy of development upholds the position that development is a task/mission more important than any other, and economic growth must be strived for at all costs. As such, the social and ecological costs of megaprojects (or for that matter any energy, mining or urban transformation project) are not taken into consideration by the state. A KOS activist expresses the dominance of the developmentalism discourse in the following words:

> The biggest challenge is the developmentalism discourse [. . .] the discourse constitutes one of the main axes of the system, whether Right or Left. It is very difficult to get past that discourse of developmentalism. It has now become so identified with the government [. . .] the developmentalism discourse has a hold on different sectors of society. (Author interview, 14 March 2016)

The above words show how powerful the developmentalism discourse is, how it is associated with the government and generates consent, even for destructive projects such as the megaprojects.

The state elite also seeks and offers grandeur through megaprojects. For instance, the third bridge was presented at its launching ceremony by the then Prime Minister Erdoğan as a 'civilisation project', the construction of which was a service by the AKP.[17] Similarly, the third airport, described as 'the most genius project in the world' by the CEO of Turkish Airlines, is also endorsed by President Erdoğan as one of the most prominent investments to help reach the 2023 targets of Turkey, the centennial of the foundation of the Republic.[18] It is projected to be the biggest airport in the world and will symbolise the power of the Turkish state and Istanbul as a global city, according to former Prime Minister Davutoğlu. President Edoğan underlines the international prestige aspect as well in talking about various megaprojects including the third bridge and the third airport, which he expects to increase the respectability of Turkey in the world.[19] Thus, the discourse on the greatness of the state makes use of civilisations that came before the Republic, and Istanbul as the cradle of these civilisations, which is preparing to assume its global role through the megaprojects.

Allusions to the centennial of the Republic symbolise the projected future of Turkey whose economic standing as a developed country will be reinforced by the megaprojects. Moreover, the hegemony built through the discourse of grandeur is reinforced by a 'cult of personality' element created around the figure of Erdoğan. It is telling that the Minister of Transportation and Communications gave instructions to complete the construction of the third airport for Erdoğan's birthday in 2018.[20] The allusions to grandeur and the direct link drawn to the Erdoğan's leadership work to convince the masses of the unquestionable capacity of the state, thereby strengthening the hegemony of the AKP.

Indispensable to the developmentalism discourse is the 'politics of serving'. This is built on presenting megaprojects as services for the people, regardless of their possible social and ecological costs. Megaprojects are used to underline the AKP position that what the government does is that it delivers and works for the people. The AKP defines its rule as politics of serving, and distinguishes itself from other political parties by differentiating between politics of serving and politics of whatever it deems opposition parties are doing (e.g. politics of identity, politics of wardenship). It especially sets itself up in stark contrast to the Republican People's Party (*Cumhuriyet Halk Partisi* – CHP), the main opposition and the founder political party of the Republic. According to the AKP, the CHP represents the main shortcomings of the regime before they came to power. The AKP has criticised preceding governments for using top-down, despotic state power to impose their developmentalist agenda in the previous Kemalist period, concomitantly maintaining that infrastructural power of the state was mobilised under the AKP rule to serve the people. Even though developmentalism under Kemalist rule offered infrastructural projects as services, the AKP uses its infrastructural power to consolidate its hegemony by creating a stark distinction between its politics and alternative political positions to undermine the latter. Megaprojects are especially useful in the politics of serving since they are presented as the epitome of services delivered to the people.

Finally, developmentalism under the AKP is constructed on self-proclaimed environmentalism. The AKP representatives declare that they are the 'real' environmentalists, the first and foremost environmentalist being President Erdoğan. He in fact announced that he is the 'best environmentalist [...] the real environmentalist'.[21] Each time the government is criticised for disregarding the ecological costs of megaprojects, it responds by competing over the definition of environmentalism to divert attention from the source of criticism. In that regard, the most often cited indication for their environmentalism is the number of trees planted under the AKP rule.[22] Recently, in reference to tree-planting projects, Erdoğan endorsed the '5,000 forests in 5,000 villages action plan' as a civilisational project while simultaneously reprimanding environmental activists for conservation efforts. He has alluded to grandeur, repeated his claim of environmentalism and criticised the opposition all at once, reproducing the developmentalism discourse in the following words:

> The plane tree planting action plan is not just about planting trees but reviving a civilisation [...] With this project, 200,000 plane trees will be planted in all of our cities, especially Istanbul [...] We have introduced 3.5 billion saplings to the earth until today. They [environmentalists] had wanted to create chaos using trees as an excuse at Istanbul Gezi Park, Middle Eastern Technical University, now in Artvin [...][23]

The presentation of tree-planting as a form of environmentalism is problematic because planting trees does not replace an extinguished ecosystem or immediately start a new ecosystem, a point often made by environmental activists (author interview, 14 March 2016). The developmentalism discourse juxtaposes trees with the AKP, presenting a false green image that completely glosses over the ecological costs of megaprojects. This is how the AKP co-opts environmentalism and turns it into an empty signifier that may mean anything and everything. This is also how the AKP strengthens its hegemony, since claims of environmentalism help fend off criticisms based on ecological arguments and create the perception of the government as an actor that addresses environmental concerns.

Combined, these four pillars make for a very powerful developmentalist discourse, the questioning of which often lead to accusations of treason, as many environmental activists have found to their detriment. This discourse may be harder to resist because it entails the 'politics of service', which emphasises the idea that the state is working for the good of the people. The AKP can incorporate new elements in its discourse more successfully to create the illusion that the state serves the people through its various megaprojects. Hence, it is also easier for the AKP to marginalise groups who contest these projects on account of their social and ecological costs, as 'traitors who want to obstruct the progress of the nation'.

The way the megaprojects are strategically situated in hegemony building cannot be fully grasped without taking into account another aspect of the process; that of integration into the neoliberal global economy. Two dimensions of neoliberalism are constitutive in so far as they pervade diverse geographies through a similar process, albeit in varying versions contingent on history and context: support for policies that facilitate integration into competitive globalisation, and restructuring of the state to accommodate the extension of competition and market forces.[24] This has been accompanied by the intensified commodification of water, forests and other commons.[25] It is beyond the scope of this chapter to address the growing scholarly work on neoliberalisation as a process and its contingent and context-specific character or to discuss forms of neoliberalisation in Turkey as yet another case of 'actually existing neoliberalisms'; however, it is essential to underline the hegemonic use of infrastructural power to generate consent for neoliberal transformations.[26] The fact that the state plays an essential role in designing neoliberal policies has already been shown by pointing to the 'roll-out' phase of neoliberalism in which state structures, regulatory mechanisms and practices are transformed to accommodate expanding markets and commodification.[27] In that regard, Peck and

Tickell argue that neoliberalism from the 1990s onward has entered a period of restructuration, in which neoliberalised economic management and authoritarian state forms co-exist.[28] Moreover, the neoliberal reorganisation of the state has led to the emergence of corporations as a key actor, thanks to the state support for the private sector in strategic industries such as energy and construction.

Major neoliberal policies such as deregulation, privatisation, re-regulation and commodification have all been endorsed under the AKP period.[29] This has crystallised especially in relation to water and the generation of hydroelectric power. With 721 planned, 133 under construction and 537 completed hydroelectric power plants (HEPPs), rivers in Turkey have become commodified alarmingly fast as the state privatised the generation of hydroelectric power and introduced new regulations and institutions, such as the Energy Market Law, which allows the sale of water rights to private companies, and the licensing agency called the Energy Market Regulatory Authority.[30] The newly acquired role of corporations in the construction and production of hydroelectric power, the commodification of water and the regulations introduced to facilitate it, and the evaluation of the nature-human relationship only in economic terms signify the neoliberal transformation of state institutions and practices. While neoliberal transformations have given rise to a substantial ecological struggle against the commodification of rivers, hydroelectric power generation is not predominantly contested in the framework of neoliberal policies undertaken by the state. As corporations take over energy and construction projects, they have become the main culprit. Locals reprimand the state for standing with the corporations, turning a blind eye to their violations of regulations and using its armed forces to protect corporate interests; nevertheless, they more often than not adopt conciliatory attitudes toward the state.[31] This attests to the strength of the hegemony built under the AKP, as the state manages to reproduce consent using the developmentalism discourse, the politics of service, allusions of grandeur and self-proclaimed environmentalism. Exceptions certainly exist since in some localities, the state is criticised precisely for its role in neoliberal restructuration.[32]

With respect to the megaprojects, the fact that the airport city is to be designed by the architectural consortium Nordic Architecture is perceived by those mobilised against the megaprojects as accommodating the interests of global capital at the expense of the collective good of the residents of Istanbul. Civil society actors re-frame the developmentalist discourse of the state as an extension of neoliberal policies.

However, the government uses its developmentalist discourse to pre-empt criticisms based on the social and ecological costs of integration into the global neoliberal economy. In this regard, the primacy of growth, the politics of service and the emphasis on becoming a part of the global North are crucial to generate consent in favour of the neoliberal reorganisation of the state. The state uses its hegemony to frame its neoliberal policy decisions, e.g. the construction of megaprojects, as services while it simultaneously takes 'roll-out' measures that protect corporate interests rather than the commons. Hegemony building makes use of not just infrastructural power but also despotic power. It has been noted that the implementation of neoliberal measures has involved the use of coercive state power, despite illusions of a market society free from state intervention of any kind.[33] The state in Turkey also uses its armed forces to protect construction sites (be it HEPPs or the third airport) against locals who mobilise to stop the construction of these projects.

The neoliberal transformations in Turkey have been bolstered by a high degree of arbitrariness that undermines rule of law and hence, democratic process. Arbitrariness in this context refers to the tendency of the state to disregard existing laws, environmental standards and procedures to push through investments and projects on behalf of corporations. The arbitrariness that characterises state power in Turkey is evident in the inconsistencies in the decisions made by policy makers. None of the megaprojects were included in the 1/100,000 scaled Istanbul Environmental Plan approved in 2009; they were introduced by the Prime Ministry out of the blue, so to speak.[34] In fact, Erdoğan had objected to plans for the third bridge, calling it the murder of Istanbul and its Northern Forests back in 1995, when he was the mayor of the city.[35] The EIA reports prepared for the airport project acknowledged the ecological demise that it would bring about; nevertheless, it was approved. In fact, the tender for the airport was made without a favourable EIA report. The number of trees (to be cut down) is mentioned in the first EIA report (March 2013) but was removed from the second report (March 2014). Even though the final EIA report states that there will be no land reclamation along the shoreline, this has been disregarded during construction.[36] Furthermore, the third airport runways will have to be filled up substantially to ensure flight safety. The planned elevation of 70 metres requires 420 million cubic metres of land to be poured; the original elevation that was set as 105 metres – requiring almost six times more land to be poured – was lowered due to cost cutting reasons, a decision that raised flight safety concerns.

Overriding the legal framework by executive decisions has been possible by relying on the consent generated through the four pillars of the developmentalist discourse expounded at length above. This kind of direct violation of the existing legal and institutional framework in Turkey has been noted as a change of practice that is part of the neoliberal transformation under the AKP.[37] In the past, the state breached laws through indirect channels such as patronage and corruption.[38] Even though direct intervention through deregulation and arbitrariness has become widespread, corruption is not altogether ruled out. For instance, allegations of corruption were made and brought to the attention of Parliament by a CHP parliamentarian in relation to the third airport project, because one of the partners in the consortium was being tried for bid rigging when it participated in the tender for the project.[39] The arbitrariness that pervades the megaprojects is exacerbated by the lack of participation in decision-making processes by organised civil society, as well as citizens whose lives and livelihoods are affected by these policies. These polices prioritise growth to such a degree as to leave no room to address social and ecological concerns raised by various social groups.

Challenging the 'Environmentalism' of the AKP: Civil Society and the Megaprojects

The AKP had initially advanced a critique of the Kemalist modernisation project that pervaded political power in Turkey, specifically on the grounds of its suppression of (Muslim) identity-related demands; however, once it consolidated its rule, it ironically became the single most powerful actor to endorse the modernisation agenda. The AKP claims that they are at the service of the people without violating the rights of any group. Moreover, they have supported the politics of service by the infrastructural projects they have undertaken, including and especially the megaprojects, as argued above. However, the claim that the AKP rule has reformed the exclusionary agenda of the state and put an end to the alienation created by an elite-defined modernisation mission is most explicitly challenged in relation to ecological issues. The AKP has successfully adopted the state tradition of top-down impositions, pushing its own understanding of growth and development as unquestionable national interest. Yet the claim that megaprojects represent the national interest reinforces a divided and polarised context, rendering state capacity to govern across diverse groups weak.

Against the claims of national interest, international prestige and the environmentalism of tree planting, environmental mobilisations against hydroelectric, thermal and nuclear power plants as well as urban renewal and mining projects and megaprojects have emphasised the importance of the environmental commons, democratic participation and the sustainability of their way of life.

Contention over the megaprojects started first when the plan to construct the third bridge was given the green light, as this was the longest-standing project. Residents initially organised at the neighbourhood level, then expanded to form a broader platform that included various neighbourhood organisations, national environmental organisations and professional chambers. The route of the bridge was relocated several times, shifting the focus of the mobilisation from the neighbourhood of Arnavutköy to Sarıyer, finally ending up at its current location of the Northern Forests. With each relocation, the framework of contention changed slightly; however, three remained central to each wave of contention: environmentalism, Istanbul as common value and democratic participation. The environmentalism framework underlined sustainability, alternative and ecological practices such as public transportation (as opposed to the bridge which will encourage the use of cars) and conservation of the Northern Forests, a critical ecosystem. Participants of the anti-bridge campaign also made references to Istanbul as a common value and global heritage, thereby demanding voice in the decisions regarding their city. This ties into the last framework that marked the mobilisations against the third bridge; that of democratic participation. Discontent resulted from the undemocratic and exclusionary decision-making processes with respect to the megaprojects, which did not take into account the demands and concerns of the residents of Istanbul, whose lives are to be directly affected. After several campaigns and protests, the mobilisation subsided with the start of the construction of the bridge.[40]

The ecological degradation caused by the construction of the third bridge and the growing threat to the Northern Forests with the pending construction of the third airport, revitalised the contention against the megaprojects pioneered by KOS. KOS is one of the spin-off movements of the Gezi protests that took place in the summer of 2013. It advocates conserving the ecosystem of the Northern Forests in their entirety and identifies the megaprojects as the biggest threat to them. KOS argues that the megaprojects threaten not only the ecosystem but also the sustainability of Istanbul.

The megaprojects will push beyond the natural thresholds of the city, making it uninhabitable for its residents. In addition to actively campaigning and organising protests against the megaprojects, KOS is in solidarity with ecological struggles around the country, seeing their activism as part of the broader struggle to defend life against the hegemonic stance of new developmentalism.[41] National environmental organisations such as TEMA and WWF-Turkey also advocate against the megaprojects, although they differ from KOS in that the latter uses direct action as a form of resistance. These environmental organisations and groups also remain alert to any step taken for Canal Istanbul and perceive its impact to be just as ecologically destructive and threatening to sustainability of the city. The use of these megaprojects by the state as part of its neoliberal developmentalism and their contestation by environmental civil society can be comprehended as a process of hegemony building, which is both disputed and subverted.

Notes

1. Theda Skocpol, 'Bringing the state back in: strategies of analysis in current research' in P. Evans, D. Rueschemeyer and T. Skocpol (eds), *Bringing the State Back In* (Cambridge, 1985), pp. 3–43.
2. Michael Mann, *The Sources of Social Power, The Rise of Classes and Nation-States, 1760–1914* 2 (Cambridge, 1993).
3. Here, the term 'the state elite' is used interchangeably with the ruling party AKP. Although the government and the state need to be treated differently, the AKP rule has infused with and transformed state institutions during the past 12 years it has continuously been in power. Thus, interchangeable use of the state elite and AKP was purposefully chosen to underline the link between the use of state power and the process of hegemony building under the AKP.

4. Nicos Soulioitis, John Sayas and Thomas Moulatas, 'Megaprojects, neoliberalisation, and state capacities: assessing the mid-term impact of the 2004 Olympic games on Athenian urban policies', *Environment and Planning C: Government and Policy* 32/4 (2014), pp. 731–45.
5. Kiran Asher and Diana Osheda, 'Producing nature and making the state: Ordenamiento territorial in the Pacific lowlands of Columbia', *Geoforum* 40 (2009), pp. 292–302.
6. This is a list prepared by the World Wildlife Foundation. Detailed information on the flora, fauna and endemic species of the Northern Forests as well as related ecosystems can be found in the TEMA report on the megaprojects ('İstanbul'un Geleceğini Etkileyecek 3 Proje: 3. Köprü, 3.- Havalimanı- Kanal İstanbul [The 3 projects that will impact on the future of Istanbul: 3. Bridge- 3. Airport- Canal Istanbul]', http://www.tema.org.tr/folders/14966/categorial1docs/1244/BUYUKPROJELER20032014data.pdf, TEMA Foundation, accessed on March 2014). For a short piece on the nine environmental hotspots in Turkey, one of which is the Northern Forests, see http://www.hurriyetdailynews.com/turkeys-nine-environmental-hotspots.aspx?pageID=238&nID=69042&NewsCatID=340, accessed August 2016.
7. Seyfettin Gürsel and Tuba Toru-Delibaşı, 'Mega Havalimanının kaderi büyümeye bağlı [The Future of Mega Airport Depends on Growth]', Research Note 13/150 (Bahçeşehir University, 2013, http://betam.bahcesehir.edu.tr/wp-content/uploads/2013/06/ArastirmaNotu150.pdf, accessed March 2016).
8. Gürsel and Toru-Delibaşı, 'Mega Havalimanının'.
9. http://www.yapi.com.tr/haberler/tasarimcisi-3-havalimanini-anlatti_125285.html, accessed March 2016.
10. 'The Third Airport Project *vis-à-vis* Life, Nature, Environment, People, and Law', KOS report; (Istanbul, 2015).
11. 'The Third Airport Project'; TEMA report, 'İstanbul'un Geleceğini Etkileyecek 3 Proje'; author interviews 25 February 2016; 14 March 2016.
12. 'The Third Airport Project'. Acknowledgment of the existence of bodies of water in later EIA reports is significant because the first EIA report at times labelled them as 'ponds', thereby downplaying the ecological impact of the airport.
13. http://www.kuzeyormanlari.org/2016/04/14/torba-yasayla-sermayeye-kiyak-kanal-istanbula-yasal-altyapi/, accessed 20 April 2016.
14. http://www.yapi.com.tr/haberler/kanal-istanbulun-ayrintilari-netlesti_128852.html, accessed 20 April 2016.
15. http://dunyalilar.org/bakin-rafa-kaldirin-demedim-unutun-dedim.html, accessed 20 April 2016.
16. Developmentalism has always been hegemonic in Turkey owing to its status as 'founding ideology'. It is a well-documented fact that since its foundation, the Republic of Turkey built its hegemony on a modernisation mission. İlkay Sunar, 'State, society and democracy in Turkey', in V. Mastny and R.C. Nations (eds), *Turkey between East and West: New Challenges for Arising Regional Power*

(Boulder, 1996); Metin Heper and Fuat Keyman, 'Double-faced state: Political patronage and the consolidation of democracy in Turkey', *Middle Eastern Studies* 34/4 (1998), pp. 259–77; Aykut Çoban, 'Community-based ecological resistance: The Bergama movement in Turkey', *Environmental Politics* 13/2 (2004), pp. 438–60; Fuat Keyman and Ahmet İçduygu (eds), *Citizenship in a Global World: European Questions and Turkish Experiences* (London, 2005); and Fikret Adaman, Bengi Akbulut and Murat Arsel, 'Türkiye'de kalkınmacılığı yeniden okumak: HES'ler ve dönüşen devlet-toplum-doğa ilişkileri [Re-reading Turkey's developmentalism: Hydropower plants and changing society-environment relationships]', in C. Aksu, S. Erensü and E. Evren (eds), *Sudan Sebepler: Türkiye'de neoliberal su-enerji politikaları ve direnişleri [Watery Reasons: Neoliberal Water-Energy Politics in Turkey and Resistance]* (İstanbul, 2016).

17. http://www.sabah.com.tr/Ekonomi/2013/05/29/3-bogaz-koprusunun-temeli-atiliyor, accessed 29 March 2016.
18. http://www.yapi.com.tr/haberler/3-havalimaninin-ilk-etap-finansmanina-4-5-milyar-euroluk-kredi-saglandi_137578.html?utm_source=link&utm_medium=bulten&utm_campaign=bulten-0677-20102015; http://www.yapi.com.tr/haberler/ucuncu-havalimani-dunyadaki-en-dahice-akillica-proje_133945.html, accessed 28 March 2016.
19. http://www.haber7.com/siyaset/haber/1825943-erdogan-mega-projelerdeki-son-durumu-acikladi, accessed 28 March 2016.
20. http://www.aktifhaber.com/3-havalimani-icin-erdoganin-dogum-gunu-talimati-1280413h.htm, accessed 29 March 2016.
21. http://arsiv.ntv.com.tr/news/457078.asp, accessed 29 March 2016.
22. http://www.sabah.com.tr/ekonomi/2013/05/29/3-bogaz-koprusunun-temeli-atiliyor; http://arsiv.ntv.com.tr/news/457078.asp, accessed 29 March 2016.
23. T24, 21 March 2016; http://t24.com.tr/haber/erdogan-nevruzu-bayram-degil-kan-dokmek-olarak-telakki-edenleri-lanetliyorum,332943, accessed 4 April 2016.
24. Bob Jessop, 'Liberalism, neoliberalism, and urban governance: A state-theoretical perspective', *Antipode* 34/3 (2002), pp. 452–72; and Jamie Peck and Adam Tickell, 'Neoliberalising space', *Antipode* 34/3 (2002), pp. 380–404.
25. Noel Castree, 'Neoliberalising nature: the logics of deregulation and reregulation', *Environment and Planning A* 40 (2008), pp. 131–52; and Eric Swyngedouw, 'Dispossessing H2O: The contested terrain of water privatisation', *Capitalism Nature Socialism* 16/1 (2005), pp. 81–98.
26. Neil Brenner and Nik Theodore, 'Cities and geographies of "actually existing neoliberalism"', *Antipode* 34/3 (2002), pp. 349–79.
27. Peck and Tickell, 'Neoliberalising space'; and Brenner and Theodore, 'Cities and geographies'. Brenner and Theodore identify these transformations at the urban level as establishing new networks between business and politics as well as among businesses, creating new forms of cooperation in what used to be areas of local state policy and using community-based programmes to ease social exclusion.

28. Peck and Tickell, 'Neoliberalising space'.
29. Changes to laws that concern forests, mining, meadows and nature conservation as well as the use of EIA reports underline the neoliberal transformation towards less conservation, less regulation and more commodification (Adaman et al., 'Türkiye'de kalkınmacılığı yeniden okumak').
30. Sinan Erensü, Erdem Evren and Cemil Aksu, 'Giriş: Yeğin sular daim engine akar [Introduction: Strong Streams Always go to the Horizon]', in Aksu et al., *Sudan Sebepler.*
31. Sıla Pelin Oğuz, 'The Politics of Nature and Neoliberalism: An Assessment of the Impact of Hydro Electric Power Plants on Local Populations', MA thesis, İstanbul: İstanbul Bilgi University, 2016.
32. Adaman et al. 'Türkiye'de kalkınmacılığı'.
33. Peck and Tickell, 'Neoliberalising space'.
34. 'The Third Airport Project'; and 'İstanbul'un geleceğini etkileyecek 3 proje'.
35. http://t24.com.tr/haber/tansu-cillerin-3-kopru-istegine-erdogan-cinayet-diye-karsi-cikmis,261072, accessed on 18 April 2016; author interview 25 February 2016.
36. http://www.denizticaretgazetesi.org/o_gemi_3_havalimani_icin_dolgu_yap iyor_haber8054.html, accessed on 18 April 2016; author interview 25 February 2016.
37. Adaman et al. 'Türkiye'de kalkınmacılığı yeniden okumak'.
38. Ibid.
39. 'The Third Airport Project'.
40. See Hande Paker, 'Contesting the 'third bridge' in Istanbul: Local environmentalism, cosmopolitan attachments?' (forthcoming 2017), for a detailed analysis of the mobilisation against the third bridge.
41. Author interviews 25 February 2016; 14 March 2016.

CHAPTER 5

TURKEY'S HYDROPOWER RENAISSANCE: NATURE, NEOLIBERALISM AND DEVELOPMENT IN THE CRACKS OF INFRASTRUCTURE

Sinan Erensü

Introduction

Construction, ribbon cutting, foreign credit, cement, energy, extraction, asphalt, grandeur, real estate, speculation, groundbreaking and expropriation... These are some of the keywords that have come to define the AKP's (Justice and Development Party) reign since 2002 and Turkey's contemporary political economy. Smothered in a sauce of developmentalism and funded by foreign finance, Turkey's construction frenzy took myriad forms but always left visible spatial footprints: a renewed wave of real-estate boom in cities (through forms of urban renewal projects, middle and upper class housing, shopping malls, theme parks, landfills, etc.) accompanied by transportation, extraction and energy investments in the countryside.[1]

While such spatial interventions boosted the party's popularity, produced mass consent, and ignited dreams and imaginations, they also turned into sites of mass discontent, augmented ecological degradation and led to the emergence of new forms and geographies of urban and environmental activism – the Gezi Uprising in the summer of 2013 being the most well-known of all.[2] Despite its popularity at the national level, the appeal of the AKP's infrastructural politics met discontent as the projects unfolded in neighbourhoods, valleys, forests, public parks, villages, and so on. Infrastructures characterised the scope, appeal and eventual success of AKP developmentalism, proved to be the Achilles' heel of its power and thus came to define its limits.

This chapter discusses how the generative capacity of infrastructures in Turkey is maintained politically and economically despite their weaknesses, contradictions, vulnerabilities as well as social and environmental limits. By looking at a key dimension of the AKP-orchestrated construction frenzy, Turkey's hydropower renaissance, the chapter opens a window into the newly emerging fields of power and relationships of dependency in contemporary Turkey through the cracks of energy infrastructures. The chapter also aims at providing an alternative neoliberalisation narrative that accounts for Turkish studies by discussing the legal, financial and (re)distributive dimensions of the hydropower boom within their historical continuity; one that is as aleatory, parochial, diffused and contested, as much as it is planned, universal and singlehandedly imposed.

The chapter has six sections. Following this short introduction, the first section discusses the political role and scholarly relevance of energy and hydropower politics in Turkey. The second section provides a history of energy and electricity reform, an overview of key (de)regulations and illustrations of how certain aspects of the energy law have seeped into other fields of governance as useful tools. The third section differentiates small hydropower projects from the large and elaborates on the impact of this material difference on the industry and energy geographies. The fourth section outlines the birth of the private hydropower industry and dwells upon the dynamics behind the hydropower boom. The fifth section asks what happens to the idea of developmentalism and its redistributive promise with the rise of privatised infrastructure. Finally, the conclusion discusses how the peculiarities of Turkey's hydropower renaissance help us understand the country's unique experience with neoliberalism.

A New Source of Energy for a 'New Turkey'

Energy is a unique form of infrastructure. Not only is it realised through complex infrastructures (coalmines, dams, pipes, grids, etc.), it also fuels other forms of infrastructure (roads, bridges, shopping malls, city lights, etc.). More importantly, energy generates power, symbolically as well as materially. Energy infrastructures are translated into industrial production and economic development, but they also form markets, establish sustained connections among the business and political elite and transform geographies. While this article provides a snapshot of rich web of energy politics in twenty-first-century Turkey to provide an alternative perspective to the AKP reign, its intention is not to reduce the AKP's construction frenzy and infrastructural economics to energy. By tracing energy infrastructures, the article rather aims at making visible some of the relationships that made the AKP's political economy so potent yet vulnerable.

In particular, the chapter focuses on one form of energy, electricity and a particular aspect of electricity production, hydropower. Yet in fact, Turkey's last decade and a half has witnessed tremendous transformations in all forms of energy as well as a wide range of energy-related disasters and scandals. Between 2008 and 2015, investments in the energy industry surpassed US$ 50 billion.[3] An average of US$ 6 billion is poured into new electricity production infrastructures annually.[4] During the same period, the total installed capacity in electricity more than doubled, rising from 31,800 MW to 69,500 MW. The country expects to attract US$ 120 billion in investments to meet its goals for the centennial of the Republic in 2023.[5] Wind energy, almost non-existent a decade ago, now accounts for 6 per cent of total installed capacity.[6] Despite considerable delay, the first set of solar farm licenses were distributed in 2015. Additionally, in 2010 the country's first nuclear power plant deal was sealed with Russia's state-owned corporation Rosatom, only to be followed by a second agreement in 2013 with a Japanese–French consortium.

The other side of the coin, however, is not as bright and presentable. In May 2014, an underground fire in the Soma coal mines took 301 lives, earning the embarassing title of the deadliest mining disaster of the twenty-first century. Energy-related accidents account for a significant portion of work-related injuries and deaths.[7] A few months after the mining disaster, 6,000 olive oil trees that belonged to farmers of Yırca – a village just a few miles west of Soma – were cut down to clear an area for the construction of a coal-power plant. Turkey's unrestrained energy boom is also cited as one of the factors underneath its biodiversity crisis.[8]

In terms of habitat and biodiversity protection Turkey performs scandalously low, ranking 177 out of 180 countries by the Yale University's Environmental Performance Index (EPI).[9] Turkey is also considered to be one of the worst performers in mitigating carbon emissions,[10] and anticipated to become one of the world's coal leaders alongside China and India if and when the proposed 80 coal-power plants are completed.[11] Despite all these investments, the entire country experienced a day-long blackout on 31 March 2015.[12] Turkey has also been implicated in the black market trade of Syrian oil, arguably extracted by ISIS.[13]

Hydropower, which also experienced an exceptional growth in the last decade, is obviously not the root cause of all the successes and failures of the energy sector in Turkey. However, a few factors make hydropower a good lens to understand and critically assess exactly what energy infrastructures are capable of setting in motion. To begin with, there is the sheer volume of the hydropower market. By adding 21.85 GW of new capacity, Turkey scored the fourth fastest growth rate in the world in 2014, behind China, Brazil and Canada. Following a series of new laws and regulations that are discussed in the following section, hydropower had embarked on an unprecedented growth trend by the mid-2000s with the involvement of new private actors. Between 2003 and 2015, Turkey's installed capacity in hydropower jumped from 12,000 MW to 24,000 MW. In other words, to copy the language that the AKP governments love, the installed capacity operationalised within 12 years exceeded the total amount operationalised prior to the AKP's reign.[14] According to projections made for the Republic's centennial, with the completion of projects that are in the planning phase, total hydropower installed capacity is expected to double once again, and reach 48,000 MW. This means the total number of hydropower plants (HEPP), which were at 531 in August 2015, will hit almost 1,400 by 2023 with the completion of 133 projects currently under construction and another 721 projects that are in the planning stage (see Table 5.1).

The main pillar of the hydropower renaissance is based on small hydropower plants (SHP)[15] built on small streams; they are individually small in capacity yet voluminous in numbers. Although considered low-impact and renewable on paper, SHPs have been particularly significant for the Turkish countryside, as well as agricultural structures, rural livelihoods and local economies. Yet Turkey's experience with

Table 5.1 Development of Turkey's Hydropower Potential (August 2015)

PROJECTS	OWNERSHIP	NUMBER OF PLANTS	CAPACITY (MW)	
IN OPERATION	SHW	65	12,369	
	Private	396	10,599	%54.8
	Other	76	2,333	
	Total	537	25,301	
UNDER CONSTRUCTION	SHW	4	1,940	
	Private	129	4,901	%14.8
	Total	133	6,841	
PLANNED	SHW	82	1,582	
	Private	639	12,429	%30.4
	Total	721	14,011	
TOTAL PROJECTED (2023 TARGETS)	***SHW***	*151*	*15,891*	
	Private	*1,164*	*27,929*	*%73.2*
	Other	*76*	*2,333*	
	TOTAL	***1,391***	***46,153***	

Source: State Hydraulic Works (SHW) Department of Hydroelectric.

hydropower is not entirely new, rendering a historical reading of political–economical categories such as developmentalism and neoliberalism possible. Beyond all these factors, anti-hydropower activism alone is a good reason to focus on Turkey's hydropower renaissance as well as its social and ecological impact. The surge in energy infrastructures has created new energy geographies by turning rural environments into energy landscapes, which host unprecedented environmental activism at the grassroots level. The geographical scope and sheer number of hydropower infrastructures translate into an anti-hydropower activism that has been pervasive and influential in the formation of a new wave of environmental activism in the country. Doing justice to the curious case of anti-hydropower activism is beyond the scope of this chapter; it does not have a dedicated section in the chapter. However, as the hydropower business is often redesigned in response to the opposition, anti-hydropower activism inevitably operates in the background throughout the chapter. The section below focuses on the legal arena as one of the pillars of the energy field that constantly had to renew itself and discusses how it became one of the battlefields where the logic of liberalism and its discontent confronted each other.

Liberalising Energy: A Never-ending Adventure

The liberalisation of Turkey's energy sector is one long story. Parallel to Turkey's overall experience with neoliberalism, the opening-up of its energy markets was initiated quite early, yet took decades to be realised. The first systematic efforts to liberalise the sector started in the first quarter of the 1980s. The process progressed piecemeal on a highly tortuous path and met with bureaucratic and judicial resistance throughout the 1990s until it was framed as an inescapable necessity to recover from the economic downturns (and also demanded by the IMF as a precondition to financial assistance) by the turn of the century. This process was eventually operationalised and implemented in the 2000s by consecutive AKP governments. The current state of Turkish energy, therefore, was shaped not only by a neoliberal blueprint, but also carries the marks of its unique and elongated history as well as the political and economic preferences of the AKP. The hydropower renaissance, particularly the inflation of SHPs, can be best understood at this juncture where AKP politics meets Turkey's meandering history with neoliberalism.

Law no. 3096, enacted in 1984 and self-explanatorily titled *Authorisation of Enterprises Other Than the Turkish Electricity Administration to Produce, Transmit, Distribute and Trade Electricity*, was the first attempt to invite private actors to partake in the energy industry. Its purpose was to create a framework in which private entities could build and/or operate power plants without completely leaving the management of the energy field to the market. It was followed by a series of other laws, each of which sought to ease the entry of entrepreneurs to the industry by introducing and/or strengthening early privatisation schemes such as the transfer of operating rights (TOOR), build-operate-transfer (BOT), build-operate (BO) and auto-production. All of these schemes were, in effect, nullified by higher courts, despite the fact that their legal status was meant to be strengthened through multiple revisions and additional laws.

The rationale behind their subsequent annulment, in fact, refers to a genuine political–economical debate, although it was conveniently cast as a typical bureaucratic delay. The Constitutional Court saw the contracts signed thanks to Law no. 3096 as concessions given by the state to private entities over the service of a public good, electricity.[16] This interpretation meant that under the newly introduced schemes, electricity production contracts would be subject to public law and reviewed by the Council of State, and thus fall outside the jurisdiction of international arbitration.[17] Both the governments of the time and investors thought otherwise. The latter was concerned with the slow pace and diligence of the oversight, while governments did not want to lose their singlehanded authority over bids and contracts.[18] Moreover, the absence of protection through international arbitration was unwelcoming for potential foreign investors.

Quarrels over the legal status of electricity production lasted 15 years, during which both public and private investments in hydropower stagnated. When it finally became clear that bypassing the legal framework through special investment schemes was unlikely to yield the desired results, the Electricity Market Law no. 4628 (EML) was passed in 2001 with the aim of creating a truly private market from scratch. The EML aimed to unbound industry activities (state monopoly), privatise public assets (power plants) and establish a 'financially strong, competitive, efficient and transparent' market; one that is subject to private law and overseen by an autonomous body, the Energy Market Regulatory Authority (EMRA).[19] It should be noted, however, that the 1999 constitutional amendment that granted privatisation a constitutional legitimacy was the key to solving the political economy riddle and acted as the legal basis of the EML.

The AKP, which came to power in November 2002, certainly did not play much of a role in either the energy controversies of the 1990s or the enactment of the EML. However, it not only embraced the perspective set by the EML, but also has been unapologetically proactive in encouraging private agents to invest in the energy sector and in passing countless legislations that completed the energy reform. One critical legislation that strengthened the legal basis of private HEPPs, for example, was the Water Usage Right Agreement Bylaw that allowed the General Directorate of State Hydraulics Works (SHW) to lease sections of rivers and streams (often for 49 years) to private entities intending to build HEPPs. Another legislative field that deserves mention is the bylaw that regulates the Environmental Impact Assessment (EIA) management, which has been revised 14 times during the AKP's 14-year rule. Although the revisions expanded the type of HEPPs that must be subject to regulation, EIA management has been rendered utterly ineffective for between 1993 and 2016, the Ministry of Environment and Urbanisation rejected only 43 EIA cases out of a total of 56,071.[20]

The new legal framework that the hydropower renaissance owes its existence to is not limited to energy and environmental deregulations. Perhaps the most consequential shift that impacted hydropower-related disputes came from the Administrative Law. As the number of contested HEPP projects increased and more and more projects and their EIA reports were taken to the courts, project finance cycles faced serious delays. Complaints from the private sector coupled with the legacy of the 1990s, where many power plant projects were halted by higher courts and pace of investments became a key issue the AKP strived to address.

There are two main aspects of the Administrative Law that have been utilised to accelerate the pace of energy investments. The first is the Urgent Expropriation (UE) procedure. With origins going back to 1940, the UE is in fact a war-time effort. It was initially intended to provide the cabinet of the time exceptional measures to confiscate private land and property for strategic purposes in response to possible foreign invasion.[21] Thanks to the UE, the government was given the authority to by-pass detailed confiscation procedures that both took a long time to finalise and were contestable in a higher court. Despite its extraordinary power, the UE had only been used a handful of times up until the early 2000s. Its rediscovery by AKP governments on the basis of the country's emerging need for energy offered a temporary solution to energy-related land disputes. This new broad interpretation of the law enabled the state to appropriate private lands, often from small-scale rural owners, and lease them to energy infrastructure entrepreneurs for extended periods of time. While there had been only six UE cases in the 1980s and four in the 1990s, UE decisions skyrocketed under the AKP rule, reaching an unprecedented 104 decisions only in the last six years of the 2000s.[22] The decade between 2004 and 2014 witnessed a total of 1,785 UE decisions; some 1,500 of them were directly related to energy production.[23] The exception soon became the norm for a variety of infrastructure investments: the law was first applied to energy-related projects (particularly SHPs), and later expanded to water management, disaster preparedness, allocation of land for tourism investments, urban renewal projects and, most recently, to suppress Kurdish insurgency and redesigning Kurdish cities,[24] and most recently more than 2,000 UE decisions were signed in the last two years. Overwhelmed by the volume of UE decisions, the cabinet has had to share its authority over taking UE decisions with other regulatory bodies. The SHW and EMRA were thus authorised to make appropriation decisions that are not easily appealable in courts.

Despite its power, the UE targets only one aspect of energy disputes: conflicts over land-grabbing. The majority of SHP projects examined by the courts, however, pertain to EIAs, which are often found superficial, incomplete and even illegal. To circumvent close scrutiny of EIAs and the slowing pace of investments, the government resorted to another acceleratory measure entitled Urgent Judicial Proceedings (UJP). Although the act that introduced the UJP was promoted as a European-style legal reform to lower the judicial workload, it made it difficult to litigate administrative actions pertaining to land-related disputes and restricted the ability of judges to suspend administrative decisions.[25]

It should be noted that components of the new legal framework summarised here (except for the Water Usage Right Agreement Bylaw) are not hydropower-specific; they (de)regulate other forms of electricity production as well. Those that transform the Administrative Law are not even energy-specific; they come in handy, for instance, in accelerating urban renewal efforts. The sheer number and sudden spread of HEPPs, however, have been a crucial trigger in the emergence of fast-track shortcut solutions and their eventual spread to other realms of governance. To appreciate the role of this catalyst, we need to examine the infrastructures of the hydropower renaissance more closely. By putting emphasis on the characteristics SHPs, the next section aims to illustrate that Turkey's energy renaissance was shaped part and parcel by the type of infrastructures that received investment as much as it was conditioned by a series of other factors.

Small is the New Large: How Infrastructures Matter

Up until the late 2000s, there was only one word in the Turkish vernacular to describe the infrastructures of hydropower. *Baraj* (adapted from French *le barrage*; dam in English) was used indiscriminately to refer to a large variety of hydraulic structures whether they were for irrigation, consumption or energy. The last decade, however, has witnessed the introduction of a new term to everyday parlance. *HES*, short for *hidroelektrik santrali* (hydroelectric power plant) is now the new name given to structures that convert river power into electricity. While it was always the preferred form of referring to HEPPs by the State Hydraulic Works, adoption of the term HES by the general public is new and unexpected.

This seemingly trivial change in terminology, in fact, tells much about Turkey's hydropower renaissance. In the last decade-and-a-half, what shaped the country's hydropower portfolio has been a sharp ascent in run-of-the river SHP infrastructures that do not require a large reservoir – which is what makes a hydropower plant a *baraj*. Small in size, run-of-the river hydropower plants did not need a new name as they looked nothing like a *baraj*, which had a well-established image in the collective memory as well as on the now defunct, 1 billion Turkish Lira bill of old. The transition from *baraj* to HES, however, is not simply a change in size and image. It also has impacted the entire energy industry and the unfolding of its privatisation led to the emergence of new energy geographies in Turkey, which explains some of the reasons beneath the emergence of the anti-SHP movement.

The difference between small HEPPs (SHPs) and large HEPPs is hard to demarcate. The European Small Hydropower Association (ESHA) defines SHPs as 'a plant with an installed capacity of up to 10 MW'.[26] The SHW, on the other hand, differentiates HEPPs according not to size, but to type of structure, and recognises two categories: HEPPs with dams and run-of-the river HEPPs. All SHPs are run-of-the river HEPPs, but not all run-of-the river HEPPs are small. The yardstick for the Turkish case could be seen as the EIA Bylaw that requires an EIA review for HEPPs with installed capacity larger than 10 MW. However, that threshold was as high as 25 MW up until recently, and many HEPPs were built without ever being subjected to environmental assessment.

No matter how we categorise them, what becomes crystal clear when we analyse HEPP licenses by their installed capacities is that there are very many plants with little cumulative addition to the country's electric production capacity (see Table 5.2). Almost half of all HEPP licenses are for projects smaller than 10 MW installed capacity, while their contribution to the country's total hydropower capacity is only 6.5 per cent. The smallest 451 SHPs combined do not equal one Atatürk Dam (the largest HEPP in Turkey) in terms of the capacity to generate electricity. Given that most future projects are small in installed capacity, it is fair to suggest that Turkey's HEPP portfolio will be even more dominated by SHPs once 2023 targets are met.

Table 5.2 HEPP Licenses by Capacity (2003–16)

	Number of Plants	% in Total Number Plants	Capacity (MW)	% in Total Capacity
<9.9 MW	451	%49.40	2162.01	%6.42
10–24.9 MW	227	%24.86	3619.96	%10.75
25–49.9 MW	115	%12.60	4004.97	%11.90
50–99.9 MW	55	%6.02	3851.70	%11.44
100–499.9 MW	54	%5.91	9843.57	%29.24
500–999.9 MW	8	%0.88	4644.10	%13.80
1000<MW	3	%0.33	5535.00	%16.44
TOTAL	*913*	*%100.00*	*33661.36*	*%100.00*

Kaynak: Energy Market Regulatory Authority (EMRA) – Electricity License Data.

As a senior SHW bureaucrat told me, 'The SHW understandably preferred to complete the most ambitious, the largest projects' in the 1960s, 1970s and 1980s, as a strategic choice. Therefore, 'it should not be surprising that what got left behind, with some notable exceptions, are smaller projects' (personal interview, January 2015). However, the sheer number of those small projects is what drives the current hydropower frenzy, because the social and environmental footprints of these projects is, in a sense, larger than the generated output. It is important to note that this is not an argument that is made only by anti-SHP activists. The then Minister of Environment and Urbanisation,

Erdoğan Bayraktar, also acknowledged once that SHPs are not worth it and they, in fact, 'destroy small streams'.[27] He went even further to declare that they 'would not permit HEPPs producing energy under 10 MW'.[28] Although the Minister's statement was considered a blunder, the 64th Government Program, which was announced on 25 November 2015, included remarks on not allowing 'on principle, HEPPs with installed capacity below 10 MW'.[29] These promises have not been kept. This is not surprising, because given their predominantly small character, such a ban would not really hurt the country's hydropower capacity, but would certainly damage the hydropower market.

The size distribution of the current HEPP boom may be understandable, as suggested by SHW officials, on the basis of planning priorities. It made sense to develop hydropower potential in a descending order according to size. However, the sheer size boom itself – the number of SHPs that have been built at an astonishing speed in the past decade – must be questioned further. How can, for example, a valley (Solaklı, Trabzon) with a depth of 55 km host a total of 36 SHPs that are planned on it? Or what is the planning logic behind approving more than a hundred small hydro projects in Rize, a province that is much smaller than the US state Delaware in comparison?[30] Why are back-to-back SHPs allowed, which channel the river into a new pipe system right after it is discharged by the previous plant? According to which master plan were hydropower licenses distributed? To what extent was Turkey's SHP boom envisioned by the state authorities?

The answer I received from a former SHW General Director to these questions reveals much about how neoliberalisation could unfold unexpectedly at the intersection of infrastructures and nature:

> It was before the 2000s; I was still in charge of the SHW. We were going over long-term investment plans with one of my branch managers. He wanted to go over the Rize Province plans and projections and asked me when we should start building some of them. I told him, 'look, why would we use precious SHW resources and the time to bother with these small projects?' We knew that privatisation was imminent. 'Let the private sector deal with it', I said. But do you know how many projects the SHW had planned for Rize back then? The great SHW, with all its resources and expertise, had planned to build 32 HEPPs in Rize [. . .] Do

> you know how many total projects Rize has right now? 136! Now calculate the amount of money and energy we saved for the country! (Personal interview, April 2013)

What the former SHW General Director was proud of, and fascinated by, was this: the liberalisation of the energy industry was, in actuality, more than the privatisation of energy infrastructures. What was up for bidding was not only the *existing infrastructure* or *projected infrastructures* but an unspecified, unconstrained *space* to build infrastructures.[31] In the absence (or in some cases disregard) of master plans, watershed planning, grid integration projections and adequate environmental regulation, private actors from all walks of the business world scrambled to find an unclaimed river section to draw a SHP project on. As a SHW engineer specialised in the hydroelectricity branch of the institution told me, 'After the lost years of 1990s – and there is the strong will of the government – the SHW did not really intend to check these projects to see whether they added up. Honestly, if it had some calculations on it, we authorised it; never checked if it adds up' (personal interview, March 2013).

Shortcomings of the highly deregulated nature of the energy liberalisation and problems with the sudden inflation of private HEPPs are now being acknowledged by many, including energy bureaucrats and investors, in varying degrees. Bureaucrats tend to put the blame on entrepreneurs' greed; investors complain about red tape. My objective, however, is not to provide yet another apologetic explanation that 'privatisation could have been done better' or to point to a couple of areas of legislation that could have been regulated for an equitable energy policy. I am rather interested in illustrating how capital, state and society are intertwined not only through legislation but also through nature and infrastructures when a new market is constructed and experimented with.[32] By overviewing the birth and growth of the private hydropower market in Turkey, the next section not only introduces some of the new actors but also attests to its unorthodox and irregular development that defies economic projections, plans and regulations.

Plans in the Briefcase: The Birth of the Hydropower Market

As noted above, private investments in hydropower picked up speed in the second half of the 2000s, when the sector was finally made truly 'business-friendly'. Back in 2003, for example, well before the transition to the licence distribution system in hydroelectricity, only one-tenth of the country's hydropower capacity was owned and operated by private companies. The private sector-state ratio for installed capacity skyrocketed from 1:10 in 2003 to 1:1 in 2014. It is projected that this ratio will be 3:2 in favour of the private sector by 2023. According to SHW data, private entrepreneurs spent approximately US$ 16 billion for the 362 new SHPs that became operational in the 11 years that followed 2003. The magnitude of the investment planned by the private sector to complete the SHPs that will go into operation until 2023 is expected to be around US$ 60 billion. In early 2015, the number of HEPPs that were being built by the private sector was 139, while the SHW was building only four new HEPPs.

If there is something more interesting than the sheer volume and speed of investment in hydroelectricity infrastructures, it is how the new private hydropower sector, which invested so much in so little time, came into being and what motivated it to invest in hydro-energy. Though its ownership structure is changing rapidly (and the why and how is explained below), Turkey's emerging hydropower market was fairly diverse, especially in the early years.[33] One could find denim companies, textile giants, appliance producers, engineer-cum-entrepreneurs, real-estate developers and even soccer clubs amongst HEPP owners along with the usual suspects, the leaders of infrastructure and construction businesses, as well as a limited number of international players.

The hydropower renaissance came at a time when one of the leading sectors of capital accumulation in Turkey – textiles – entered a deep crisis primarily due to stiff competition from Chinese manufacturers. Thanks to this overlap, it is common to find ex-textiles giants in hydro-energy. This explains why the provinces of Denizli and Gaziantep, two textiles powerhouses, follow Ankara and Istanbul in the number of hydropower companies they host, despite the fact all four cities are poor in rivers and streams. SANKO textile industries, the leading Gaziantep-based cotton and synthetic yarn manufacturer in Turkey since 1945, holds eleven HEPP licenses, installed capacities of which range between 8 MW and 130 MW. Recalling the closing down of its Adıyaman factory in 2008 and eventual laying off of 7,000 workers, Eberliköse points out that SANKO's investments in energy was at the expense of its divestments in textiles, a labour intensive sector.[34] Although reading the energy boom in Turkey as a fix to certain crises of capital accumulation provides valuable insights, it is also worthwhile to note that hydropower investments attract a diverse set of motivations. Many individual investors, I was told in multiple interviews, see SHPs as cash cows that are ideal for retirement or as investments to pass on to family members. The initial optimism was replaced by a deep disappointment for some as nature, social resistance and markets themselves surfaced as unexpected risk factors.

The heterodoxy in HEPP ownership is not surprising for those who are familiar with the argument that renewable energy stimulates a more open and competitive market. The newly emerging renewable energy markets, the argument goes, require flexibility, speedy decisions and the capacity to adopt new technologies that put small and new companies in a more advantageous position. For Turkish hydropower, we need to add access to the SHW expertise into the mix. Compared to other forms of renewable energy, HEPP-building (particularly SHP-building) is less technology-intensive; it is mostly a matter of construction. The crucial knowledge required to build any HEPP, however, is detailed data regarding seasonal stream flows. Due to the state monopoly on hydro-energy, only the SHW had this kind of data. Yet, even it was incomplete and unreliable beyond major river basins, the SHW personnel (along with hydropower experts of the broader energy bureaucracy) played a key role in making this data available and accessible to the private sector. Many civil servants left the SHW in the mid-2000s and embarked on careers in the private sector. When I asked about the magnitude of the desertion, one senior SHW engineer told me 'The SHW used to be the best engineering school in the country, now it is like an MBA program and people want to get their degree quickly and leave' (personal interview, March 2013).

The transfer of the SHW expertise took different forms as well. Some of its staff were recruited as chief engineers or project managers by a small number of Ankara-based companies that had been in hydropower as contractors of the SHW projects before the privatisation of the industry. Others were offered large shares in newly formed energy companies. Concerned with establishing healthy communication with the SHW and EMRA during the cumbersome licensing and construction processes, almost all hydro-energy companies seek to employ ex-SHW personnel. As one SHW retiree jokingly remarked, 'even the SHW janitors are now on the payroll of energy companies; well, almost' (personal interview, January 2015).

The most striking business practice that connects capital, state and nature together in the form of hydropower has been the energy brokers referred to as *çantacı* (briefcase dealers). They have access to a HEPP license or what is referred to as a ready project that needs to be submitted to the EMRA and the SHW for a production license. Often energy bureaucracy insiders (public servants or retirees), they not only secured sizable commission fees from license trading, but also facilitated in maintaining an unruly hydropower black market, roughly from 2007 to 2013. During this boom period, which is retrospectively traceable by the unprecedented 'HEPP for sale' ads in national newspapers, investing in hydropower was in every entrepreneur's mind. Thanks to this eagerness, many projects changed hands at their early planning stages, creating a vibrant market while inflating start-up expenses and causing delays in electricity capacity growth. Although there were some vocal complaints from the government that *çantacı* activity threatened energy security,[35] it was unclear if actually being one was illegal. An energy executive that I interviewed, for example, thought that the underlying reason of all the talk was the need to respond to the public outcry against the HEPP boom: 'They are looking for a scapegoat! Did you privatise this activity? Yes! Is this a commodity now? Yes! Then I am sorry, but you should perceive it as normal if a bunch of licenses are traded' (personal interview, February 2014).

The obvious reason why there is so much entrepreneurial interest in hydropower is simply that it is a very lucrative business. According to energy finance experts, average annual income from a single HEPP is around US$ 1.5 million per MW installed capacity. Companies are expected to cover around 25 to 30 per cent of capital costs, the rest is financed. After the initial loan payback period, there are few fixed costs beyond employing an engineer, a couple of technicians, security guards and conducting routine maintenance. With different expected loan payback periods, however, the lucrativeness of the business could become questionable. While most of the early projects were able to pay their loans back in five to seven years, nowadays this period has doubled, putting serious pressure particularly on small players. The SHW routinely reduces the number of projected HEPPs and many small-to-mid-size projects are being offered to bigger players.

The reasons underlying the stagnation in the market are manifold. What is striking is that some of these reasons are in fact the very factors that made the hydropower renaissance possible. To begin with, many licensed projects, experts argue, have proved to be unprofitable. It turns out that not all *çantacı* were reliable: while some were crucial for the sector to acquire quality data and projects, others designed flawed projects based on optimistic forecasts, often without even visiting project sites. Even many good-intentioned projects were based on the SHW data that was not up-to-date. Many investors found out only after the fact that a stream section that they had taken out a US$ 10-million loan for had dried out years ago. These errors were overlooked in the speculative hype of the boom period. The draught of 2014 made these errors unbearable for many projects and the number of projected projects decreased significantly. But the most important reason that caused unforeseeable delays and complicated the project finance cycle has been public opposition and litigation processes. Many banks, which flooded the industry with money a few years ago, are now increasingly hesitant to offer loans to SHP projects as it is hard to predict what kind of relationship investors (and their subcontractors in the field) will establish with the local population. The next section tackles this uneasy relationship and attempts to answer how infrastructures are justified through discursive and material tools of development when the traditional role of the state as the distributer of development is undermined.

Whither the Developmentalist State?

The link between development and hydroelectricity is almost self-evident. In concrete terms, like all power plants, HEPPs power industry, light up residences and charge everyday life. Beyond their primary tasks, large dams in particular are second to none in propagating images and ideas of improvement, achievement and grandeur. Especially in the global South, hydroelectricity is tightly linked to politics. It has been the material and symbolic carrier of the idea of development and the dream of catching up with 'modernity' throughout the second half of the twentieth century. In India, Jawaharlal Nehru referred to large dams as the 'temples of modern India', while in Turkey, Süleyman Demirel – former prime minister and president – owed some of his popularity to his SHW background and nickname as 'the king of dams'. Yet although hydropower sets a myriad of ideas and desires in motion, it also touches on potential areas of tension, disrupts local livelihoods, causes large-scale environmental change and re-shapes rural landscapes. As a result, hydroelectricity (alongside coal and oil) is not surprisingly an important subject in investigating how ideas and policies of development unfold.[36]

The South-eastern Anatolia Project (*Güneydoğu Anadolu Projesi – GAP*), Turkey's long-running integrated regional strategy that revolves around 22 dams (19 of which are HEPPs), attracted scholarly interest precisely because it 'offers an excellent laboratory to study the paradoxical and difficult nature of developmentalism'.[37] As critical as they have been about the ambiguities, unintended consequences and failures of the project, researchers were also overwhelmed by its ambitious scope. After all, while the GAP project was initiated solely for electricity production back in the 1960s, in time it first incorporated a complex agricultural development component, then evolved into a colossal multisector sustainable development undertaking that aims at alleviating regional socio-economic disparities. Despite its shortcomings, deleterious effects, top-down high modernist approach and perhaps highly problematic assumptions (including that the project would miraculously solve Turkey's decades-long Kurdish problem), the GAP project always had a developmentalist claim that has proudly been rephrased by generations of politicians to garner political support.[38] Against this background, one cannot help but wonder how the privatisation of hydroelectric production impacted the legacy of hydropower-fuelled, state-led developmentalism.

In an article written more than a decade ago, and just a few years before the boom of Turkish hydropower renaissance, Kaygusuz and Arsel sought to explain the Turkish state's 'insistence [. . .] on favouring hydropower' while there was so much to gain from diversifying energy production through renewables.[39] If one reason was to covert the spectacle of large-scale development into a political advantage, the other was using the Tigris and the Euphrates as a foreign policy tool, through the elaborate dam system built on them.[40] As noted above, the majority of the hydropower developments since then lack the spectacularity of large dams; most are built on streams that do not cross borders and only a handful are built and owned by the state.[41] Yet this transformation did not change the government's interest in turning the ground-breaking and ribbon-cutting ceremonies related to hydropower structures, large or small, into political rallies. In fact, the AKP and its leader Erdoğan have doubled down on emphasising the link between energy and development. His ambition to revise the notorious proverb 'water flows, Turk stares' as 'water flows, Turk builds' is one of the catchiest political mottos of the AKP's 14-year long reign. More recently and particularly after the Gezi Uprising, which successfully devised an oppositional language agitated by urban and environmental justice tones, energy developments now have a new discursive role. According to this political spin, the success of hydro-energy (along with other infrastructure and extraction) investments are the reasons why AKP governments are criticised by international powers that are jealous of, and determined to stop, Turkey's development.[42]

However, there are non-discursive elements that bind Turkey's hydropower renaissance to development that are less straightforward and more fragile. Sustaining developmentalism needs constant reworking and negotiation at the local level in the absence of the welfare state, even though pleasant poses of government members with energy businesspeople may suggest otherwise. No matter how hegemonic the national development discourse is, it could be politically costly to neglect local welfare and livelihoods entirely in each case. A pro-government energy bureaucrat explains this challenge as follows:

> When we [the state] were building these [HEPPs], we used to settle down. Citizens were able to see the entire state with all its might there. We used to have hundreds of workers, run a huge cafeteria for them, employ tens of engineers, build a kindergarten or improve the primary school for their kids if necessary, repair the roads and the minaret of the mosque, and stay for many years. That was not efficient and that is why things needed to be privatised. But citizens are disappointed if they don't see all this. The private sector is only concerned with getting it done quick and cheap. They don't even hire a cook from the village; instead they work with a caterer from the city. Look, citizens need to change their mentality but our entrepreneurs should take good care of the locals, too. We advise

> them along these lines all the time; some follow our advice, some don't. (Personal interview, April 2013)

Spending some time in the new energy geographies of Turkey guarantees that one comes across many fascinating stories on 'how local citizens are taken good care of', although the scope and meaning of the concepts may differ depending on whom you are talking to. Anti-SHP activists from resistance sites tell you how aggressively companies try to bribe locals and buy out elected village chiefs. Meanwhile, companies with operational SHPs complain about being the unofficial sponsor of villages and small towns, which range from providing needy students with scholarships to covering heating expenses of the local primary school. Yet often, local residents are caught between struggling for a campaign that is losing ground and securing some sort of compensation before it is too late.

Erdem Evren's rich ethnography, for example, discusses the role of waiting in infrastructure disputes and how the strong resistance in Yusufeli, Artvin (the town that will be inundated by the under-construction Yusufeli Dam), encumbered the almost decade-long process.[43] Waiting in uncertainty, Evren argues, first transformed the resistance of Yusufeli into a negotiation with the municipality (backed by the government) over terms of compensation and then all-out surrender. The idea of development, understood as the desire to have a better life with the help of large infrastructure projects, does not (cannot) entirely wither away under neoliberal developmentalism. Citizens, in contrast to welfare-state developmentalism, are now expected to seize opportunities that neoliberalism haphazardly offers them. A form of entrepreneurial citizenship that speculates and takes chances, as many have argued,[44] emerges to survive in the uneven and uncertain field of neoliberalism. Parallel to the character of the contemporary form of Turkish neoliberalism, however, citizens feel the need to perform a type of entrepreneurship that is not only self-fashioned but somehow authoritarian, too. Ekrem, a 33-year-old beekeeper-cum-anti-SHP-activist in rural Artvin, explains why he is now on the payroll of an SHP run by an Ankara-based company:

> Look, I was against it [SHP] from the very first day. We struggled, I led the struggle, but we failed, they won. Now it is here splitting our village in two. I can't change this [...] So if you are making

> money in my village, if you are turning this stream into money, my friend, I will not let you exploit me. Now we are running the plant, we control it. You know, some days we fight with the boss if necessary. He knows that I am not afraid to speak my mind [. . .] Just like Tayyip [Erdoğan] scolding businessmen on TV, the boss here is in our palm you know [. . .] (Personal interview, August 2014)

Ekrem's boss might be benevolent and/or clever enough to employ Ekrem and his 11 friends and give them certain autonomy in managing the daily routine of the plant that is adjacent to their village. Yet it is hard to believe that a bunch of extra employees and their relaxed work routine could hurt the boss and the profit margin of his SHP in any substantial way. Nor is there much reason to believe that entrepreneur citizenship practices could alter the highly uneven and unpredictable nature of neoliberal developmentalism and replicate the welfare state in any meaningful way.

In its new format, development projects do have a twisted yet undeniable impact on local politics as million dollar businesses flourish in provincial towns. Logistics giant MNG, for example, holds three SHP licenses in Arhavi, Artvin, a small seashore town in the Eastern Black Sea Region. Arhavi is one of the strongholds of the anti-SHP struggle and has actively mobilised against MNG's SHPs and 12 other projects over the past four years, none of which have yet been completed. MNG lost two legal battles against the opposition so far, but revitalised the project by acquiring new EIA reports approved from Ankara, and more critically, work permits from the Arhavi Municipality. MNG, whose founding CEO is from Arhavi, coincidentally distributes many scholarships through the municipality, sponsors Arhavi's one and only summer festival, and singlehandedly undertook the rehabilitation project of the underutilised landfill between the city and the sea. In turn, Coşkun Hekimoğlu, Arhavi's AKP-affiliated mayor is a staunch SHP supporter. So much so that in the fall of 2014 he organised the country's first pro-SHP rally under the banner 'Arhavi embraces its local values', in which values refer to local businesspeople of Arhavi (such as MNG) who are interested in investing in the town along with the SHPs.[45] Mayor Hekimoğlu's unapologetical support for MNG's SHP project did not go unnoticed. MNG group's donations to the municipal projects as well as scholarships they provide for the students of Arhavi are larger than ever now.[46]

Despite their smallness in terms of installed capacity, the infrastructures that mark Turkey's hydropower renaissance cast a shadow much larger than their actual size. This shadow is not limited to the country's changing hydropower inventory and conversion of rural livelihoods into new energy geographies. The sheer volume and aggressiveness of the contemporary hydropower boom generate new markets and establish new fields of penetration for both the capital and political power. They, at the same time, establish new market-based relationships in the periphery and recruit new participants into AKP's game of speculative economics, while rendering beekeepers (such as Ekrem) as well as small town mayors (such as that of Arhavi) as self-entrepreneurs. While the aggressive intrusion of energy infrastructures to the Turkish countryside continues to displace local populations and destroy the rural fabric, the speculative promise of growth economics is still appealing and/or understandable for many.

Concluding Remarks

Brenner et al. describe neoliberalism as a 'rascal concept', one that is 'promiscuously pervasive yet inconsistently defined, empirically imprecise and frequently contested'.[47] Reasons vary. On the one hand, there is not much that escapes the cynically broad definitions of neoliberalism. On the other, neoliberalism is a dynamic process, one that is constantly redefined in response to social or ecological obstacles. Therefore, rather than an ultimate policy prescription, we can only talk about neoliberalisation as a dynamic process, one that is willing to renew itself. Moreover, no matter how amorphous neoliberalism may seem, it moulds into a concrete form as it gets traction at particular sites at the local level. Neoliberalisation finds a new definition as it meets with and transforms through other political rationalities; local, spatial and temporal realities.

This chapter reflects on Turkey's neoliberalisation experience by examining its transforming energy domain. Yet it does not treat energy merely as a policy era. To do justice to the messiness of neoliberalism, the chapter travels on the back of a particular form of infrastructure, hydropower plants, as they move from SHW offices to courthouses, from investment bank corridors to the valleys of the Eastern Black Sea Coast. The inconsistencies of neoliberalism are perhaps more pronounced when it encounters 'unruly' environments, as nature matters to neoliberalism not only in terms of its significance to humans but also in terms of its materiality.[48]

All this search for complications in the neoliberalisation experience is not to deny the existence of power dynamics and relationships of dependency that the chapter aims to address. On the contrary, Turkey's hydropower renaissance has created clear winners and losers. But addressing the riddle of infrastructural boom that marked the past decade-and-a-half in Turkey can only be done by taking these infrastructures seriously.

Notes

1. Conceptualising the construction-led political economy of the AKP reign has been on the agenda of Turkey scholars for the last few years. Some notable examples include Bengi Akbulut and Fikret Adaman, 'The unbearable appeal of modernisation: The fetish of growth', *Perspectives: Political Analysis and Commentary from Turkey* 5 (2013), pp. 14–17; Fikret Adaman, Bengi Akbulut, Yahya Madra and Şevket Pamuk, 'Hitting the wall: Erdoğan's construction-based, finance-led growth regime', *The Middle East in London* 10/3 (2014), pp. 7–8; Ayşe Buğra and Osman Savaşkan, *New Capitalism in Turkey: The Relationship between Politics, Religion and Business* (Cheltenham, 2014); Erinç Yeldan and Burcu Ünüvar, 'An assessment of the Turkish economy in the AKP era', *Research and Policy on Turkey* 1/1 (2016), pp. 11–28; and Tanıl Bora (ed.), *İnşaat Ya Resullulah {Construction, Dear Prophet}* (İstanbul, 2016).
2. On the link between Gezi and environmental activism, see Sinan Erensü and Ozan Karaman, 'Work of a few trees: Gezi, space and politics', *International Journal of Urban and Regional Research* (forthcoming).
3. 'Enerji sektöründe iflas kaygısı' ['Bankruptcy anxiety in energy sector'], *Enerji Panorama*, 25 July 2005, pp. 33–5; p. 33.
4. Ibid.
5. 'Turkey needs to invest 120 billion in energy until 2023', *Hurriyet Daily News*, 20 January 2015, http://www.hurriyetdailynews.com/turkey-needs-to-invest-120-billion-in-energy-until-2023-says-erdogan.aspx?pageID=23ID=77197&News CatID=348, accessed 10 June 2016.
6. Turkish Electricity Transmission Co (TEIAS). Contemporary stats and figures, available at http://www.teias.gov.tr/ [in Turkish], accessed 20 May 2016.
7. Bir Umut Derneği, *İş Cinayetleri Almanağı 2015 {Labour Murders Almanac 2015}* (İstanbul, 2016).
8. Çağan H. Şekercioğlu et al., 'Turkey's globally important biodiversity in crisis', *Biological Conservation* 144/22 (2011), pp. 2752–69.
9. While EPI fails to capture many aspects of environmental degradation, yet Turkey's extreme low performance in certain indicators (for example, ranking

177 in biodiversity and habitat measure among 180 countries) is particularly worthwhile. The report is available at http://epi.yale.edu/country/turkey, accessed 1 May 2016.

10. 'Turkey among the worst performers in dealing with greenhouse gas emissions', *Hürriyet*, 10 December 2014, available at http://www.hurriyetdailynews.com/turkey-among-the-worst-performers-in-dealing-with-greenhouse-gas-emissions.aspx?pageID=238&nID=75449&NewsCatID=340, accessed 20 April 2016. For a critical account on Turkey's climate change policy, see Ethemcan Turhan et al., 'Beyond special circumstances: Climate change policy in Turkey 1992–2015', *Wiley Interdisciplinary Reviews: Climate Change* 7/3 (2016), pp. 448–60.
11. Damian Carrigton, 'Is it too late to stop Turkey's coal rush?', *The Guardian*, 6 August 2015, available at http://www.theguardian.com/environment/2015/aug/06/is-it-too-late-to-stop-turkeys-coal-rush, accessed 20 May 2016.
12. 'Turkey's blackout caused by line maintenance, hydro production oversupply – TEIAS', *ICIS*, 16 April 2015, available at http://www.icis.com/resources/news/2015/04/16/9876979/turkey-s-blackout-caused-by-line-maintenance-hydro-production-oversupply-teias/, accessed 20 May 2016.
13. Maria Tsvetkova and Lidia Kelly, 'Russia says it has proof Turkey involved in Islamic State oil trade', *Reuters*, 15 December 2015, available at http://www.reuters.com/article/us-mideast-crisis-russia-turkey-idUSKBN0TL19S20151202, accessed 20 May 2016.
14. The first hydroelectric power plant in Turkey was a primitive one constructed in Tarsus in 1902 while the Ottoman Empire was still intact. One had to wait until 1956 for the first modern hydroelectric power plant that was planned and constructed by the State Hydraulic Works: The Sarıyar Dam on River Sakarya (80 MW installed capacity). Therefore, the history of hydropower in Turkey is contingent on the origin story one prefers.
15. Throughout the chapter, I use the initialism HEPP to refer to all sorts of hydropower plants, while I reserve the initialism SHP only for small run-off-the-river HEPPs. Arif Hepbaşlı, 'Development and restructuring of Turkey's electricity sector: a review', *Renewable and Sustainable Energy Reviews* 9 (2005), pp. 311–43.
16. İzak Atiyas, Tamer Çetin and Gürcan Güler, *Reforming Turkish Energy Markets: Political Economy, Regulation and Competition in the Search for Energy Policy* (New York, 2002).
17. Ibid.
18. For a report that reveals some of the ideological debates on the energy reform, see TÜSİAD, *21. Yüzyıl'a Girerken Türkiye'nin Enerji Stratejisinin Değerlendirilmesi {Evaluation of Turkish Energy Strategy at the Dawn of 21st Century}*, TÜSİAD Publication No: T/98–12/239 (1998).
19. On the features of Electricity Market Reform, see Atiyas et al., *Reforming*; Hepbaşlı, *Development*; and Erkan Erdoğdu, 'Regulatory reform in Turkish energy: An analysis', *Energy Policy* 35 (2007), pp. 984–93.

20. Ministry of Environment and Urbanisation Statistics on Environmental Impact Assessment (EIA), available at http://www.csb.gov.tr/db/ced/icerikbelge/icerikbelge2910.pdf, accessed 20 May 2016.
21. Law no. 6830, which introduced urgent expropriation procedures, directly refers to a state of war or state of emergency as a condition that defines urgency. Some of the concrete examples that the law provides include bakeries, factories, medical tools and facilities that could be utilised by military forces. As such, this special law only targets services and properties needed for their technical features. See Buket Karaman, 'Acele Kamulaştırma [Urgent Expropriation]', unpublished MA thesis, Ankara University (2015).
22. Alp Yücel Kaya, 'Neoliberal mülkiyet ya da acele kamulaştırma nedir? [What is neoliberal property, or the urgent expropriation?]', *Toplum ve Bilim* 122 (2011), pp. 194–236, p. 200.
23. Alp Yücel Kaya, 'Sermaye-emek kutuplaşmasının yeniden üretimi: acele kamulaştırma kararlarında HES'ler [Reproduction of capital-labour bifurcation: HEPPs in urgent expropriation decisions]', in C. Aksu, S. Erensü and E. Evren (eds), *Sudan Sebepler: Türkiye'de neoliberal su-enerji politikaları ve direnişler {Watery Reasons: Neoliberal Water-Energy Politics in Turkey and Resistance}* (İstanbul, 2016).
24. On 23 March 2016, the AKP government signed a UE decision that confiscated 6,300 parcels in historic Sur District of Diyarbakır, the political and cultural heartland of the Kurdish region. Prior to the decision, Sur remained under a 24-hour curfew for three months during which it was shelled by tanks and raked by armed vehicles and machine guns to uproot the young PKK militia and their barricades. The government promised that Sur residents will be given modern units and a new police station once the renewal is completed.
25. Nazile I. Yeşilyurt, 'İdari yargıda yürütmenin durdurulması ve ivedi yargılama: Hukuka sermayeye koşut hız ayarı [Suspension of execution and urgent judicial proceeding in the administrative law: Legal speed up for the capital]', *SBF Dergisi* 70/2 (2015), pp. 403–33.
26. ESHA brochure, available at http://www.esha.be/fileadmin/esha_files/documents/Policy/ESHA-Policy_sheets_-_new.pdf, accessed 20 May 2016.
27. Erdoğan Bayraktar, 'HES'lerle işin altından kalkamayız, nükleer şart [Erdoğan Bayraktar: We cannot surmount this by SHPs, nuclear is a must]', 21 November 2013, available at https://t24.com.tr/haber/erdogan-bayraktar-heslerle-isin-altindan-kalkamayiz-nukleer-sart,244474, accessed 20 May 2016.
28. Ibid.
29. Platform of the 64th Government, http://www.basbakanlik.gov.tr/docs/KurumsalHaberler/64.hukumet_programi.pdf, accessed 20 May 2016.
30. Rize is 1,513 square miles while Delaware, the second smallest state of the USA, is 1,954 square miles.
31. In fact, the SHW differentiates between state-planned and privatised HEPPs, and privately-planned HEPPs, according to their well-known Table-5.1,

Table-5.2 classification. Available at http://www2.dsi.gov.tr/ska/ska.htm, accessed 20 May 2016.

32. Fabian Muniesa, Yuval Millo and Michel Callon, 'An introduction to market devices', *The Sociological Review* 55/2 (2007), pp. 1–12; Michel Callon 'What does it mean to say that economics is performative', in D. MacKenzie, F. Muniesa and L. Siu (eds), *Do Economists Make Markets? On the Performativity of Economics* (Princeton, 2007); and Koray Çalışkan and Michel Callon 'Economisation, part 2: A research programme for the study of markets', *Economy and Society* 39/1 (2010), pp. 1–32.
33. Although the hydropower market includes a diverse set of sectors such as EIA reports and project finance consultants, turbine importers and producers, construction vehicle dealers and local subcontractors, which are all crucial to appreciate the size of the pie, in this chapter I will limit the analysis to license-holding firms.
34. Mustafa Eberliköse, 'Enerji sektörünün dönüşümü ve HES sürecinde birikim, devlet ve sınıflar [Accumulation, state and classes in the process of transformation of the energy sector and the construction of HEPPs]', *Praksis* 30–1 (2013), pp. 129–45; p. 142.
35. Frustrated with the black market, the government passed a series of measures, such as a pre-licensing, higher license fees and most important, license cancellations if companies failed to start construction within a given period of time. These changes eliminated some of the small players, decreased the number of HEPP licenses, yet increased the revolving door type of relationship between the energy market and the bureaucracy.
36. On energy preferences and political power see, Timothy Mitchell, *Carbon Democracy: Political Power in the Age of Oil* (New York, 2011); and Erik Swengedouw, *Liquid Power: Contested Hydro-Modernities in Twentieth-Century Spain* (New York, 2015).
37. Ali Çarkoğlu and Mine Eder, 'Development alla Turca: The Southeastern Anatolia project', in F. Adaman and M. Arsel (eds), *Environmentalism in Turkey: Between Democracy and Development?* (Aldershot, 2005).
38. On the ambivalence related to the South-eastern Anatolia Project and its developmentalist perspective, see Leila Harris, 'Modernising the nation: Postcolonialism, postdevelopmentalism, and ambivalent spaces of difference in Southeastern Turkey', *Geoforum* 38 (2008), pp. 1698–708.
39. Kamil Kaygusuz and Murat Arsel, 'Energy politics and policy', in Adaman and Arsel (eds), *Environmentalism in Turkey*, p. 161.
40. Ibid.
41. With the notable exception of hydropower projects in the Çoruh Valley, which are both large and built on a river that crosses into Georgia.
42. At a political rally in Yusufeli, President Erdoğan stated: 'Why is the West jealous of us? Because of dams like this (referring to Yusufeli Dam), Yavuz Sultan Selim Bridge (the third Bosphorus bridge), the Bosphorus underwater

tunnel and the Marmaray Subway line'. Erdoğan, 'The west is jealous of our dams, bridges and subways', *Turkish Sun*, 23 May 2016, available at http://theturkishsun.com/erdogan-the-west-is-jealous-of-our-dams-bridges-and-subways-19364/, accessed 25 May 2016.

43. Erdem Evren 'The rise and decline of an anti-dam campaign: Yusufeli Dam project and the temporal politics of development', *Water History* 6/4 (2014), pp. 405–19.
44. Aihwa Ong, *Neoliberalism as Exception: Mutations in Citizenship and Modernity* (Durham, 2016).
45. Sinan Erensü, 'İnşaat ekonomisinin Arhavi eşiği [The Arhavi threshold of the construction economy]', *Evrensel*, 31 August 2014, available at http://www.evrensel.net/haber/90953/insaat-ekonomisinin-arhavi-esigi, accessed 20 May 2013.
46. MNG is the main sponsor of the largest municipal project in Arhavi which consists of turning the underutilised landfill strip between the town and the highway running by the shore into a multi-purpose recreational facility. My informants also reported that MNG recently donated a large sum to ISTAD (Arhavi kinship association in Istanbul) to be spent fort the needy Arhavian students studying away from their home town.
47. Neil Brenner, Jamie Peck and Nik Theodore, 'Veriegated neoliberalisation: geographies, modalities, pathways', *Global Networks* 10/2 (2010), pp. 182–222.
48. Noel Castree, 'Neoliberalism and the biophysical environment 1: What neoliberalism is, and what difference nature makes to it', *Geography Compass* 4/12 (2010), pp. 1725–33; p. 1731.

CHAPTER 6

ENVIRONMENTAL CONCERNS IN TURKEY: A COMPARATIVE PERSPECTIVE

Ali Çarkoğlu

Introduction

The standard explanation for the rise of environmental issues on the public agenda is typically linked to rising 'post-material values' in the post-World War II era.[1] The fact that environmental issues gained priority is deemed to be partially responsible for the rise of environmental movements and the ecological green parties in many Western European party systems. A similar development is expected from developing democracies, in particular, when their economic development reaches a stage where basic survival motivations leave their impact on mobilisation to post-materialist values that question and remain sceptical about economic development, especially when it touches upon environmental issues. As a result, modern democracies witness the rise of political movements that emphasise the need for environmental regulations that could impose limitations even on economic development objectives, should the accomplishment of these objectives require unsustainable environmental balances in certain localities or globally. These developments are relatively well-traced in the Western democracies. However, for developing democracies where neither the socio-economic dimension nor the political institutions are fully developed and functional, our knowledge remains limited.[2]

The above outlined causal mechanism has popular environmental concerns at its root. Rising public concerns about the environment due to changing public priorities that shift from basic material needs to post-materialist concerns are expected to bring regulatory interventions that may restrict achieving material objectives for the sake of environmental protection, which finds support not only amongst the public but ultimately in policy priorities reflected in party manifestos. Consequently, if public concern about the environment is on the rise, there should be a corresponding rise in how parties treat this issue and a corresponding emphasis in their election manifestos. Obviously, besides political parties, other civil society and non-governmental organisations, interest groups and the like would also be responsive to the same rising popular concerns. However, in this chapter I will solely focus on the responsiveness of political parties to rising environmental concerns.

I focus on this simple expectation concerning public preferences and elite emphases for electoral competition. I first show in a comparative framework as to how public and elite concerns about the environment developed between 1993 and 2010 by using the International Social Survey Program (ISSP) data on environmental attitudes and Comparative Manifestos Project (CMP) data. I expand these analyses by focusing more in-depth on the Turkish case and illustrating how different party constituencies and socio-economic groups differ in their approach to the environment, blurring the simple causal picture linking the elite to the masses. My objective in this exercise is to demonstrate how difficult it is to find a clear socio-economic foundation that persistently supports or opposes environmentally sensitive issues. When there is a clear partisan divide on these issues, the political elite is likely to use this to its advantage to bypass serious resistance that blocks materialist policy initiatives.

Tracing the Elite Rhetoric and Preferences in Election Manifestos: 1950–2015

Tracing the development of environmental concerns in the elite rhetoric of post-World War II party systems can be accomplished with reference to party manifestos. The CMP uses individual coders who apply a common set of rules and definitions to measure policy positions of all relevant parties in a given democracy.[3] Manifestos are taken as an authoritative policy statement of the parties and hence, reflective of their policy preferences at a given point in time. The CMP content analysis framework aims to discover party stances by quantifying their manifesto statements and messages to their electorate.

The CMP coding framework includes a particular category under the *Welfare and Quality of Life Domain* that aims to capture environmental protection appeals. This should prove useful in tracing the development of environmental concerns among the party elites in Turkey after 1950, for which we have complete data for 56 countries.[4] This category (501) is described in the *Manifesto Coding Instructions* (4th edition) by Annika Werner, Onawa Lacewell and Andrea Volkens as follows:

General policies in favour of protecting the environment, fighting climate change and other 'green' policies. For instance:

- general preservation of natural resources;
- preservation of countryside, forests, etc.;
- protection of national parks;
- animal rights.

May include a great variance of policies that have the unified goal of environmental protection.

Accordingly, this coding category aims to capture the essence of rising environmental concerns in modern democracies. From protection of the environment in all its guises, to detrimental policies at the highest macro-level in energy production using nuclear technology, to the very bottom of social interaction in the form of how household waste should be disposed, this category can be used to depict the policy positions of political parties in all its detail. In Figure 6.1a to 6.1c, I use the occurrence of this category (501) as the percentage of the total number of statements in a given political party manifesto in a given election year, aggregated over three decades across party systems for which we also have public concern measurements from the 1993, 2000 and 2010 ISSP surveys for 18 to 30 countries. Country figures here represent average space as percentage of manifesto emphases allocated for the 501 category across all parties in a given country. The larger its share, it is assumed that emphasising this category is deemed more important and hence the issue is considered more important. We see from this figure that 10 of the 24 countries experienced an

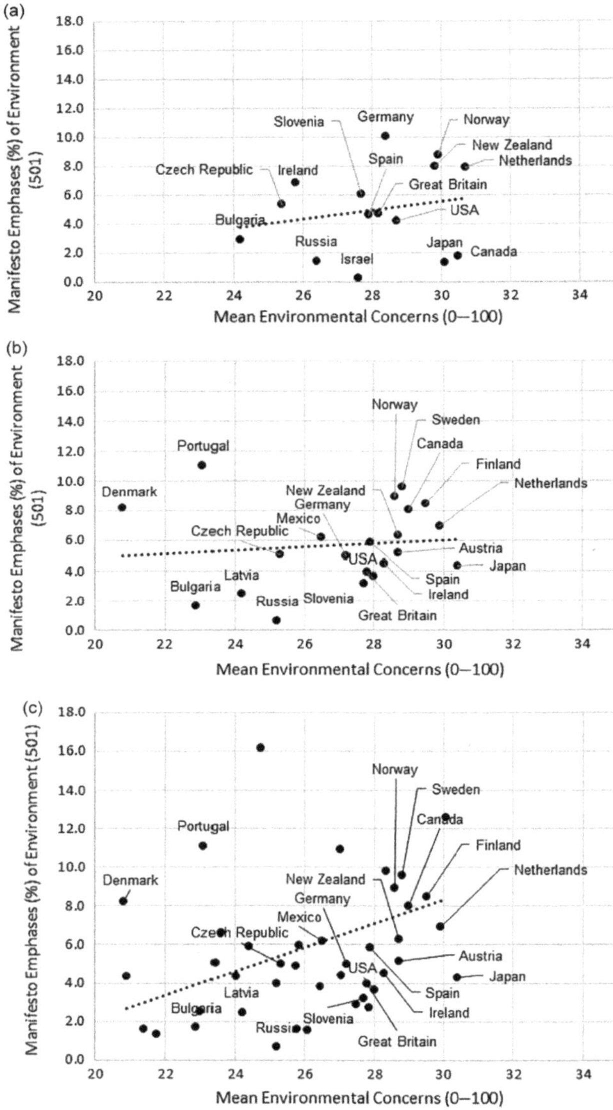

Figure 6.1 **a.** Environmental Concern and Manifesto Emphases on Environment, 1990–9. **b.** Environmental Concern and Manifesto Emphases on Environment, 2000–9. **c.** Environmental Concern and Manifesto Emphases on Environment, 2010–15

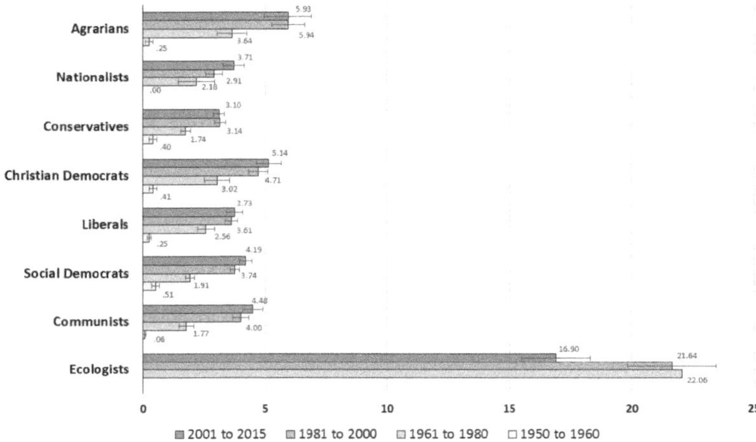

Figure 6.2 Manifesto Emphases on Environment by Major Party Families, 1950–2015

increase in the space allocated to environmental issues in election manifestos during the 1990–2015 period. We also see that the space allocated to environmental discussions ranged between 1 per cent and 16 per cent of total manifesto space and thus was not amongst the top most important issues in the electoral debates of the relevant countries.

Figure 6.2 shows in greater detail how the space allocated to environmental issues progressed over the past nearly 65 years. Among the eight major party families – including the relative latecomer ecologist parties – we observe a marked progression in the allocation of greater space for environmental issues. For example, social democrats had almost no discussion of environmental issues in the 1950s. However, in the period from 1960 to 1980, there is marginal space set aside for the environmental concerns in their manifestos, about 2 per cent, which rises to about 3.7 per cent and then to 4.2 per cent over the most recent 2000–15 period. A similar upward trend is observed for all party families, surprisingly except for the ecologists.

However, since the ecologist parties allocate more than three times the space typically allocated by other party families, the space they set aside are observed to drop in the same period. Nevertheless, during the most recent 2000–15 period, the ecologist parties allocated, on average, nearly 17 per cent of their manifestos to the discussion of environmental issues. The observed drop in environmental emphases may hence be taken as an indication that these parties are spending more time on other mainstream issues concerning governance, economic policy, welfare policy, security and discussions on various identity issues, which replace the emphasis on the environment.

The horizontal axis in Figure 6.1 depicts the environmental concerns measurements after Franzen and Meyer, which use the ISSP 1993 and 2000 data to create an environmental concern index.[5] Table 6.1 summarises the index questions for Turkey, South Korea, Germany, Japan and the United States. The same summary can be found for the United States, Japan and Germany for the earlier two rounds in 1993 and 2000, again in Franzen and Meyer,[6] while Turkey did not participate in these rounds. We observe that nearly one-fourth of the Turkish sample is willing to pay 'much higher prices in order to protect the environment', while this figure was about 60 per cent in South Korea and 39 per cent in Japan. Similarly, only about 22 per cent of the respondents in Turkey were willing to pay 'much higher taxes in order to protect the environment', compared to some 50 per cent of the respondents in South Korea. While about 17 per cent accepted 'cuts in their standards of living in order to protect the environment' in Turkey, this group constituted 37 per cent in Germany and 43 per cent in South Korea.

A similar pattern is observed in other attitudinal evaluations concerning the role of science in resolving environmental problems, economic growth and its linkage to the environment, and the necessary sacrifices individuals need to make to protect the environment. For example, while about one-third of the sample disagreed with the statement 'we worry too much about the future of the environment and not enough about prices and jobs today' in Turkey and in Japan, this figure was 47 per cent in Germany and 64 per cent in South Korea. Through these nine items that are assessed on a scale from 1 to 5, Franzen and Meyer formed a simple additive environmental concern index that ranges between 9 and 45. Cronbach's alpha for the whole data is 0.69 and appears to be higher for European democracies compared to other regions.[7]

Returning to Figures 6.1a to 6.1c, we observe that over the three periods for which we have data for both the ISSP environmental concern index as well as the CMP data on party manifestos, there is a clear positive link between public environmental concerns and those emphasised in the manifesto of the elite. What is also striking is that compared to the 1990s and 2000s, there is a much more pronounced link between the two variables in the most recent period from 2010 to 2015: a unit increase in public concern about environmental issues leads to a much higher positive influence on the space allocated to environmental issues in election manifestos.

This alone could be taken as a signal that the elite have been more responsive to public concerns in this period. The fact that the elite have been more responsive to rising public concerns about the environment can be an indication that electoral benefits associated with being responsive has also been increasing over the years. The salience of the environment as an electoral issue over which parties position themselves strategically is hence likely to be on the rise over the period in concern from the 1990s through to 2015.

When we turn our attention to the Turkish case and trace the extent to which parties have increased their emphasis on environmental issues over the past 65 years, we see that environmental concerns were simply not in the forefront in the early years of multi-party competition (Figure 6.3). This may be hard to conceive; however, this was a time when the country was at the turning point of modern history following the end of World War II and a new world order was being established with Turkey participating in the process by aligning itself with its Western allies, and issues other than the environment were being emphasised; issues that were more linked to economic and social development as well as security. In this context, the environment was often seen as a resource to be exploited in order to meet the mass demands for development, which generated increased consumption and easier access to markets irrespective of their costs for the country's environment. Sustainability was simply not part of the Turkish vocabulary at the time.

There is no mention of environmental protection in the election manifestos of the 1950s and of the first post-coup election of 1961. Only in the 1965 electoral campaign do we see some concerns, voiced by the Republican People's Party (*Cumhuriyet Halk Partisi*, CHP). However, this emphasis cannot be considered a conscious effort by the CHP to bring these issues to the forefront in competition with the

Table 6.1 Environmental Concern in Turkey, Germany, South Korea and the United States, 2010

	Turkey	Germany	South Korea	US	Japan
How willing would you be to pay much higher prices in order to protect the environment (% very and fairly willing)?	24.3	35.6	58.8	44.5	39.4
How willing would you be to pay much higher taxes in order to protect the environment (% very and fairly willing)?	21.9	21.1	49.9	32.1	22.1
How willing would you be to accept cuts in your standard of living in order to protect the environment (% very and fairly willing)?	17.2	37.4	43.0	34.0	26.6
I do what is right for the environment, even when it costs more money or takes more time (% agree strongly and agree)	54.2	49.2	57.5	53.4	38.3
Modern science will solve our environmental problems with little change to our way of life (% disagree strongly and disagree)	20.2	39.7	51.9	45.5	58.1
We worry too much about the future of the environment and not enough about prices and jobs today (% disagree strongly and disagree)	33.5	46.8	63.6	40.1	32.1
People worry too much about human progress harming the environment (% disagree strongly and disagree)	28.6	43.3	33.4	40.4	36.7
In order to protect the environment, the country needs economic growth (% disagree strongly and disagree)	10.5	24.7	18.5	20.1	6.8

It is just too difficult for someone like me to do much about the environment (% disagree strongly and disagree)	49.2	45.1	36.1	51.7	47.1
Number of cases	1665	1407	1576	1430	1307
Mean of the index for environmental concern	23.0	25.7	27.9	26.1	26.0
Standard deviation of the environmental concern index	6.1	6.5	5.3	6.5	6.8
Cronbach's alpha of the environmental concern index	0.54	0.71	0.57	0.73	0.71

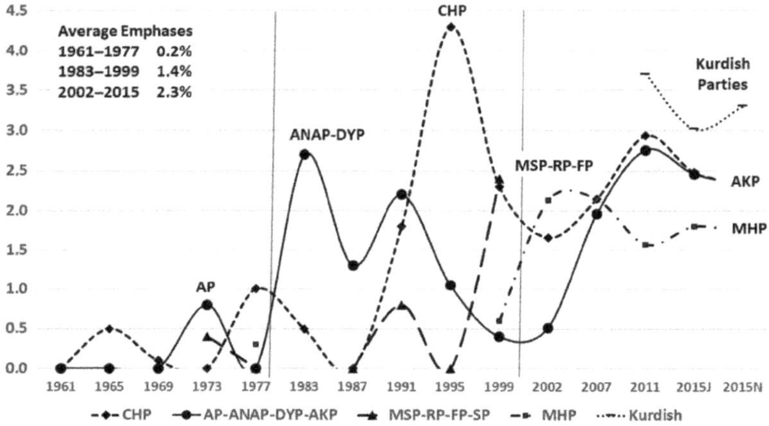

Figure 6.3 Party Manifesto Emphases on Environmental Protection, 1961–2015

Justice Party (*Adalet Partisi*, AP) at the time.[8] We observe no sustained continual emphasis on these issues for more than a decade until the 1977 election. In turn, the AP picked up on environmental concerns in 1973, when the CHP made no reference to them. In the 1977 general elections, the CHP spared only about 1 per cent of its manifesto emphasis on environmental protection, this did not find much of a matching emphasis by the AP, despite having slightly emphasised the issue earlier.

In short, while the 1950s remained completely silent on environmental concerns, these issues were on average only fractionally emphasised in political manifestos in the following two decades. Nevertheless, as of the late 1970s, the Turkish party system had already recognised the relevance of environmental concerns for Turkish politics. On the basis of fundamental democratic motivations, we can conjecture that these elite movements had their bearing among at least some constituencies of the Turkish electorate at the time. Otherwise, utility maximising elites would not have touched these issues at all. However, we simply are not in a position to test this assumption that the elite of the time were associated with the masses based on survey data for the 1970s.

The period between the 1980 military coup and 2002, when the Justice and Development Party (*Adalet ve Kalkınma Partisi*, AKP) came to power, witnessed the rise of environmental concerns in the Turkish party system. The Motherland Party (*Anavatan Partisi*, ANAP)[9] used this issue in its first post-coup election campaign in 1983 more than ever, allocating 3 per cent of its manifesto emphasis on the protection of the environment. Yet in the 1990s, as the ANAP and its nemesis the True Path Party (*Doğru Yol Partisi*, DYP) competed for supremacy of the Turkish peripheral centre-right, their attention slowly shifted away from environmental concerns. By the end of the 1990s, the emphasis on environmental concerns in the manifestos of both parties had dropped, on average, to fractional levels. However, it appears that their attention on the environment triggered the pro-Islamist Welfare Party (*Refah Partisi*, RP)[10] and eventually the Nationalist Action Party (*Milliyetçi Hareket Partisi*, MHP), which appear to have followed these issues at levels that were unprecedented in their respective party traditions. In other words, as the data surfaces, it appears that parties in the party system took steps in reaction to one another rather than undertaking the role of a pioneer, persistently owning this issue and following it to its full potential.

In the early stages of the post-1980 period, the CHP did not emphasise the environment; but in the 1991 and 1995 elections, a successively increasing share of its manifestos was devoted to environmental protection. It appears that as the CHP tradition leaned more towards the left of the Turkish ideological spectrum, its emphasis on environmental issues also increased. Although this level of emphasis was not maintained in the ensuing elections in the two decades that followed, this marks a time when environmental issues were accorded an exemplary level of priority within the Turkish party system, which still remains unprecedented.

During the period of the AKP's electoral dominance, starting from 2002, we see that both the AKP as well as its main competitor the CHP remain relatively low in their emphases compared to the level of importance attached by the Kurdish electoral tradition. While the Turkish nationalist MHP remained low in its emphasis on the environment, it nevertheless hit a higher average emphasis than the previous decade. The overall average of environmental issue emphases rose to about 1.4 per cent of total manifesto space available in the 1980s and 1990s, and then to 2.3 per cent in the post-2002 period. As such, the emphasis on environmental issues reached a peak in the latest period, although the importance attributed to these issues was still at relatively marginal levels. In the 1990s, the ANAP followed by the CHP appear to have set the tone for environmental concerns in the party system at large. The CHP of the 1990s focused its attention more on the environment, which appears to be owned primarily by the Kurdish tradition parties in the latest period. Overall concern remained low, if not marginal, never exceeding about 3-to-5 per cent of the total of manifesto emphases.

From a comparative perspective, compared to CMP data averages across party families for the post-2000 period, we see that Turkish political parties emphasised the environment much less compared to all other party families. In the post-2000 period, CMP data averages were 4.2 per cent for the social democrats, 5.1 per cent for the Christian democrats, 3.7 per cent for the nationalists and 3.1 per cent for the conservatives. In other words, the non-Kurdish parties in the post-2000 period emphasised environmental concerns the least compared to any other major party family.

In order to evaluate how environmental issues fare in comparison to other issue areas, we need to look into their components under the main issue categories. Environmental protection (501) is placed within the Domain 5: *Welfare and Quality of Life*, which occupies about one-fifth of the election emphases in the 2002–15 period. This is only second to Domain 4: *Economy*, that has nearly a 30 per cent share. However, environmental protection only covers about 11 per cent of the total emphases within the *Welfare and Quality of Life* domain or 2.3 per cent of the total manifesto emphases in this period. Within the same domain, *Welfare State Expansion* occupies about 31 per cent (or 6.3 per cent of the total) and positive mentions of equality about 26 per cent (or 5.5 per cent of the total). In other words, environmental protection is not a manifesto priority even within Domain 5. Although we see a historical upward trend in the emphasis on environmental protection since 1965, when it first appears in Turkish party manifestos, it remains part of a set of marginally important issues that occupy relatively little space in election manifestos.

Mass Electoral Perspective

From the perspective of the mass electorate, environmental concerns occupy nearly no space among the issues that shape and move electoral campaigns. When the top two most important issues on the country's agenda was questioned in the five consecutive election studies in 2002, 2007, 2011, and the general elections in June and November 2015, environmental concerns were not among these issues in any one of these studies. This is most likely due to the open-ended format that was used, since in the 2010 ISSP survey – which uses a closed-ended format – a few answers (1.3 per cent of the respondents) were related to the environment. In other words, even when the environment was one of the options available, only a handful of respondents picked it and placed it amongst the top two most important problems facing Turkey.

Protection of the environment was specifically questioned as part of the evaluations for the incumbent AKP government only for the pre-June 2015 survey. Although this issue was not mentioned by anyone as amongst the two most important issues facing Turkey, the performance of the incumbent government was found to be successful by about 37 per cent of the respondents and 39.5 per cent found the incumbent government unsuccessful.

The 2010 ISSP survey also distinguished between the most important environmental problems that impact Turkey as opposed to respondents and their families. Table 6.2 depicts an analysis of these two questions by cross-tabulating them against one another. While air pollution (24 per cent) and genetically modified foods (18 per cent) topped the lists for Turkey, respondents were of the opinion that genetically modified foods (21 per cent) and air pollution (14 per cent) impacted them the most in terms of themselves and their families. In other words, although their priority changes, these two items – air pollution and genetically modified foods – top the lists related to impacts at both the individual and the country levels.

We see that very few people actually give the same answer to both questions. Hence people do separate the impact of different environmental threats on their immediate family as opposed to the country at large. Whatever the answer might be for the question about the impact on Turkey overall, we observe that 'genetically modified foods' is the response given for the impact on one's immediate life surrounding family and friends. Not surprisingly, people whose response was 'water shortage' to the question concerning Turkey most prominently said 'climate change' was the problem that faces them personally. Similarly, if their focus was on air pollution or domestic waste disposal, then the most frequently given answer for the impact on family was 'air pollution'. If 'genetically modified foods' was the response in terms of the country, then the 'depletion of natural resources' was the answer at the more personal level.

Table 6.2 Which problem, if any, affects you and your family the most?

Which problem, if any, do you think is the most important for TURKEY?	Air pollution	Chemicals and pesticides	Water shortage	Water pollution	Nuclear waste	Domestic waste disposal	Climate change	Genetically modified foods	Using up our natural resources	None of these	Can't choose		Total
Air pollution	4.7	7.7	9.4	17.8	4.2	7.7	9.2	22.8	10.6	4.2	1.7	100	24.3
Chemicals and pesticides	10.3	3.2	10.9	6.4	8.3	5.8	5.8	36.5	9.0	1.3	2.6	100	9.4
Water shortage	15.2	9.3	3.3	13.2	3.3	7.9	19.9	11.9	7.3	2.6	6.0	100	9.1
Water pollution	28.0	5.3	6.7	3.3	5.3	10.7	10.0	16.7	8.7	2.0	3.3	100	9.0
Nuclear waste	15.8	7.0	8.8	7.0	1.8	5.3	10.5	31.6	8.8	0.0	3.5	100	3.4
Domestic waste disposal	26.0	6.0	8.0	10.0	6.0	4.0	10.0	14.0	14.0	0.0	2.0	100	3.0
Climate change	23.7	8.6	5.4	9.7	4.3	2.2	1.1	24.7	19.4	0.0	1.1	100	5.6
Genetically modified foods	20.5	12.3	4.6	11.9	3.6	3.6	6.6	5.6	25.5	3.6	2.0	100	18.1
Using up our natural resources	13.5	12.5	5.3	4.8	2.4	4.8	6.7	43.3	1.0	3.8	1.9	100	12.5
None of these	0.0	2.1	0.0	0.0	0.0	0.0	0.0	0.0	0.0	66.0	31.9	100	2.8
Can't choose	0.0	0.0	0.0	0.0	0.0	0.0	0.0	4.3	0.0	0.0	95.7	100	2.8
Total	14.1	8.2	6.5	10.3	4.0	5.8	8.2	21.0	11.4	4.6	5.9	100	100

Which problem, if any, do you think is the most important for TURKEY?	Air pollution	8.1	22.6	**34.9**	**42.1**	**25.4**	**32.3**	**27.0**	**26.4**	22.6	22.4	7.1
	Chemicals and pesticides	6.8	3.6	15.6	5.8	19.4	9.4	6.6	16.3	7.4	2.6	4.0
	Water shortage	9.8	10.2	4.6	11.7	7.5	12.5	21.9	5.2	5.8	5.3	9.1
	Water pollution	17.9	5.8	9.2	2.9	11.9	16.7	10.9	7.2	6.8	3.9	5.1
	Nuclear waste	3.8	2.9	4.6	2.3	1.5	3.1	4.4	5.2	2.6	0.0	2.0
	Domestic waste disposal	5.6	2.2	3.7	2.9	4.5	2.1	3.6	2.0	3.7	0.0	1.0
	Climate change	9.4	5.8	4.6	5.3	6.0	2.1	0.7	6.6	9.5	0.0	1.0
	Genetically modified foods	**26.5**	**27.0**	12.8	21.1	16.4	11.5	14.6	4.9	**40.5**	14.5	6.1
	Using up our natural resources	12.0	19.0	10.1	5.8	7.5	10.4	10.2	25.8	1.1	10.5	4.0
	None of these	0.0	0.7	0.0	0.0	0.0	0.0	0.0	0.0	0.0	**40.8**	15.2
	Can't choose	0.0	0.0	0.0	0.0	0.0	0.0	0.0	0.6	0.0	0.0	**45.5**
		100	100	100	100	100	100	100	100	100	100	100

To examine how these problems are viewed from the personal to the country level, we can look at the bottom half of Table 6.2. Here we see that at the country level 'air pollution' and 'genetically modified foods' are the only two answers predominantly given for any environmental problem. For example, if at a personal level the answer is 'air pollution' or 'chemicals and pesticides', then the genetically modified foods item is the most frequent answer at the national level. For all other environmental problems, we see that air pollution is the most frequent response at the country level. In other words, individuals do distinguish between being impacted by the environment at a personal level versus the national level. For any type of environmental problem at the national level genetically modified foods come to mind at the individual level. Air pollution, however, appears more often as the dominant problem that comes to mind at the national level for six out of nine environmental problems at the individual level.

Besides differentiating between problems of influence at the individual level as opposed to the national level, individuals also appear to be seriously concerned about environmental issues. Although Turkey ranks at the very bottom according to the Franzen and Meyer index that compares perspectives on environmental concerns on a 9-item index, we see that respondents express a great deal of concern about the environment when directly asked about the issue. As Figure 6.4 shows, as of 2010, only about 21 per cent of the respondents appear to be unconcerned about environmental issues while about 51 per cent are clearly concerned. The Franzen and Meyer environmental concerns index and this direct question as to the degree to which individual respondents are concerned about the environment ('Generally speaking, how concerned are you about environmental issues?') is correlated only at 0.16 level. Hence, there is more to both of these questions that is not captured by the other question, deserving a separate analysis. Table 6.3, however, indicates that only the level of education is positively linked to these concerns. There appears to be no gender or age cohort or urban-rural difference in the levels of concern people feel about the environment; nor are there any statistically significant differences between party constituencies. Religious practices that differentiate between different value systems also appear to be ineffective in differentiating between different levels of concern about environmental issues.

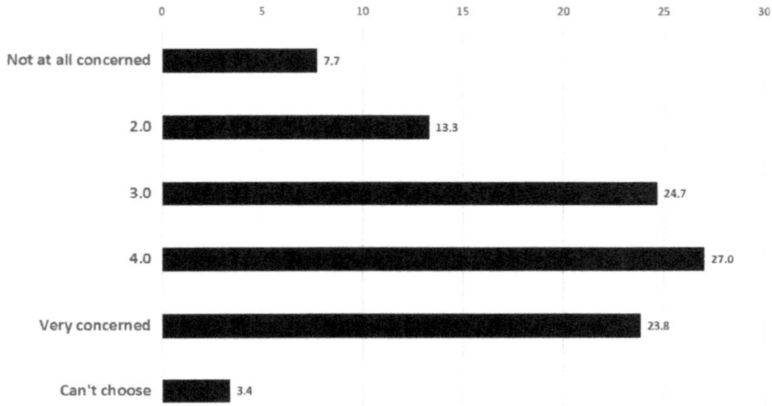

Figure 6.4 Generally speaking, how concerned are you about environmental issues?

From a purely subjective perspective, we observe that respondents also do not appear to be knowledgeable about the causes of environmental problems. Nearly one-third stated they had no knowledge, while a slightly lower percentage were self-confident about their knowledge about the causes of environmental problems (Figure 6.5). From Table 6.3, we also observe that this almost symmetrical distribution of self-ascribed knowledge concerning the causes of environmental problems is structured according not only to level of education, but to party constituency as well. The highest level of self-ascribed knowledge appears amongst the CHP constituency, followed by constituencies of both the AKP and then the Kurdish Peace and Democracy Party (*Barış ve Demokrasi Partisi*, BDP), while MHP voters appear insignificantly distant in their self-ascribed knowledge compared to CHP voters. Once again gender, age cohort, religious practice and urban–rural differences appear to be non-significant in explaining self-ascribed knowledge about the causes of environmental problems.

Respondents were also asked about the degree to which they believed different phenomena were dangerous for the environment. Figure 6.6 shows that people judged the detailed descriptions of various phenomena as being very detrimental for the environment. Air pollution caused by industry topped the list, followed closely by genetically modified foods.

Table 6.3 Concern and Knowledge about Environmental Problems

	How concerned are you about environmental issues?		How much do you feel you know about the causes of environmental problems?	
	Estimate	Sig.	Estimate	Sig.
(Ordinal level (concern/subjective knowledge) = 1)	**– 1.99**	**0.00**	**– 1.16**	**0.00**
(Ordinal level (concern/subjective knowledge) = 2)	**– 0.85**	**0.00**	0.12	0.67
(Ordinal level (concern/subjective knowledge) = 3)	0.33	0.26	**1.95**	**0.00**
(Ordinal level (concern/subjective knowledge) = 4)	**1.63**	**0.00**	**3.92**	**0.00**
Sex (Female = 1)	0.10	0.32	−0.03	0.80
Age	0.00	0.18	0.00	0.38
Education in years	**0.06**	**0.00**	**0.15**	**0.00**
DV for urban dwellers	−0.07	0.53	−0.03	0.81
Religious practice (0 to 6)	−0.02	0.37	0.00	0.95
DV for AKP voters	−0.28	0.06	**– 0.40**	**0.01**
DV for MHP voters	0.28	0.19	0.30	0.17
DV for BDP voters	−0.05	0.86	**– 0.85**	**0.00**

DV for those who would not vote for any party	0.07	0.74	**− 0.52**	**0.01**
DV for undecided	0.36	0.10	−0.28	0.20
DV for Others	0.51	0.17	0.08	0.83
Pseudo R-Square				
Cox and Snell	0.04		0.15	
Nagelkerke	0.05		0.15	
McFadden	0.01		0.05	
Test of Parallel Lines [a]				
Chi-Square	44.51		44.45	
Sig.	0.09		0.09	

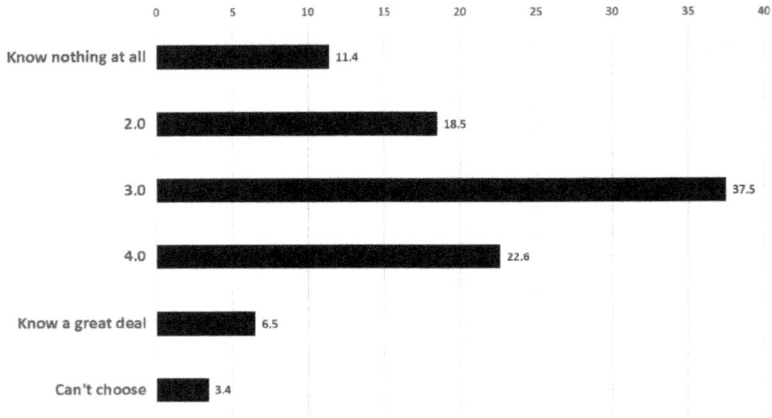

Figure 6.5 How much do you feel you know about the causes of these sorts of environmental problems?

These two issues were also the topmost ranked environmental problems listed as having the most impact on lives at the individual and national levels. It is noticeable that while Turkish citizens seem to consistently worry about genetic modification and air pollution, nuclear power or climate change are relatively low in their priority list about environmental problems.

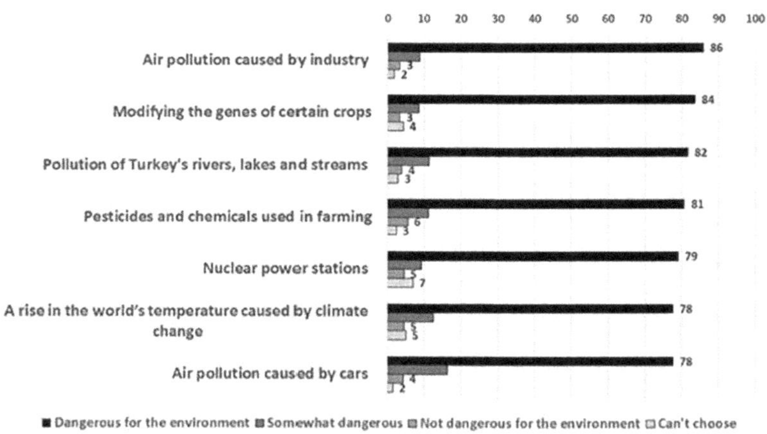

Figure 6.6 In general to what extent do you think the following are dangerous for the environment?

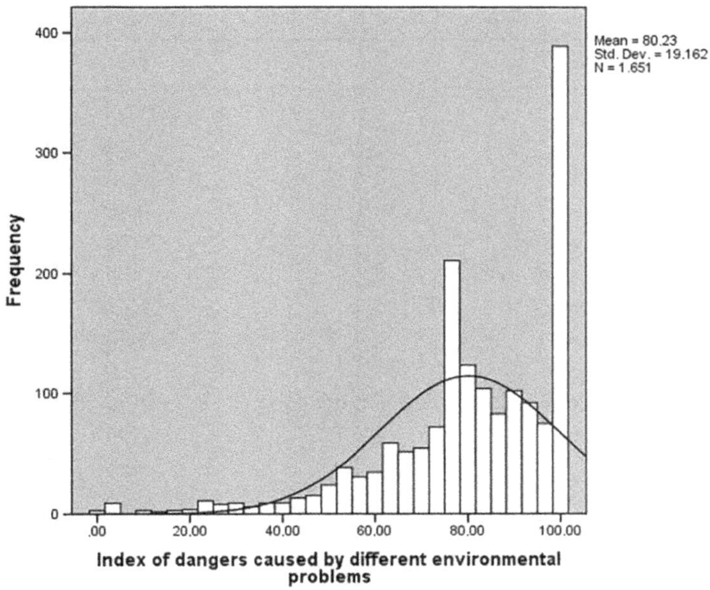

Figure 6.7 Distribution of Perceived Dangers Caused by Environmental Problems

An additive index was formed on the basis of these seven assessments. If respondents said all seven phenomena were dangerous for the environment, then the corresponding index value would be 100; if they picked none of these items, then the index value would be 0. An increasing number of answers that indicate environmental threat is reflected as an index value that rises towards 100. In this sample, nearly one-fourth of the respondents obtained an index value of 100 and the distribution of the index is skewed to the left; few respondents obtained low values (see Figure 6.7). Only about 8 per cent obtained an index value of 50 or below, while about 40 per cent obtained an index value between 50 and 80. In other words, most respondents seem to be not only worried about the environment but also judge that many of the phenomena presented to them are detrimental for the environment.

Table 6.4 reports a simple regression equation that depicts the determinants of the distribution of our index of dangers caused by

Table 6.4 Index of Dangers Caused by Different Environmental Problems

	B	Sig.
(Constant)	75.22	0.00
Sex (Female=1)	3.02	0.00
Age	0.10	0.01
Education in years	0.43	0.00
DV for urban dwellers	0.77	0.53
Religious practice (0 to 6)	−0.05	0.86
DV for AKP voters	− 5.32	0.00
DV for MHP voters	− 4.46	0.04
DV for BDP voters	1.39	0.64
DV for those who would not vote for any party	− 7.50	0.00
DV for undecided	− 1.93	0.39
DV for Others	0.86	0.82
R Square	0.04	
Adjusted R Square	0.03	
Std. Error of the Estimate	18.86	

different environmental phenomenon. We see here that not only women, but also older and more educated respondents scored higher on this index. A similar differentiation between partisan groups is also apparent in the table. CHP voters obtained the highest index score, indicating that they judged various phenomena as being dangerous more so than other partisan groups. Similar to earlier findings about the state of self-ascribed knowledge or lack thereof, AKP voters scored lower than CHP voters, followed this time by respondents who reported they were voting for none of the existing parties. There was no difference between the scores of BDP voters and CHP voters.

Lastly, Table 6.5 shows a similar analysis of the determinants of the Franzen and Meyer environmental concern index for Turkey. Like the single question version in Table 6.3, we see here again that education is positively linked to environmental concerns. However, in this version of the environmental concern index we observe that religiosity also renders an individual more concerned. The partisan divide is similar to earlier observed patterns where the CHP constituency exhibits the highest level of concern and the AKP and BDP constituencies are relatively less concerned. In addition, we observe that those who do not report any party choice – the

Table 6.5 Determinants of Franzen and Meyer (2010) Environmental Concern Index for Turkey, 2010 ISSP

	Unstandardised Coefficients		Unstandardised Coefficients	
	B	Sig.	B	Sig.
(Constant)	**19.81**	**0.00**	**18.16**	**0.00**
Sex (Female = 1)	−0.43	0.19	−0.50	0.11
Age	0.02	0.13	0.00	0.71
DV for urban dwellers	−0.43	0.24	0.64	0.10
Education years	**0.44**	**0.00**	**0.41**	**0.00**
Religious practice (0 to 6)	**0.18**	**0.04**	0.08	0.35
Dummy Variable for AKP voters	**− 1.43**	**0.00**	**− 1.10**	**0.02**
Dummy Variable for MHP voters	−0.60	0.37	−0.41	0.53
Dummy Variable for BDP voters	**− 3.18**	**0.00**	**− 2.53**	**0.01**
Dummy Variable for those who would not vote for any party	−0.89	0.16	−0.32	0.60
Dummy Variable for undecided	**− 1.74**	**0.01**	**− 1.75**	**0.01**
Dummy Variable for Others	0.26	0.82	0.51	0.64
Dummy Variable for Aegean Region			**3.23**	**0.00**
Dummy Variable for Mediterranean Region			0.60	0.30
Dummy Variable for South Eastern Anatolia Region			0.96	0.12
Dummy Variable for Western Anatolia Region			−1.28	0.06

Table 6.5 *Continued*

	Unstandardised Coefficients		Unstandardised Coefficients	
	B	Sig.	B	Sig.
Dummy Variable for Marmara Region			3.86	0.00
Dummy Variable for Black Sea Region			2.69	0.00
Dummy Variable for Central Anatolia Region			2.48	0.00
Dummy Variable for Eastern Anatolia Region			3.53	0.00
R Square	0.12		0.18	
Adjusted R Square	0.11		0.17	
Std. Error of the Estimate	5.74		5.55	

undecided – appear to also be less concerned compared to the CHP constituency.

Table 6.5 also reports the same equation estimated with regional fixed effects, which also shows a significant degree of geographic differentiation in environmental concerns. The reference category is Istanbul, and the Mediterranean region together with South-eastern Anatolia are the two regions that do not differ from Istanbul in a statistically significant way in terms of fixed regional effects. However, the NUTS 5 region composed of Ankara and Konya appear to have a lower fixed effect, but only at the $p < 0.06$ level. Other regions all had a higher fixed effect compared to Istanbul, and among all regions, Marmara had the highest followed closely by provinces in the Aegean region. In other words, regional differences appear to be significant even after controlling for basic demographic and socio-political variables.[11]

Conclusion

Several patterns emerge from the analyses so far. One concerns the responsiveness of party elites to rising public concerns about the environment. We clearly observe that not only is there a positive link between increasing public concerns and elite emphases on the environment in election manifestos for the last nearly two decades, but that this link also appears to have grown stronger in the most recent period. In terms of party elites' responsiveness to environmental issues, ecological parties are in the lead. However, although at a much lower rate, all party families appear to have emphasised environmental issues more over the past few decades. Obviously, reverse causality might also be at play here; elite emphasis might be driving the concerns of the masses. Although there is little historical evidence that backs this reverse link, our data does not allow us to test this hypothesis.

Together with Russia, Turkey ranks at the very bottom of the environmental concerns index for the 2010 ISSP survey data. When the environmental concern question is directly asked, social conformist pressures appear to push answers up to a level that reflects some public concern, at least at face value. However, a composite index that takes willingness to make economic sacrifices into account while remaining sceptical to scientific solutions as well as classical developmentalist approaches clearly shows how much the Turkish population lags behind global trends.

What is also striking in these analyses is a clear reflection of a partisan divide that shapes how the masses react to environmental concerns. The larger conservative constituency of the AKP together with the Kurdish electoral constituency of the BDP appear to lag behind the main opposition party CHP constituency in terms of knowledge, environmental threat perceptions and environmental concerns. Given the observation that the BDP is the party that allocates the largest space for environmental issues in their election manifestos (between 3 and 4 per cent), this is a clear dilemma for the party. However, this level of emphasis is low enough for the party to keep it as an issue of secondary importance, especially compared to ethnic identity debates on the basis of which the party forms its main rhetoric and policy positioning.

The fact that the CHP has a significantly more reactive and sensitive constituency compared to the AKP when it comes to environmental debates, and that it maintains more or less the same level of environmental emphasis compared to the AKP is puzzling. Clearly, an immediate explanation might be that the CHP finds this issue as ineffective in its overall electoral strategy competing against the conservative AKP and hence keeps its commitment to this cause limited.

Although the emphasis on environmental issues in the Turkish party system has been increasing over the long-term, this issue is clearly not very salient and hence of little electoral importance. The driving force behind this insensitive stance of the party elite towards the environment is clearly the deep partisan divide and most importantly the overall low level of concern on the part of the electoral masses. Given that sensitivity to the environment is quite lacking, political parties are not very likely to deliver much on the environmental policy front. Priority is most likely to be given to old-fashioned developmentalist policies at the expense of real effective environmental regulations that aim to maintain global and local environmental sustainability.

There also appears to be significant regionality when it comes to environmental concerns in Turkey. In terms of geographical differences, Istanbul – a hub where people from all over the country come together – does not surface as a centre with the highest level of environmental concern. Provinces in the Marmara Region display the highest average level of environmental concern, followed by provinces in the Aegean Region. Obviously, regional sensitivities play a significant role here in driving popular concerns around the country. Unfortunately, our data does not differentiate between regional, national and global sources for environmental concerns. This issue needs to be addressed in future research.

Notes

1. See Ronald Inglehart, *The Silent Revolution, Changing Values and Political Styles among Western Publics* (Princeton, 1977); Ronald Inglehart, 'Post-Materialism in an environment of insecurity', *American Political Science Review* 75/4 (1981), pp. 880–900; Ronald Inglehart, 'Public support for environmental protection: Objective problems and subjective values in 43 societies', *Political Science and Politics* 15 (1995), pp. 57–71; and Paul C. Stern, Thomas Dietz, Troy D. Abel, Gregory A. Guagnano and Linda Kalof, 'A value-belief-norm theory of support for social movements: The case of environmentalism', *Huxley College on the Peninsulas Publications* (1999). Paper 1. http://cedar.wwu.edu/hcop_facpubs/1, accessed 8 March 2017. For an alternative perspective, see Stephen Cotgrove and Andrew Duff, 'Environmentalism, values, and social change', *British Journal of Sociology* 32/1 (1981), pp. 92–110.
2. See Phil Macnaghten and Michael Jacobs, 'Public identification with sustainable development Investigating cultural barriers to participation', *Global Environmental Change* 7/1 (1997), pp. 5–24; and Andrew Jamison, *The Making of Green Knowledge, Environmental Politics and Cultural Transformation* (Cambridge, 2001). On an early study in Turkey, see Andrzej Furman, 'A note on environmental concern in a developing country: Results from an Istanbul survey', *Environment and Behavior*, 30/4 (1998), pp. 520–34; Anja Kollmuss and Julian Agyeman, 'Mind the gap: Why do people act environmentally and what are the barriers to pro-environmental behavior?', *Education Research* 8/3 (2002), pp. 239–60. For more recent evaluations, see Russell J. Dalton 'Waxing or waning? The changing patterns of environmental activism', *Environmental Politics* 24/4 (2015), pp. 530–52; Ali Çarkoğlu and Çiğdem Kentmen-Çin, 'Economic development, environmental justice, and pro-environmental behavior', *Environmental Politics* 24/4 (2015), pp. 575–97; Paul Chaisty and Stephen Whitefield, 'Attitudes towards the environment: Are post-Communist societies (still) different?', *Environmental Politics* 24/4 (2015), pp. 598–616.
3. See https://manifestoproject.wzb.eu/ (accessed 8 March 2017) for more details about the CMP coding procedures and data.
4. All ensuing analyses use the latest version of the CMP data; see Annika Werner, Onawa Lacewell and Andrea Volkens, *Manifesto Coding Instructions* (4th edition) (2016). Available at: https://manifestoproject.wzb.eu/datasets, accessed 14 June 2016.

5. Axel Franzen and Reto Meyer, 'Environmental attitudes in cross-national perspective: A multilevel analysis of the ISSP 1993 and 2000', *European Sociological Review* 26/2 (2010), pp. 219–34.
6. Ibid., p. 225.
7. Note that Cronbach's alpha is a measure of internal consistency. Its value varies from 0 to 1, and as a rule of thumb, a reliability of 0.65 or higher is required before an instrument can be used. For the 2010 ISSP, Cronbach alpha values for European party systems were about 9 per cent points higher than the rest of the ISSP sample countries. In other words, the environmental concern index appears to work better in European party systems than anywhere else.
8. Note that in the 1961–80 period, the CHP and the AP were the two main parties, the former representing the centre-left and the latter, the centre-right.
9. The centre-right party that was formed after the 1980 coup, which largely relied on the AP's constituencies. Erdoğan's AKP would later capture them to a great extent.
10. *Milli Selamet Partisi* (MSP), *Fazilet Partisi* (FP) and *Saadet Partisi* (SP) are all pro-Islamist parties with similar ideological position to that of the RP, each active in a different period of time.
11. It is also worth noting that when regional effects are taken into account, religiosity ceases to be significant and urban-rural differences appear to have a positive influence on environmental concerns, though only at the $p<0.1$ level. All other variables maintain their significance and magnitude of influence on environmental concerns.

CHAPTER 7

THE RADIOACTIVE INERTIA: DECIPHERING TURKEY'S ANTI-NUCLEAR MOVEMENT

Bengi Akbulut, Fikret Adaman and Murat Arsel

Introduction

According to an opinion poll conducted by Greenpeace Turkey in 2011 84 per cent of the people in Turkey think that nuclear risks should not be shouldered in meeting energy demands and 64 per cent would oppose the construction of a nuclear plant if a referendum was held.[1] A survey conducted by the international research company IPSOS the same year similarly finds that 80 per cent of the Turkish society think the state should not carry on with its plans to build a nuclear power plant. Furthermore, a 2012 study by KONDA, a national research company, reveals that the incidence of opposition to nuclear power has increased from 56.8 per cent to 63.4 per cent between 2011–12.[2] Yet currently the anti-nuclear movement in Turkey remains surprisingly weak with meager public visibility and influence.

Indeed, quite a long tradition of anti-nuclear mobilisation exists in Turkey, dating back to the 1970s when the news of a nuclear plant first became public. It gained momentum especially in the 1990s and a national level anti-nuclear platform was formed in 1993. The first ever demonstration carried out by Greenpeace in Turkey was a protest against nuclear power, after which they collaborated actively with local campaigns. Anti-nuclear summer camps with the participation of thousands were organised in several consecutive years. From rural mobilisations to numerous petitions and public campaigns, from rallies to mass mailing actions and direct interventions, the movement had remained dynamic throughout the 1990s. In many ways, however, that dynamism seems to have lost steam in the more recent era, paradoxically as the proposed plans of nuclear plants are as (or more) concrete as ever. Moreover, relatively robust regional and transnational anti-nuclear campaigns against Turkey's nuclear ambitions continue to exist in neighbouring countries such as Cyprus.

The weakness of the anti-nuclear movement in Turkey becomes more striking when juxtaposed against the wave of struggles opposing energy projects more broadly that swept the country for the past decade and a half. Spurred by the liberalisation of the electricity market and the systematic relaxation of environmental regulations, the country witnessed the construction of hundreds of small-scale hydro-dams, tens of thermic power plants, dozens of wind-energy farms. Discontent with and open opposition to these projects are strong both at local and national levels. Given that a louder and more visible environmental movement is growing in Turkey in this sense, this chapter focuses on the seeming, yet puzzling, decline of the anti-nuclear movement. In tackling this decline, the chapter provides an analysis in terms of both local dynamics and the specific features of nuclear power as a form of energy investment, and points to their general implications for understanding the state-environment-development nexus in Turkey.

The Radioactive History of Turkey

First steps towards developing a nuclear power plant in Turkey date back to 1965, when preliminary exploratory studies were undertaken by the State Electricity Research Unit and Istanbul Technical University's Nuclear Energy Institute. The prospect of nuclear energy development later found its way into the second 5-year national development plan (1967–70), and the Bureau of Nuclear Energy was established under the Turkish Electricity Authority in 1972. Following the feasibility studies conducted in the early 1970s for identifying suitable locations, Akkuyu (Mersin) was selected as the first site to develop a nuclear power plant in 1974 with a siting permit for construction issued in 1976. While the decision was made for two Swedish companies to build the plant, the project was cancelled after credit guarantees were revoked by Sweden. The plans for developing nuclear power resurfaced in the early 1980s and the Atomic Energy of Canada Limited (AECL), Siemens-Kraft Werk Union (KWU) of Germany and General Electric (GE) of the United States were asked to submit bids (without a tender process) for two nuclear plants in Akkuyu and İnceburun (Sinop) in 1982. Although negotiations were initiated, this attempt failed as well because a consensus could not be reached due to Turkish government's insistence on the build-operate-transfer model and financing difficulties.

Yet nuclear power remained to be the state's major objective in the 5th national development plan together with the Atatürk Dam. While the Chernobyl Disaster in 1986 put the plans on hold, the proposed plant in Akkuyu was identified as a prioritised developmental project and included within the state investment programme in 1993. A state tender for international bidding was made in 1997 with the participation of three consortia from Canada, Germany–France, and USA–Japan; yet the final auction date was postponed six times for technical and economic reasons. In 2000, the prime minister of the time announced the cancellation of the project due to corruption allegations regarding the bidding process.

With the Justice and Development Party's (AKP) coming to power in 2002, nuclear power took the stage once more, with the government's reiterations on the inevitability of nuclear power investment given the energy need of the country. At the end of 2005, the Ministry of Energy announced plans for the construction of three nuclear plants (of 5000 MW in total) to be started in 2007 and put in operation by 2012, which was soon pushed to 2015. Following the declaration of İnceburun as the first plant to be developed, the government initiated talks with various stakeholders (private sector, academia, bureaucracy, etc.) primarily on appropriate technology and investment models, as well as focusing on the legal infrastructure for licensing and nuclear fuel deals.[3] In 2008, a tender for Akkuyu was opened, for which only one proposal was filed, while the licensing process for İnceburun was ongoing. Following the annulment of the tender by the Supreme Court and the suspension of various articles within the tender regulation, the AKP government opted to bypass the tender procedures by signing bilateral agreements at the governmental level for nuclear plants, the first of which (Akkuyu) was signed with Russia in 2011 and the second (İnceburun) was signed with Japan in 2013.

A parallel history of anti-nuclear mobilisation can be traced throughout the same period. Siting and feasibility studies of 1976 in Akkuyu sowed the seeds of a local mobilisation spearheaded by the head of the village (fishery and agriculture) cooperative in a neighbouring town (Taşucu), which started organising local farmers and fishers, and reached out to national media to publicise the issue. During the ensuing few years, numerous meetings, petition campaigns, panels and rallies were organised in Akkuyu with the participation of influential national NGOs (such as the Union of Chambers of Turkish Engineers and Architects), trade unions, associations as well as local groups. The anti-nuclear movement also began to make some transnational connections at this stage. For instance, 25 Swedish non-governmental organisations denounced Sweden's interest in building a nuclear power plant in Turkey as an attempt to prop-up a failing national corporation.

After a period of hibernation following the *coup d'état* in 1980, the mobilisation started gaining momentum again in the post-Chernobyl era of the early 1990s. This period was marked by the higher visibility of national-level actors such as the Green Party, who spearheaded the organisation of the broad anti-nuclear front *SOS Akdeniz* (SOS Mediterranean), and Greenpeace, whose first action in Turkey was an anti-nuclear demonstration. Various anti-nuclear local publications such as *Akkuyu Postası, Git* and *Ağaçkakan* were initiated in the same period. With actions organised by the national level anti-nuclear platform founded in 1993, the movement acquired a wider base. In addition to anti-nuclear meetings held in Istanbul, Ankara, İzmir, Bursa, Zonguldak and Mersin, mass mailings of the members of parliament and the prime minister, petitions, street demonstrations and 'counter-congresses' to coincide with nuclear energy congresses were organised from 1993 onwards. The strength of local organising in the project areas was also sustained with the annual anti-nuclear summer camps/festivals in Akkuyu in addition to regular demonstrations and meetings. Notably among these was the founding of *Yeşil Ev* (the Green House) in Büyükeceli village (the nearest community to the proposed power plant) by the anti-nuclear platform and the visit of Bergama villagers, who had waged an effective resistance against a gold-mine project,[4] for sharing experiences and organising a joint demonstration. In addition, a symbolic referendum was held by Greenpeace and Büyükeceli municipality in 1999, which resulted in 84 per cent of votes against the nuclear plant.

The reinstatement of the Akkuyu project by the AKP government in the mid-2000s prompted a second phase of mobilisation in Mersin. This post-2006 period is marked by the weakened opposition of villagers and the low levels of engagement by national actors, while a Mersin-centred (urban) movement emerged to be stronger than before. Among the numerous actions organised and operationalised by the urban core of the movement, the most notable ones are the re-initiation of the anti-nuclear camps (albeit with significantly less participation and visibility) and the 159 km-long human chain formed in the aftermath of the Fukushima accident.

The anti-nuclear mobilisation in Sinop, on the other hand, started much later with the announcement of İnceburun as a site for nuclear power development in the mid-1990s. The first local actions to this end included a large meeting with the country-level participation in the spring of 1997 and an anti-nuclear festival organised in the summer of the same year. While local organisation largely waned with the cancellation of the Akkuyu project in 2000, it gained new impetus in 2006 with the AKP's retabling of nuclear power development. Between 2006 and 2007, the newly formed Sinop Anti-Nuclear Platform had kept an office for informational and organisational purposes and organised regular weekly demonstrations in the city centre in the form of the symbolic act of standing guard. The well-attended anti-nuclear summer camp in 2007 was doomed with internal strife among the participating groups (the social democrats/municipality versus the radical left) as well as the tragic death of three young radicals by drowning in the Black Sea. With the exception of the crowded 2009 rally, the movement had weakened considerably: the city seems to be silent on the nuclear agenda nowadays, apart from a handful number of locals.

More generally, the anti-nuclear opposition at the national level visibly declined compared to its earlier stages. Apart from few notable examples, such as the 2015 rally attended by some 30 thousand people, participation in calls and actions by the movement was dismal and left no major trace behind them. Even the news of a possible third plant was not much of a stimulus: as the construction was ongoing in Akkuyu and the preparations for İnceburun were moving forward, the possibility of yet another plant in İğneada started to circulate, following an implicit statement by the Minister of Energy and Natural Resources in 2015. Yet anti-nuclear opposition at both local and national levels remains poor and ineffectual. The next section delineates the reasons underlying the decline of local mobilisations in Akkuyu and İnceburun. This is followed by an analysis of challenges inherently associated with nuclear power as a form of energy investment.

Delineating Decline: Akkuyu and İnceburun

In Mersin, the more recent over-politicisation of the urban leg of the opposition appears to have become a major obstacle. The overtly leftist tone adopted is stated to be undermining the possibility of forming a broad-based anti-nuclear front in the city centre, sparking divisions and alienating newcomers as well as estranging the villagers in the project area. While the left-leaning character of the movement's urban base was always pronounced, it has sharpened in the aftermath of Gezi protests of 2013. It was claimed that the broader support that Gezi protests acquired led some constituents to instrumentalise the anti-nuclear mobilisation for narrowly defined political agendas. The broader political climate has also dictated diverging priorities for the varied groups that constitute this urban base, as the ongoing-armed conflict became the most important urgency for Mersin's considerable Kurdish population and the Kurdish Movement.

More generally, the diverse and growing population of central Mersin, a metropolis compared to 30 years ago, implies lower predictability in terms of the appeal of actions and strategies adopted by the movement. The specific composition of the urban leg of the movement, the Mersin Anti-Nuclear Platform, has presented challenges as well. As the more institutionalised constituents of the anti-nuclear platform are local branches of national level non-governmental organisations, such as professional associations and unions, their local agendas and priorities are shaped significantly by decisions taken at central administrations. Activists express concern over how the anti-nuclear agenda and environmental struggles more broadly are still seen as secondary to the 'genuine' political issues in most of these organisations and thus cannot find their way easily into their focus. Within a context marked by reactionary politics and a failure to become proactive (to be discussed below), such particular political priorities more easily hijack the broader anti-nuclear agenda.

What distinguishes the case of Sinop is perhaps the visibly lower participation of the villagers from the project area (Soğucak and Abalı) in the opposition movement. In addition to the fact that these villages are markedly conservative compared to the broader region, state intimidation to deter the participation of villagers seems to have been more intense as the gendarmerie is reported to follow-up after every visit the urban activists made to the villages. According to the activists, the social conservativism and religiosity have effectively been translated into a culture of fatalism and obedience within the context of the nuclear opposition. This is explained by the broader process of the withdrawal of the social (secular) state functions (e.g. the closing down of the hospital as well as the school at the town) and at the same time religion's filling of the void as the basis of social organisation and social support mechanism. Although the village women have been more sympathetic and have responded to the activists' outreach, they too have quickly backed down.

The opposition movement in Sinop seems to be disadvantaged in terms of lack of municipal support as well. The urban activists often compare the lack of support they received from (social democratic) Sinop municipality to the instrumental role that a neighbouring mayor played in the successful resistance against a coal project in the neighbouring town of Gerze.[5] While the Sinop municipality cannot be said to have actively prevented local organising efforts, it has hardly been a facilitator and avoided taking an active stance against the project. The ambivalent position of the municipality is often linked to the internal divisions within the movement. Manifested especially during the anti-nuclear camp in 2007, the sharpened differences between the (more moderate) social democrats and the (more radical) socialist left undermined local organising efforts as well as the participation of outside groups such as the Black Sea in Rebellion Platform (*Karadeniz İsyandadır Platformu*).

The difficulties encountered by the urban activists in relating to and linking with villagers from the project areas, and the more general failure to garner the active participation of a broader (urban and rural) social base emerge as major challenges in both Mersin and Sinop. Although the villagers were initially (until the 2000s) mobilised against the nuclear plant and open to aligning with urban activists in Mersin, the tide seems to have turned. The company behind the power plant had been exceptionally attentive to delivering the developmental promises of the project. It has been pointed out that employment needs were met locally in all project phases from exploratory studies to construction, and that the project had indeed stimulated the local economy as 'the Russians were careful to shop from the locals'. The role played by the overstatement of ideological motives mentioned earlier in alienating the villagers was also highlighted. The strained relationship between the urban activists and the villagers was further weakened by the closing down of the Green House, which had provided a space of contact until then.

In Sinop, on the other hand, the villagers remained suspicious of the urban-centred opposition movement and were never actively engaged with it. Besides, the villagers' (mostly presumed) ignorance, religiosity and fatalism that reproduce a culture of obedience, activists discussed how relating to the villagers solely on the basis of the anti-nuclear agenda acted as an impediment on forging an effective alliance. Within a context shaped by a broader and historical disconnect between the villagers and the progressives from the provincial centre (except at electoral periods), this has projected an opportunistic image of the movement and estranged the village residents – rather than building a consistent relationship on everyday issues, needs and demands.

The disconnect between the urban bases of opposition and the rural communities is coupled with the more structural trend of declining viability of rural livelihoods and the eradication of the basis of an environmentalism of the poor type of opposition.[6] Many villagers prefer to sell their land and move to urban centres as their link to land and rural livelihoods erode and as further integration into the commodity economy increases their dependency on cash incomes. On the other hand, the urban mobilisations in both Sinop and Mersin suffer from a general failure to acquire a broader social base. The main obstacle in Sinop emerges to be the massive outmigration of the recent years, whereas over-politicisation in Mersin seems to be a more decisive factor.

Common Threads and Inherent Challenges

While specific locales of resistance encounter different contextual obstacles, some emerge to be cross-cutting challenges faced by the anti-nuclear opposition more generally. We argue that an important fraction of these pertain to the specific nature of nuclear plants as a form of energy investment. Nuclear power plants are fraught with an ambiguity quite unlike dams, small-scale hydropower or coal plants. There is widespread misinformation, or at best lack of information, regarding the exact extent and nature of the impacts of a nuclear spill, as well as of environmental risks associated with nuclear waste disposal and the plant's seawater-based cooling system. Even when the implications of a potential accident are clearly grasped, such an event is often seen as a distant probability and its risks are underestimated. While the impacts of coal or hydropower plants are more directly observable and thus have a more immediate connection to the everyday lives of the concerned communities (e.g. the smoke and chimneys of coal plants are easily connected to air pollutants emitted and to health impacts; the covered pipes of hydropower plants concretise loss of access to water), the implications of a nuclear power plant in terms of access to resources, livelihoods, health, ecological sustainability and social cohesion are seldom as concrete. Indeed, such comparisons between anti-hydro and anti-coal resistances were drawn by activists themselves in highlighting the unique difficulties they face. Thus, the movement organisers find it hard to mobilise people (both the immediate locals inhabiting the project areas and the residents of the broader provincial region) around the realised or expected impacts of the projects.

An important factor that perpetuates this inherent vagueness and lack of immediacy of the impacts of nuclear plants is the typical indeterminacy and long duration of completion associated with such large-scale developmental projects.[7] As discussed earlier, the idea of a nuclear plant in Akkuyu was first proposed in the early 1970s and took countless back and forths until it was tendered in 2011. The most recent development that cast doubt on the process and postponed its completion was the altercations in Turkey–Russia relations in late 2015. In Sinop, on the other hand, the construction process was postponed indefinitely after the contracted Japanese company pulled out following the Fukushima disaster, after being on and off the table for almost 20 years. Even in the absence of conjunctural incidents such as these, it is typical for such mega projects to take longer completion terms than planned, often with developments that render the entire project uncertain at times, as financing and investment, technological and technical capacity-building, and legal and regulatory processes related to such huge undertakings are cumbersome and lengthy.

This characteristic, also largely unique to nuclear plants among energy projects more broadly, holds two inter-related implications for movements opposing them. The uncertainties related to the actual realisation of the project erode the sense of urgency that often provides a spark for a heated and sustained mobilisation. The elongated project durations and the time-lags between the announcement and the various phases of the project imply a general fatigue and lack of morale within the opposition. Activists complain that it becomes 'harder to get people out on the street and to keep them there' and that 'less and less people attend to demonstrations' when it is not clear what people are called to demonstrate against. Some of the key figures within the movement thus point to the need for proactively building an agenda independent of actual developments in the projects, rather than reproducing the reactive politics of an opposition movement.

A parallel idea is evoked by some of the key activists when they claim that 'if something had happened here, something major and visible, then the movement would get a boost and things would start to roll' and by their expectation that the groundbreaking in Sinop or the announcement of the actual date of operation in Mersin would provide this much needed impetus. Such an event is believed to be helpful in materialising the potential impacts (at least with regards to the expropriation of space by the plant) and installing a sense of urgency. Some activists further link this relative (and somewhat inherent) absence of stimulating events in the course of a nuclear plant development to the lack of a transformative stimulus that would produce different, perhaps more radical, subjects within the movement. A frequently invoked comparison is with the anti-coal resistance that took place in the Black Sea town of Gerze in 2011–12,[8] which is known not only for its success in stopping the planned coal plant in the area but also for the highly dynamic struggle of the locals, even in the face of police and gendarmerie brutality. In the words of an activist from the anti-nuclear platform in Sinop, 'the women in Gerze, who lay down in front of the police vehicles, were not always as courageous, as active. They became so during the course of the resistance. This is the key point, becoming. People should not be taken as they are, they become something else *through* the movement. We need to create that here.' In other words, the types of action that the movement is capable of taking and sustaining seems to be endogenous to the very course of the movement, in particular how concrete events shape different positions, capacities and subjectivities within it. The course of the movement, however, is hardly ever determined by the anti-nuclear mobilisation, but rather conditioned by the acts of the state-capital nexus. It is in this sense that it is almost wished by the activists, ironically, that the state would take aggressive steps, such as street confrontation with activists or expediting the project construction phases, so that a process of becoming (radical) subjects can finally take place.

The specific nature of nuclear plants also shapes the type of spatiality and the connected social relationships that can be produced within and through the movement. Such spatiality would in turn serve as a base to support and further the mobilisation. Within this context, the 'resistance tent' and the act of guard-watching (to spot and blockade company vehicles) are worth mentioning as key notions that emerged within environmental resistances in the contemporary era. Arsel et al. argue that the resistance tent in Gerze served as a ground where villagers from the planned project site (and their grievances) could link up with the activists from the neighbouring town (and their grievances). The tent and the collective act of standing guard organised around it thus helped conjoin the seemingly disparate motivations of these two groups within the resistance, as well as to build relations of solidarity and trust between them.[9] It was around the physicality of the tent that a public space could be constructed and maintained, which served as a forum of discussion as well as an invitation for supporters to join. Guard-watching, on the other hand, engaged the actors of the movement in the collective production of a service and generated a shared memory and sense of belonging. Çoban et al. further elaborate on the notion of the tent and trace it through various environmental resistances.[10] They claim that the existence of the tent and the production of the citizen–subject standing guard to defend the commons in question have effectively produced a public space that brings together common concerns, desires and actions. The formation of such a public space has also served to move these resistances beyond a defense of space/resources towards re-constituting the defended space with the new meanings of the life desired in common. A similar role can be (and has been) assumed by different physical spaces, e.g. the village coffeehouse or the public school building.[11]

Such acts of producing space where disparate motivations and concerns can meet in mutual ground and new (and synergistic) relations of collectivity and solidarity can be fostered are likely to be more challenging in the case of anti-nuclear resistances. It seems that the sense of urgency plays a facilitating, even a constructive, role for the production of such space: that guard-watching is often the initial constructive practice that forms such spatiality is more than a coincidence. The imminent and concrete threat of company vehicles or state forces initiating construction is often the first, if not the most important, reason that mobilises opposition movements to reclaim space for guard duty and sustains it. While site-specific setbacks were also present (the municipality in Sinop did not allow the platform to pitch a tent in public space, the collective house in the village in Mersin had to be shut down due to financial and bureaucratic problems), the lack of such urgency in relation to nuclear power projects (discussed above) acted as an impediment in this regard as well. In a related vein, the production of such spatiality goes hand-in-hand with the discourse of defending living spaces threatened by the proposed projects, which is utilised especially by the anti-hydropower plant and anti-coal mobilisations. The appropriation of resources and living spaces as well as the eradication of associated forms of life emerge as a prime mobiliser for activists to engage in the counter-activity of guarding, reclaiming and producing space by their own means. The anti-nuclear opposition, on the other hand, has primarily mobilised around the involved risks and potential impacts rather than a defense of space/resources and the displacement of associated forms of life. In this sense, organising efforts have mostly focused on disseminating information on risks and impacts where defending and reclaiming space (against an uncertain and postponed threat of appropriation) became a much less emphasised issue.

The implications of the absence of such spatiality, either in the form of a durable structure or generated in an *ad hoc* manner like the resistance tent, were concretely articulated by some of the local activists during interviews. In Sinop, the importance of a space shared and produced by the movement for aligning different motivations and fostering durable relations, which would produce the motivation and desire to be together for reasons other than day-to-day developments of the project, was emphasised. A space to ground the movement, it was claimed, would also help produce effective counter-agendas as the movement's strength would be less dependent on the course of the project. In Mersin, on the other hand, the role that would be played by such a space in (re)building relationships between urban activists and villagers from the project area was highlighted. The Green House that was maintained by the urban anti-nuclear activists in Büyükeceli between 1997 and 2000 is often referred to as the key example in how a public space could function as a ground where different groups could overcome feelings of distrust, conjoin agendas and thus build a broader social base of opposition.

The distance that marks the relationship between urban activists and locals/villagers becomes a particularly exacerbated challenge within the context of anti-nuclear opposition. This is admittedly a more general issue faced by many local environmental mobilisations in Turkey, as they are increasingly relying on an uneasy alliance between urban and rural communities. So is the adverse and alienating impact of traversing this distance only with the anti-project motivation on the possibility of effective alliances. However, how this challenge has unraveled in the context of anti-nuclear mobilisation was shaped by the dynamics specific to nuclear investments. The uncertain and elongated processes inherent to nuclear power development seem to allow more space for coopting and/or acquiring consent of the rural opposition by delivering developmental promises or systematic reproduction of defeatism. On the other hand, the lack of urgency severs the basis of an alliance between the rural and urban bases of opposition since a concrete and visible threat to force diverse groups and motivations to conjoin does not exist.

Yet another particular challenge faced by the anti-nuclear movement pertains to the strength of developmentalism attached to nuclear power as a form of energy investment. Nuclear power has a distinct lure within the broader imperative of growth-oriented modernisation, the dominant motive that has shaped state-society relationships in Turkey. Quite unlike hydropower or coal plants (or other types of infrastructural investment) nuclear power signifies the utmost criterion of becoming a truly modernised country. While much of this is related to the required level of technological advancement and technical capacity, nuclear power development also insinuates military strength, widely believed to be necessary for a country in Turkey's geopolitical shoes. In this sense, nuclear power resonates much more strongly with developmental and military might, giving the anti-nuclear opposition the weakest hand among all environmental struggles delegitimised by the appeal of developmentalism.

The persistent push and pronounced determinism of the Turkish state for nuclear power goes hand-in-hand with this particular developmental appeal. While mobilising against private energy investments has proven to be relatively legitimate, state-led or backed initiatives are challenges in themselves.[12] Not only does state involvement signify an image of collective benefit and reciprocity of compromises: seen in the historical setting of state-society relationships in Turkey, state undertakings of such projects signal the idea of the 'father state' that is supposedly a fair arbiter of the costs and benefits of developmentalism. But the visible presence of the state also instigates a sense of defeatism and pessimism as many started seeing the anti-nuclear opposition as a lost cause given the state's determinism to push nuclear power despite numerous setbacks.

Conclusion

To the extent that environmental movements are developing and gaining strength in contemporary Turkey, the anti-nuclear movement, both at the local and national level, seems to remain the exception. This is so despite the movement's rich history of (relatively) effective organisation and the existence of broad-based public opposition to nuclear power, on the one hand, and the presence of ongoing struggles against various other types of energy generation projects, on the other. This chapter sought some exploratory answers for the curious decline of the anti-nuclear movement, paying particular attention to the nature of such projects with long and intermittent planning and implementation processes, the constraints they imply in terms of spatial and transformative practices adopted within the movements, and the linkages between the (perceived) dominance of the state in Turkey and its hegemonic hold over the idea of societal development. Added to these more structural constraints are the context-specific factors such as the political and cultural predispositions of communities neighbouring the planned project sites, conflicts within core activist groups, and the types of actions taken by the project companies.

While these explanations indeed go a long way in illuminating the reasons behind the failure of a meaningful anti-nuclear movement to materialise in Turkey in recent years, our overall understanding of the genesis of environmental conflicts remains limited at best. Arguably, this is especially the case when it comes to nuclear technology, which can resonate with deep-seated historical and social dynamics as evidenced, for instance, by analyses of Germany's reluctance towards nuclear technology. This points to a more general necessity of environmental studies and social movements scholars to diversify beyond successful or visible cases of resistance in our opinion. As this chapter shows, there remains a major analytical task in investigating the unspectacular, the mundane and the unmaterialised conflicts as well as the spectacular.

Notes

1. A few academic studies also find a strong opposition to nuclear power. Adaman et al., for instance, reveal that the opposition to investment in nuclear energy within the urban population is 62.5 per cent, whereas those who supported investment to nuclear added up to a small figure of 7.2 per cent. See Fikret Adaman, Nihal Karalı, İlhan Or, Begüm Özkaynak and Ünal Zenginobuz, 'What determines urban households' willingness to pay for CO2 emission reductions in Turkey: A contingent valuation survey', *Energy Policy* 39/2 (2011), pp. 689–98.
2. http://www.greenpeace.org/turkey/tr/news/turkiyenin-yuzde-64u-nukleere-hayir-diyor-290411/, accessed 26 August 2016; https://www.ipsos-mori.com/researchpublications/researcharchive/2817/, accessed 24 August 2016; http://konda.com.tr/tr/raporlar/KONDA_CEVRE_BILINCI_MART2012.pdf, accessed 23 August 2016.
3. Şebnem Udum, 'Understanding The Nuclear Energy Debate in Turkey: Internal and External Contexts', unpublished PhD dissertation, Bilkent University, Ankara, 2010.
4. The Bergama Movement, a local environmental movement struggling against a transnational gold-mining company in Western Turkey, is considered as the first of its type that had a large impact over the society, and it became a reference point to environmentalists. See Murat Arsel, 'The Bergama Imbroglio', in F. Adaman and M. Arsel (eds), *Environmentalism in Turkey: Between Democracy and Development?* (Aldershot, 2005).
5. See Murat Arsel, Bengi Akbulut and Fikret Adaman, 'Environmentalism of the malcontent: Anatomy of an anti-coal power plant struggle in Turkey', *The Journal of Peasant Studies* 42/2 (2015), pp. 1–25.
6. Joan Martinez-Alier, *The Environmentalism of the Poor: A Study of Ecological Conflicts and Valuation* (Cheltenham, 2002).
7. James Scott, *Seeing Like a State: How Certain Schemes to Improve the Human Condition have Failed* (New Haven, 1998).
8. Arsel et al., 'Malcontent'.
9. Ibid.
10. Aykut Çoban, Fevzi Özlüer, Sinan Erensü, Özder Akdemir and Beyza Üstün, 'Türkiye'de neoliberal politikaların ekolojiyi kuşatması, direnis ve yeniden inşa [The sieging of the ecology by neoliberal policies in Turkey, resistance and rebirth]', Mimarlık Semineri (2015).

11. Murat Arsel, 'Risking Development or Development Risks?: Probing the Environmental Dilemmas of Turkish Modernisation', unpublished PhD thesis, University of Cambridge, 2006.
12. Fikret Adaman, Murat Arsel and Bengi Akbulut, 'Türkiye'de kalkınmacılığı yeniden okumak: HES'ler ve değişen doğa-toplum ilişkileri [Re-reading Turkey's developmentalism: Hydropower plants and changing society-environment relationships]', in E. Evren, S. Erensü and C. Aksu (eds), *Sudan Sebepler: Türkiye'de Neoliberal Su-Enerji Politikaları ve Direnişler* [*Watery Reasons: Neoliberal Water-Energy Politics in Turkey and Resistance*] (İstanbul, 2016).
13. Ulrich Beck, 'The anthropological shock: Chernobyl and the contours of the risk society', *Berkeley Journal of Sociology* 32 (1987), pp. 153–65.

CHAPTER 8

'A FEW ENVIRONMENTALISTS'? INTERROGATING THE 'POLITICAL' IN GEZİ PARK

Murat Arsel, Fikret Adaman and Bengi Akbulut

Gezi Park and Environmental Studies

At the height of the Gezi Park Uprising, the then Prime Minister Recep Tayyip Erdoğan, referring to his supporters who were presumably watching the events in anger, declared that he was having 'a difficult time holding back the remaining fifty per cent at home'. Equal parts a threat and a confession, Erdoğan's comment was proof of what environmental social scientists working on contemporary Turkey had known for some time, namely not only that the 'environment' is inherently political but that it provides a particularly important vantage point from which to understand the political economy of the country's transformation.

In the days that followed the Gezi Uprising, the number of scholarly interventions on the subject grew in much the same pace as the crowds that arrived in the park following the brutal attack of the police on 30 May 2013. The uprising, the underlying factors that gave birth to it, its short- and long-term significance, the socio-economic character of its participants and the tactics used by the protestors have been extensively discussed. Its parallels in terms of regional and global dynamics were considered in comparison to other events, including Tahrir Square,[1]

Occupy Wall Street,[2] Indignados[3] and other national contexts such as Greece[4] and Brazil.[5] While coming almost exclusively from a critical social science perspective, the explosive growth of the literature saw also very specific lenses brought to bear on the event: Marxian,[6] Levinasian[7] and Badiouesque,[8] just to name a few. It is remarkable, however, that very few of these interventions have been made from the vantage point of environmental studies,[9] which remains lamentably weak within the context of contemporary Turkish studies.[10] This chapter is therefore intended as a small corrective to this glaring absence.

What the protestors were demanding, at least in the short term, was relatively clear: first, the cessation of the abuse of the demonstrators by the police, and second, the abandonment of the plans to replace the park with a hotel/shopping mall complex constructed in a neo-Ottoman style to replace Gezi Park as part of the redesign of the Taksim Square. What would the 'other 50 per cent' do if they defied the prime minister and went out to the streets? Would they have uprooted the trees themselves and lent a hand to the police as they beat up the protestors? The aim of this paper is not to answer these questions. However, thinking through them as well as other related questions makes it is possible to reflect on the meaning of the concept of 'environmental politics' in contemporary Turkey, which has been misunderstood not just by Erdoğan but also by many critical social scientists.

Rethinking the significance of 'environmental politics' can also be a corrective to another extremely common misconception that has come to dominate the literature on the Gezi protests. Most of the published literature on the events begin their analysis by emphasising the 'surprise' nature of the uprising and how it would not have been possible to anticipate how the defence of 'a few trees' could explode into one of the most spectacular social conflicts in the history of modern Turkey. The period since Turkey's neoliberal turn in the 1980s, however, is replete with episodes similar to Gezi in many regards, even though they have not achieved the same level of public support or attention. Was it mainly because many of them were set in rural areas? Or was it that the Gezi Uprising is indeed a unique, surprising turn in Turkey's environmental conflicts? To this end, is it possible to link the Gezi Uprising – and its grammar of environmental politics – to other movements across the country, connecting them organically to a broader contestation over nature and development?

Answers to these questions, in turn, can help problematise the long-term significance of the Gezi Uprising. In other words, if Tuğal is correct that the spectacle of Gezi Park is ultimately marked by its 'inability [. . .] to offer alternatives to the current order',[11] is this a failure of the uprising itself (and of those who, however loosely, organised and orchestrated it)? Or is this a shortcoming, if not a failure outright, of environmental politics in contemporary Turkey?

As already mentioned, the Gezi Uprising has been covered extensively in the literature. Therefore, rather than providing another overview of its specifics, it should suffice to make a few brief observations that are pertinent to the questions set out above. While Istanbul's sustained construction boom has come at a heavy cost to public spaces, it is important to note that new green areas have also been created as part of urban transformation and beautification drives. This is not to suggest that Gezi Park is not significant. However, its spirited defence by activists and intellectuals since plans of its transformation have been announced needs to be contextualised within a broader political economy framework, one that not only recognises the class-based nature of how the city is experienced but also apprehends the material and historical processes that imbue the contemporary symbolism of the park with added value. It is within such a framework that Gezi Park's location in the Taksim Square takes on added significance. Located at the edge of the city's old European quarter, it occupies a significant place within the Kemalist modernisation project and has long been the preeminent location for political demonstrations. Put simply, Gezi Park is not just another park and Taksim Square is not an ordinary square. Finally, it is important to underscore the particularly tense political climate in which plans to transform the park and the square were put into practice. Specifically, by the time the Gezi Uprising began, the AKP had begun to lose support from its non-traditional supporters, who had suspended their scepticism as long as processes of political reform continued to crawl forward and the party's leadership did not overtly seek to leverage their considerable electoral support to achieve what many believed to be their goal of creating a more conservative and pious society. It is within this context that the protests grew in size and significance and made Gezi Park the epicentre of a confrontation between a large but highly specific segment of the society and the state.

Politics of a Few Trees

A key trope that emerges from this vast and still rapidly growing literature is that the Gezi Uprising started with the defence of something relatively trivial. For instance, Onbaşı writes that the events started 'as a local protest by a small group of environmentalists against the cutting down of *several trees* and the destruction of the public park in Taksim'[12] (our italics). In a similar vein, İnceoğlu asserts that 'the catalyst which triggered the events was an attempt by a handful of environmentalists to protect a *few trees* from being cut down'[13] (our italics). What is being suggested is that a small number of trees could not, on their own, be a sufficient cause for an uprising of this size. Or as Gül and his associates put it succinctly, a 'modest environmental protest against the redevelopment of a park and the loss of a few trees on face value would be considered trivial in mainstream national politics'.[14]

Such a reading of the Gezi Uprising is problematic on several fronts. This is not because the Gezi Uprising was solely or even mainly about the conservation of trees. As discussed already, the specific political and cultural context – neoliberal urban transformation, fears of a cultural backslide through attempts to regulate alcohol consumption, etc. – did of course play a role in the way in which the defence of trees gave rise to a significant struggle.

What is problematic here instead is the strict separation of the 'environment' from other concerns, such as 'democracy'. In other words, the implicit assumption seems to be that the defence of 'a few trees' is a fundamentally *ecological* concern and that such a concern is separate from and ranked in lower significance than other, genuinely *political*, concerns.

Several decades into the development of the literature on political ecology, such an assumption is difficult to maintain. In short, nature – and its transformations – are simultaneously political and economic. The way in which social actors perceive nature, their relationships with it and the transformations of both are fundamentally a question of power – to preserve, to transform, to represent. The acknowledgement of this fundamental axiom necessitates the recognition that it is not the quantity or quality of the trees that defines the significance of the object of a particular instance of 'environmental politics'. Rather, it is how those trees fit within broader processes of transformation that render them – and their potential and resisted uprooting – political.

It is of course not only the scholarly literature that has concentrated on the fact that the early days of the resistance movement was focused on a small number of trees. In the same speech quoted at the beginning of the chapter, Erdoğan described these trees as 'the fuse' which was lit to unleash a larger and, in his estimation, far more nefarious scenario. The study of other related conflicts in Turkey has shown that such allusions to conspiracy theories have become the staple of environmental politics in the country. Such conspiratorial thinking is not only exceedingly common but also pervasive on all sides of environmental conflicts in Turkey, bringing to surface deep-seated and dark national fears that are often expressed in racist, chauvinistic and xenophobic terms. While the 'usual suspects' – the US and Israel – often get implicated in these conspiracy theories, for reasons owing to the particularities of modern Turkish history that cannot be discussed here, Germany features very prominently as well. Thus, for the prosecutors of the State Security Court (DGM in its Turkish acronym) peasants fighting against a gold mine cannot be expected to express a 'genuine' fear of potential spills of cyanide-laden tailings; they must be agents that are either brainwashed or actively employed by Germany intelligence services. Or, the construction of a coal power plant is not 'simply' the result of the combination of short-sighted energy policies and crony capitalism but the outcome of the machinations of the German state, which, in its bid to get rid of its own supply of coal in order to reduce its greenhouse gas emissions, has contrived to get the Turkish state into investing in an out-dated technology.

In light of such conspiratorial thinking, the following exchange between Erdoğan and a reporter from Reuters is worth quoting at length. In response to her question on whether he intended to take any steps to diffuse the mounting tension, Erdoğan proceeded to examine the reporter:

Erdoğan: Let me ask you first, what is the message [to the government] being sent from Gezi?

Reporter: From education to the 'alcohol law', everyone is concerned with restrictions that affect them. The people we see in the squares [referring not just to

	Taksim but other demonstrations nationwide] are not from a particular political movement [. . .] and that's what is surprising to all the observers [. . .] Many of the demonstrators are also not the supporters of the main opposition party, the Republican People's Party [CHP in its Turkish acronym], they are not the supporters of any organisation [. . .] Perhaps, in my opinion, the anger of these people can be explained as 'why is the government not questioning [itself] as to why these people are rising up?'
Erdoğan:	Wait a second, we've arrived at a peculiar point [. . .] so [you are saying] there is no CHP [in the squares]? Very well, who is there?
Reporter:	There is of course CHP.
Erdoğan:	Who else is there? Were you able to ascertain that?
Reporter:	There are lots of young people in the streets, many university students.
Erdoğan:	They may not be supporters of CHP. Don't university students have ideals, ideologies?
Reporter:	Yes, why did they rise up? Why did housewives rise up?
Erdoğan:	Don't they have an ideology? Right now, there are people, at least fifty per cent of the country, whom we can barely keep in their homes [. . .] and we are telling them, be patient, don't fall into these traps.

The implicit assumption that Erdoğan makes is that the will to conserve trees or a park, in and of itself, cannot be an ideological position. Furthermore, since, as he continues to state in the interview, only a few trees would be cut, action taken in their name cannot be considered genuine, acceptable political practice but must be considered as a subversive activity aimed at undermining the state. In short, for Erdoğan there is no 'environmental politics' as such but merely 'environmentalism'. It is not surprising, therefore, that Erdoğan claimed that he himself and the AKP are the genuine environmentalists since they were behind the planting of more than 2.5 billion trees during ten years of power,[15] a claim which some environmentalists dispute as an exaggeration.

Furthermore, any overlap between strictly ecological considerations – e.g. conserving trees in an urban park – with other concerns – e.g.

the manner in which the decision to alter the park was taken or implemented – can only be understood as betraying the spirit of environmentalism and, by extension, something 'ideologically motivated'. Those acting for the sake of these ideologies have since been accused, at best, with being unwitting servants of various internal and external enemies of Turkey or, at worst, with working directly for them to destroy the AKP and, by extension, the country as a whole.

Returning to the scholarly literature, it is possible to detect a different type of differentiation of environmental politics from presumably higher order concerns. This is especially visible in another trope, one that is perhaps even more common than that of 'a few trees'. Analyses of the Gezi movement invariably begin with an expression of surprise, that such a movement was unimaginable. For instance, Navaro-Yashin reflects that '[s]ocial scientists in the square were surprised; so were anthropologists',[16] and Gürcan and Peker similarly argue that the 'sudden and unprompted nature of the protests took specialists on Turkey by surprise'.[17]

The underlying assumption that dominates the literature is that, to the extent that it is possible to speak of environmental politics in Turkey, this is understood as being local and small-scale. In other words, the social scientific literature on contemporary Turkey treats environmental politics primarily as a 'not in my backyard' (NIMBY) activity, failing to appreciate its critical position at the nexus of related struggles over the meaning and quality of democracy within a hugely complex and diverse society. The surprise therefore is not that the Gezi Uprising happened at the moment it did. To that end, almost all political explosions – e.g. the fall of the Berlin Wall, Tiananmen Square, Tahrir Square and many others – come as a surprise to the experts. Thus when scholars express their surprise regarding the Gezi Uprising, this refers to the fact that it somehow managed to 'jump scales [...] to the urban and the national'.[18]

In other words, it is possible to detect a type of post-materialism thesis here but in reverse. Inglehart's thesis[19] had famously classified certain political preferences and dispositions – concern for environmental quality being an important example – as post-material, or, put differently, as higher order concerns that are expressed only after material (read essential) needs have been met. This second trope of the Gezi Uprising literature regarding its surprisingness concerns the moment in which environmental politics went national. The surprise is not simply that environmental politics has a certain, unexpected potency, or that it was able to 'jump scales'. Inherent in such expressions is surprise at the fact that with the Gezi Uprising environmental politics jumped ahead of Turkey's putatively more important socio-economic and cultural challenges such as rise of Islamist conservatism, worsening oppression of Kurds, and deepening economic equalities to claim the national limelight.

The Grammar of Resistance

'Teams belonging to the metropolitan municipality cut down 60-year old trees without mercy. The park will be converted into a shopping centre and a parking lot.'[20] This headline, eerily reminiscent of the threats surrounding Gezi Park in May 2013, was in fact taken from a piece dated March 1986 published in *Ulus* newspaper. The article was entitled 'Slaughter of trees in Ankara' and it lamented the fate not only of Zafer Park but also the hugely symbolic Güven Park which awaited a similar fate as well as reporting that concerned citizens where demonstrating against the action.

The previous section argued that to a large extent both the political and scholarly discussions concerning the Gezi Uprising misread the meaning and significance of contemporary environmental politics in Turkey. But this shortcoming is not limited to analytical conceptualisation. It also reflects a failure to engage with key moments in the post-1980s development of environmental action in Turkey. Part of this can be attributed to an urban bias in contemporary Turkish studies. While the rural has to a certain extent been investigated, this has been done mainly within the context of other concerns, be it religion, ethnicity or gender. It is surprising that contemporary research has shied away from engaging with the political economy of the peasantry. Within this context, the lack of contextualisation of the Gezi Uprising within a broader historical context is understandable. It is remarkable, however, that the large body of published output concerning the Gezi Uprising has not even taken note of previous urban struggles such as the ones aiming to protect Zafer Park and Güven Park, which set the tone for contemporary struggles.

In fact, many of the facets of the Gezi Uprising that have been highlighted as well as a few that have escaped notice, can be traced back to previous struggles such as the Bergama Resistance,[21] the movement against the Gerze coal power plant,[22] the struggles against micro-hydroelectric plants in Artvin and the rest of the Black Sea.[23] While a detailed analysis of this shared grammar of resistance that developed over the past three decades is not possible here, it is nevertheless important to highlight some of the more salient ones.

One of the most commented about features of the Gezi Uprising has been the combination of humour and creativity with which the demonstrators expressed their discontent and confronted the police. Dağtaş is correct that this '[expanded] the range of the "publicly expressible" in times of fear, despair and dissatisfaction with the existing order'.[24] In such highly charged and closely monitored situations, irony, word play and creative expression of discontent can create not only a much needed emotional outlet for the activists but also a modest layer of protection since even within an oppressive political culture the boundaries of the permissible can be expanded further for humorous expression. In fact, the graffiti art that was created during the Gezi Uprising recalls the equally creative banners that were developed during the Bergama resistance against a gold mine in Western Turkey, which began in the late 1980s and continued through much of the 1990s. In that movement, one of the strategies that helped the peasant activists connect with the national public sphere was the use of creative allusions such as the one that connected foreign direct investment into natural resource extraction with the US Navy's 6th fleet that patrolled the Mediterranean.

The Bergama Resistance was especially prolific in breaking the mold of public protest and creating novel, attention grabbing forms of demonstrations. Its members marched down the streets in their underwear (to demonstrate that living with gold mining in their town would be even more embarrassing), protested outside the building that housed the inaugural parliamentary meeting of the Republic of Turkey (because they believed the new, official parliament had been sold off to the IMF and the World Bank) and, in arguably their most effective move, chained themselves to the bridge connecting Istanbul's European and Asian sides (to reject the mining company's claim that mining would bring development and, hence, Europeanisation). Considering the novel forms of dissent displayed in Gezi Park within such a repertoire (that comprises many similarly creative episodes in other movements) need not diminish the significance of the creativity and impact of acts such as that of the 'Standing Man'.[25] Rather, doing so enhances their significance, demonstrating their organic connections to related struggles that have been going on for decades.

Another much-commented feature of the Gezi Uprising has been the ways in which it featured LGBT activists prominently as well as creating an opportunity to advance the struggle for gender equality in Turkey. Yıldız, for instance, draws attention to the 'expressive and explosive political momentum'[26] that Gezi provided LGBT and feminist activists (as well as those representing or expressing solidarity with other marginalised groups). The relationship between LGBT and feminist activists can be interpreted in two ways. On the one hand, thanks due to a small but committed group of activists building on eco-feminist theory, Turkey's environmental activist community has long been attuned to the interconnections between struggles for ecological and gender justice, not least because of capitalism's organic relationship with patriarchy. On the other, the conflagration of state-society conflict also has the potential to demonstrate to the newly 'radicalised' masses (a particularly important feature of the Gezi Uprising) not only what marginalised groups had known all along – that the power of the state in Turkey is often deployed in brutal, punitive ways to silence any form of dissent – but also the need for closer links of solidarity between the 'mainstream' and the 'margins'. In other words, environmental political action provides both an opportunity for reflexive agency and for deepened solidarity. For example, it is well-documented that the activists in Gezi Park were able to engage in critical discussions regarding some of the sexist slogans that were used against the security forces. Similarly, rural environmental resistance movements in Turkey – such as Bergama, Gerze and Artvin – have frequently been led by women or were built around their strong participation. Taking place in what are relatively patriarchal settings, these movements have not only benefited from women's political agency but also promoted longer-term changes in gender relations both at the level of the household and the public sphere.

It is the third trope, the heterogeneity of the demonstrators, however, that is especially noticeable in the Gezi literature. For instance, Örs describes them as 'environmentalists, football fans, academics, workers, artists, LGBTTQ [lesbian gay bisexual transvestite transgender queer], Kurds, feminists, people from all walks of life',[27] which is not far from

Arat's list, 'Kemalists, leftists, environmentalists, feminists, LGBT activists, Kurds, Alevis, soccer fans, professionals, and workers',[28] or from Rodrik's, which is comprised of 'nationalists, secularists, Kurdish activists, environmentalists, liberals, soccer fans, gay and lesbian rights supporters, and even some Islamists'.[29] Once again, the untenable separation of 'environmentalism' from other forms of political positionality characterises these descriptions. The surprise seems to emerge as much from presumed antagonisms embodied in these descriptors as from an unwillingness to imagine the existence of – among many other possibly permutations! – a Kurdish lesbian environmentalist soccer fan. Moreover, such expressions at the diversity of the Gezi demonstrators display a lack of appreciation of environmental concern as a unifying political project, one that has considerable – though certainly not limitless – potential to serve as a boundary concept that helps activists construct efficacious political coalitions.

That environmental movements in Turkey have necessarily been built around diverse interests is readily appreciable from a review of the cases already discussed in this section. Both in Bergama and Gerze, for instance, while the early stages of the campaigns were led by seasoned leftist activists, the broader movements included various constituencies that exist also in thinly populated rural areas. The available evidence demonstrates that while shared environmental concerns can be the foundational blocks of such alliances, the environment also can work as a vehicle to articulate other political grievances. Therefore, some activists join an environmental campaign not primarily because of an *ecological* concern but because it enables them to articulate a seemingly unrelated *political* grievance. It is important, however, not to reduce these categories to monolithic and unchanging constructions. For the evidence also shows that these environmentally themed coalitions initiate a process of political reflexivity in which the ecologists become politicised while the others become environmentalised. Put differently, it is necessary to acknowledge the dynamic nature of the political subjectivity of both the building blocks of a movement as well as the totality of the movement during its life cycle. The experiences of Gerze and Bergama also show that such coalitions require extensive organisational capability and willingness to negotiate and compromise even though on their surface they might seem spontaneous and natural.

From Criticism of Construction to Constructive Criticism

How does this heterogeneity map onto a discussion of the class composition of the Gezi Uprising? This has been a relatively narrow but highly significant component of the ensuing discussions. Before engaging with this question, it is necessary to recognise that it is often invoked in relation to the overall inability of the movement to articulate a concrete agenda for change and its failure to coalesce into a sustained political alliance. Most of the commentators have argued that the Gezi Uprising is a fundamentally middle-class affair and that 'certain sections of the working class, especially of industrial labour, remained politically underrepresented among the Gezi protesters'.[30] These arguments were primarily based on the sectors in which the demonstrators worked or the modality of their relationship to capital. In other words, this 'middle class' was distinguished by its white-collar pedigree and its comparative autonomy to act independently. This independence combined with the defining concerns of this class – namely individual freedoms, environmental quality and limiting state oppression[31] – has conditioned the rise of the Gezi Uprising and structured its demands. The failure of the working class to materialise in significant numbers in the demonstrations – especially in and around Gezi Park – can then be interpreted as a function of the conflicting agendas of the middle and working classes.

Boratav[32] and others have not necessarily disputed the point that many of the demonstrators were urban professionals, especially those in the service sector. However, they have interpreted their class position not as middle class but as 'various wage-earning class fractions'.[33] In other words, the dispute centred on not necessarily who were present in the uprising but rather on how to locate the urban professionals within Turkey's class structures. The main empirically driven exception to this narrative comes from Yörük and Yüksel who argue that '[c]lass is [. . .] not effective as an explanatory variable for the Gezi protesters'[34] and that it is better understood as a political process, mainly as opposition to the AKP and Erdoğan's growing authoritarianism. However, their reading of surveys that show that the social democratic CHP received the lion's share of voters from those supporting the uprising and that the party relies heavily on urban middle-class voters shows that this discussion cannot yet be considered settled.

Class positions do have an important relationship to how the environment becomes politicised and lends itself to mobilisation efforts. It is important to recognise that rather than a 'true' environmental ethic, it is possible to link different class positions to different political conceptualisations of the environment and its transformation by global capitalism. In the defining contribution to this literature, Martinez-Alier and Guha coined the concept of the 'environmentalism of the poor' to create a conceptual ballast against the (then) hegemonic mode of environmentalism, which they rechristened as the 'environmentalism of the rich'.[35] In their parlance, environmentalism cannot be limited to the activities of the 'rich' – i.e. fighting for symbolically important types of biodiversity or against issue-specific causes that left systemic sources of the environmental crisis untouched. Therefore, attempts to defend certain resources by the poor (and the marginalised, indigenous, etc.) had to be understood as a just as if not more important type of environmental activity. However, Martinez-Alier and Guha's disentangling of these different class-based positions, or our recent attempt to show that there exist forms of cross-class alliances, which we described as the 'environmentalism of the malcontent' in the case of the Gerze movement,[36] do not have much analytical purchase to explain the overall shortcoming of the Gezi Uprising to capitalise on its unprecedented momentum to make concrete changes to the dominant political and economic structures or its inability to articulate a shared vision of transformation.

This is because whether the movement is working-class, middle-class or a combination thereof, none of these class positions have a coherent alternative position to the modernising growth ideology that has come to characterise Turkey's political economy. Moreover, while this chapter has argued that the Gezi Uprising is not especially unique or surprising and that it represents a continuity of on-going struggles that back at least to the beginning of the neoliberal phase of developmentalism in the 1980s, the environmental movement itself – arguably the best positioned political force in the country to question developmentalism – has failed to articulate a meaningful alternative to create a just, equitable and sustainable society. This is not to argue that environmental movements in general or the Gezi Uprising in particular are characterised by NIMBY responses. There is ample evidence that the root causes of the problem are conceptualised in broad and internationalist terms (for instance, a monument erected to commemorate the Bergama resistance against gold mining made explicit references to the fate of the indigenous peoples of the Americas and their suffering under imperialism). However, this has not been sufficient to articulate an alternative pathway to achieving meaningful material emancipation without resorting to top-down, authoritarian developmentalism.[37] To the extent that the Gezi Uprising has failed to advance in this regard, this is therefore best understood as a failure to put in place a vision that can replace the neoliberal version of Turkey's long standing ambition to transform itself with one that is more sustainable, democratic and egalitarian.

Notes

1 Kerem Öktem, 'Turkey, from Tahrir to Taksim', *Open Democracy* 7 (2013), https://www.opendemocracy.net/kerem-oktem/turkey-from-tahrir-to-taksim, accessed 10 July 2016.

2 Cihan Tuğal, 'Occupy Gezi: The limits of Turkey's neoliberal success', *Jadaliyya* (2013), http://www.jadaliyya.com/pages/index/12009/occupy-gezi_the-limits-of-turkey%E2%80%99s-neoliberal-succ?, accessed 10 July 2016.

3 Cihan Tuğal, '"Resistance everywhere": The Gezi revolt in global perspective', *New Perspectives on Turkey* 49 (2013), pp. 147–62.

4 Leonidas Karakatsanis, 'Radicalised citizens vs. radicalised governments? Greece and Turkey in a comparative perspective from the December 2008 uprising to the 2013 Gezi Park protests', *Journal of Contemporary European Studies* 24/2 (2016), pp. 255–79.

5 Ricardo Fabrino Mendonça and Selen A. Ercan, 'Deliberation and protest: Strange bedfellows? Revealing the deliberative potential of 2013 protests in Turkey and Brazil', *Policy Studies* 36/3 (2015), pp. 267–82.

6 Efe Can Gürcan and Efe Peker, 'Turkey's Gezi Park demonstrations of 2013: A Marxian analysis of the political moment', *Socialism and Democracy* 28/1 (2014), pp. 70–89.

7 Anna-Verena Nosthoff, 'Fighting for the other's rights first: Levinasian perspectives on Occupy Gezi's standing protest', *Culture, Theory and Critique* 57/3 (2015), pp. 313–37.

8 Özden Sözalan, 'A few remarks on the lessons of Gezi Uprising', *Badiou Studies* 2/1 (2013), pp. 146–51.

9 Begüm Özkaynak, Cem Aydın, Pınar Ertör-Akyazı and Irmak Ertör, 'The Gezi Park resistance from an environmental justice and social metabolism perspective', *Capitalism Nature Socialism* 26/1 (2015), pp. 99–114; and Ömür Harmanşah, 'Urban utopias and how they fell apart: The political ecology of Gezi Parkı', in Umut Özkırımlı (ed.), *The Making of a Protest Movement in Turkey: #occupygezi* (London, 2014).

10 Murat Arsel, 'Environmental studies in Turkey: Critical perspectives in a time of neo-liberal developmentalism', *The Arab World Geographer* 15/1 (2012), pp. 72–81.
11 Tuğal, '"Resistance everywhere"', p. 160.
12 Funda Gençoğlu Onbaşı, 'Gezi Park protests in Turkey: From "enough is enough" to counter-hegemony?', *Turkish Studies* 17/2 (2016), pp. 272–94; p. 273.
13 İrem İnceoğlu, 'The Gezi resistance and its aftermath: A radical democratic opportunity', *Soundings* 57 (2014), pp. 23–4; p. 23.
14 Murat Gül, John Dee and Cahide Nur Cünük, 'Istanbul's Taksim Square and Gezi Park: The place of protest and the ideology of place', *Journal of Architecture and Urbanism* 38/1 (2014), pp. 63–72; p. 70.
15 http://www.medyaradar.com/basbakan-resti-cekti-birkac-capulcuya-pabuc-birakmayiz-haberi-100182, accessed 10 October 2016.
16 Yael Navaro-Yashin, 'Editorial-breaking memory, spoiling memorisation: The Taksim Protest in Istanbul', 2013, *Fieldsights-Hot Spots, Cultural Anthropology Online*, https://culanth.org/fieldsights/411-editorial-breaking-memory-spoiling-memorisation-the-taksim-protests-in-istanbul, accessed 10 July 2016.
17 Efe Can Gürcan and Efe Peker, 'A class analytic approach to the Gezi Park events: Challenging the "middle class" myth', *Capital & Class*, 39/2 (2015), pp. 321–43.
18 Mehmet Barış Kuymulu, 'Reclaiming the right to the city: Reflections on the urban uprisings in Turkey', *City* 17/3 (2013), pp. 274–8; p. 275.
19 Ronald Inglehart, 'The silent revolution in Europe: Intergenerational change in post-industrial societies', *American Political Science Review* 65/4 (1971), pp. 991–1017.
20 'Ankara'da ağaç katliamı', *Ulus*, 39 March 1986.
21 Murat Arsel, 'Risk society at Europe's periphery? The case of the Bergama Resistance in Turkey', in F. Gökşen, O. Seippel, M. O'Brien, E.Ü. Zenginobuz, F. Adaman and J. Grolin (eds), *Integrating and Articulating Environments: A Challenge for Northern and Southern Europe* (Lisse, 2003).
22 Murat Arsel, Bengi Akbulut and Fikret Adaman, 'Environmentalism of the malcontent: Anatomy of an anti-coal power plant struggle in Turkey', *Journal of Peasant Studies* 42/2 (2015), pp. 371–95.
23 Fikret Adaman, Bengi Akbulut and Murat Arsel, 'Türkiye'de kalkınmacılığı yeniden okumak: HES'ler ve değişen doğa-toplum ilişkileri [Re-reading Turkey's developmentalism: Hydropower plants and changing society-environment relationships]', in E. Evren, S. Erensü and C. Aksu (eds), *Sudan Sebepler: Türkiye'de neoliberal su-enerji politikaları ve direnişler [Watery Reasons: Neoliberal water-energy politics in Turkey and resistance]* (İstanbul, 2016).
24 Seçil Dağtaş, 'The politics of humor and humor as politics during Turkey's Gezi Park protests', *Fieldsights-Hot Spots, Cultural Anthropology Online*, 2013, https://culanth.org/fieldsights/397-the-politics-of-humor-and-

humor-as-politics-during-turkey-s-gezi-park-protests, accessed 10 July 2016.

25 Erin B. Mee, 'Standing man and the impromptu performance of hope: An interview with Erdem Gündüz', *TDR/The Drama Review* 58/3 (2014), pp. 69–83.

26 Emrah Yıldız, 'Cruising politics: Sexuality, solidarity and modularity after Gezi', in Umut Özkırımlı (ed.), *The Making of a Protest Movement in Turkey: #occupygezi* (London, 2014).

27 İlay Romain Örs, 'Genie in the bottle: Gezi Park, Taksim Square, and the realignment of democracy and space in Turkey', *Philosophy & Social Criticism* 40/4–5 (2014), pp. 489–98.

28 Yeşim Arat, 'Violence, resistance, and Gezi Park', *International Journal of Middle East Studies* 45/4 (2013), pp. 807–9.

29 Dani Rodrik, 'The wrath of Erdoğan', *Juncture* 20/2 (2013), pp. 129–30.

30 Fuat Ercan and Şebnem Oğuz, 'From Gezi Resistance to Soma Massacre: Capital accumulation and class struggle in Turkey', *Socialist Register* 51 (2015), pp. 114–35.

31 Çağlar Keyder, 'Yeni orta sınıf', *Siyaset ve Toplum Bilim Perspektifinden Gezi Parkı Olayları – Çalısma Grubu Raporu {Gezi Park Events from Sociological and Political Perspectives – Working Group Report}*, 2013, http://bilimakademisi.org/wp-content/uploads/2013/09/Yeni-Orta-Sinif.pdf, accessed 10 July 2016, pp. 1–4.

32 Korkut Boratav, 'Olgunlaşmış bir sınıfsal başkaldırı: Gezi direnişi. Gezi direnişi üzerine düşünceler [An unmatured class uprising: Gezi uprising. Some Thoughts on the Gezi Uprising]', http://emekatolyesi.org/olgunlasmis-bir-sinifsal-baskaldiri#.WBYmpPorLb0, accessed 10 July 2016.

33 Efe Can Gürcan and Efe Peker, 'A class analytic approach', p. 324.

34 Erdem Yörük and Murat Yüksel, 'Class and politics in Turkey's Gezi Protests', *New Left Review* 89 (2014), pp. 103–23; p. 122.

35 Joan Martinez-Alier and Ramachandra Guha, *Varieties of Environmentalism: Essays North and South* (London, 1997).

36 Arsel et al., 'Environmentalism of the malcontent'.

37 Murat Arsel, 'Reflexive developmentalism? Toward an environmental critique of modernisation', in F. Adaman and M. Arsel (eds), *Environmentalism in Turkey: Between Democracy and Development?* (Aldershot, 2005).

CHAPTER 9

ALTERNATIVE FOOD INITIATIVES IN TURKEY[1]

Zeynep Kadirbeyoğlu and Nazlı Konya

Introduction

In today's urbanised world, having access to healthy and affordable food is a problem both for urban dwellers and for rural inhabitants who do not produce their own food. Not only access to food on the consumer side but also the ability to make a decent living by producing food crops are important areas of exclusion in the contemporary globalised and corporatised food governance regime. Departing from an urgent need to correct the injustices caused within the processes of food production, distribution and consumption, alternative food initiatives (AFIs) creatively experiment with alternative systems of production and exchange. Their main goal can be summarised as engendering agrifood systems that are 'environmentally sustainable, economically viable and socially just'.[2] To this end, multiple paths have been taken by activists on the ground, about which a great deal of academic work has been produced, such as urban/community garden projects,[3] farmers' markets,[4] consumer cooperatives and community supported agriculture.[5] The multitude of AFIs aim to 'reconnect farmers and consumers'[6] and to create a broad alliance based on mutual aid and trust between growers and consumers,[7] redistribute the value extracted within the food system,[8] maintain the 'integrity of ecosystems',[9] 'transform the oppressive trade relations and corporate control'[10] and replace them 'with socially embedded markets and democratic governance'.[11] AFIs have attracted significant academic attention over the past decade from various disciplines.[12]

Through a combination of concepts such as form of life,[13] democratic governance and resistance from within, we examine whether AFIs can bring viable alternative modalities to hegemonic neoliberal policies. It is not easy to resist the social, environmental and health damage caused by the hegemonic corporatised food regime – a system which, in the context of the economies of the global South, seems to have been unleashed ever more strongly in the neoliberal era, with the profit drive restricted by very few or no regulatory boundaries. Dissent from such inequality-deepening policies in food production, distribution and consumption requires the imagining of different modalities over and beyond a criticism of economic policies and existing institutions. These modalities should be diverse and multiple in order to allow for concrete experimentation with democracy and democratic politics when it comes to food production, distribution and consumption processes. The form of life literature suggests that food-related alternative organisations such as collectives and cooperatives can be effective only if they imagine and start to live in that form and believe that the economy is a debatable and changeable issue.

In Turkey, the mechanisms that lead to exclusion in food systems intensified in the 1990s with the entrenchment of neoliberal policies such as the cutback on agricultural subsidies and support mechanisms. There are two aspects of the exclusionary practices within the food governance regime of the past three decades in Turkey. On the one hand, these policies were combined with the increasing presence of agrifood corporations, which placed even more pressure on small peasant/family farms in a context where agricultural policy had long been depoliticised in line with IMF and World Bank recipes. There has been very little movement to re-politicise agricultural policy, with the exception of efforts by Çiftci-Sen (*Çiftçi Sendikaları Konfedereasyonu* – the Confederation of Farmers' Unions), which attempts to mobilise small farmers.[14] On the other hand, consumers are excluded from access to healthy and affordable food as a result of processes such as the unregulated use of pesticides and chemical fertilisers in agriculture, and growth hormones in livestock and poultry production. Given this state of affairs in the mainstream food regime, this chapter examines AFIs to evaluate whether they offer an alternative to neoliberal, corporatised agrifood systems. Food initiatives have not been examined in the case of

Turkey, and this chapter contributes to the literature on movements that aim to transform the economic and political realms through enactments that resist dominant models and reconstitute an alternative constellation. Although food sovereignty is a concept that is used to refer to alternative strategies employed by food initiatives willing to break away from the dominant agrifood regimes, we do not refer to this concept in this chapter as the groups we examined did not use it in their mission statements.

The next section provides a brief overview of the theoretical framework for imagining and achieving alternatives. It is followed by a short synopsis of agricultural transformation in Turkey, with a focus on the period after 1980. AFIs in Turkey are presented in the following section in order to discuss the extent to which these initiatives are able to present an alternative process of production, distribution and consumption.

Imagining an Alternative Social Order

The matter of viable resilience in the face of ubiquitous neoliberal transformation occupies the centre of contemporary social, political and philosophical debates in search of a left-critique. Furthermore, a great many social movements across the world strive to provide alternatives to the 'neoliberal attitudes, imaginaries, and practices that have come to inform everyday life in the first few decades of the millennium'.[15] However, critical theories and practices conceive the challenge as the lack of an 'outside' – namely, outside neoliberalism – that can be discovered or recuperated. Dissenting projects often find themselves trapped in despair and impotence, or charged with being incremental, partial or co-opted by the very power they seek to resist. Moreover, neoliberalism's own resilience to recurring economic crises and public cries for its dismissal intensify the challenge.

The difficulty in proposing a robust oppositional politics stems from neoliberalism's irreducibility to a mere dominant economic paradigm or to a set of economic policies. As originally theorised by influential political philosopher Michel Foucault,[16] the neoliberal doctrine goes beyond the mere restructuring of national economies for the unconstrained working of the market. Instead, it first and foremost recasts a whole new society that imitates the market relations themselves, thus redesigning the social fabric as being composed of self-entrepreneurial subjects. The new social fabric comes to be constructed on the market imperatives of interest, competition and value-enhancement, at the expense of solidarity, participation or responsibility-sharing. Therefore, neoliberalism constitutes itself as a productive political rationality, which generates new rules of conduct, new forms of socialities and subjectivities in all spheres of human existence.[17]

Such capacious reordering, then, requires multifarious politics of critique and resistance that offer diverse ways to challenge, subvert, transform or *un*do the existent operations and techniques of power in a wide web of social existence. In other words, alternative economies, socialities and sites of power should be creatively constructed through diverse relationalities that are part of everyday life.

The terrain of food politics represents one of these sites of resistance, for food is so central to sustaining the life and well-being of human and non-human beings that varied practices in its production, distribution and consumption are valuable domains for alternative imaginaries. We should note that our theoretical insights situate resistance to neoliberalism in the ongoing instances of experimentation with forms of 'living' other than what the market imperative advocates and requires.

Adopting the term 'living' is a deliberate decision made to underscore the commitment to expand the resistance out of the bounded spaces of legal/institutional change toward a full body of modes of life, where participants actively *practise* the broader economic, social and political conditions that they strive to attain. We argue for locating the political activities that aim both to change the norms in the realm of experimentation and invention, and understand dissenting politics as a world-building activity.[18] In other words, enacted actions, enlivened experiences, actualised practices of political aspirations should precede formalisation or institutionalisation. Following Honig[19] in this respect, one could claim that 'the form of life' that these political activists presuppose 'through the daily work of life' bring into being the very modality of living before it is termed. In this light, the binary between alternative social movements/politics and formal/institutional/juridical politics becomes a futile discussion, for it ignores the potentialities that stem from habituated modes of conduct, of 'liv[ing] otherwise'.[20]

Related to what was said above, our second theoretical orientation directed us to examine the democratic promises that diverse collectivities might offer in the process of enacting their governing principles. Although they might not necessarily be concerned with salient political objectives, the study of social collectivities nevertheless opens up a space where the real premises of formal enactments can be observed. To put it more clearly, we perceive democratic governance as a mode of performative enactment[21] by collectivities that do not rest on predefined imperatives: their perpetual and open-ended processes of self-constitution generate the principles and procedures that will govern social, economic and political relations in the desired future. What follows this understanding of democratic practice is another order of priority: should norms, ends, means and procedures be kept open to constant contestation, then we shall shift our focus from questions of 'what' or 'who' to questions of 'how'[22] in our conceptualisation of resistance and dissenting politics.

Finally, the third crucial aspect of our thinking is related to the need to part ways with deep-rooted investments in 'scaling up' strategies.[23] Symptomatic of the all-pervasiveness of neoliberal rationality as a 'totality', resistant imaginaries are quite often programmed to think through the lens of self-duplication: if neoliberalism is a gigantic structure, the argument goes, we must also be giants, and replace the whole economy, the whole world, the whole realm of production, consumption, distribution and exchange with our alternative structure. Such visions of dissident political projects not only mimic neoliberalism in its expansionist logic, but also suffer from (even fatalistically prophesise) an almost inevitable likelihood of failure as all grandiose attempts are wont to do. Consequently, we would like to bring in an alternative way of thinking about transformation, resistance, or world-building, in response to self-defeating and frustrating conceptualisations of resistance. For us, multiplication – instead of scaling-up – seems a promising horizon of resistance; not for the sake of humility, but for its *decorum*: as underlined above, today's nonconforming practices will emerge through multiplicity, diversity and proliferation in all realms of social existence. A viable critique of neoliberalism can be sought in infinite modalities of life through multiplying imaginations, experiments and practices, instead of attributing one certain particularity and privilege to replicate across otherwise distinctively constituted spaces and socialities.

Agriculture and Food in Turkey

Agricultural production in Turkey was traditionally small and peasant-based, although large and powerful landlords were dominant in some areas. It had already become commercialised in the western and southern regions by the 1920s, when the mechanisation of agriculture began, and reached new levels with the Marshall Plan Aid in the 1950s and 1960s. State policies during the planned growth era of the 1960s favoured industrialisation through import substitution. In the field of agriculture, the use of chemical fertilisers and tractors, and increased state support meant that most agricultural production in Turkey was marketised, and subsistence agriculture dropped to insignificant levels by the early 1980s.[24] In the 1980s, the IMF and World Bank prioritised removing the burden on the state budget caused by agricultural subsidies and support mechanisms, and introduced structural adjustment policies. Within the export-oriented development model of the post-1980s era, agriculture was no longer seen as a major contributor to growth in Turkey:[25] its contribution to national income was 40 per cent in 1950, had fallen to 26.3 per cent by 1970 and to 15.9 per cent by 1990.[26] Köymen[27] argues that this constituted a break with previous agricultural policies, where state support had been an essential element.

Initially, reliance on small-scale producers was not challenged because ruling parties wanted to maintain good ties with the rural electorate. This made structural adjustment reforms half-hearted attempts.[28] The Agricultural Reform Implementation Project (ARIP), designed by the World Bank and the Ministry of Agriculture, aimed to further the reform process in the field of agriculture.[29] Its implementation in 2001 was followed by a speedy liberalisation process; support to farmers – inputs, loans and marketing facilities – declined significantly over the course of the 2000s[30] and the quasi-governmental agricultural sales cooperative unions were privatised.[31] To mitigate the impact of the reforms on farmers, the Direct Income Support (DIS) system was implemented[32] through which registered farmers received per hectare payments for up to 20 hectares – this limit was later increased to 50 hectares.[33] While the DIS was in effect, two laws – Agriculture Law No. 5488 and Seed Law No. 5553 – were passed in 2006;[34] the former partially reinstituted government support for agriculture and the latter banned the sale of uncertified and unregistered seeds.[35] All the reforms mentioned above were part of the process to bring about a market-driven agrifood system in Turkey.[36] Although Turkey was able to complete its cadastre and create a farmer registration database through ARIP, the project and other laws had negative impacts such as the 'mounting numbers of informal and illegal lenders in the countryside who are also merchants of agricultural commodities; a growing rate of bankruptcy among small producers; a drastic drop in the rural agricultural population [...]; an escalating role for supermarkets and their dominance in food chains; and an increase in contract farming and the proletarianisation of rural agricultural workers in their own lands'.[37]

Although a mix of subsidies still exist in Turkey,[38] the majority of small-scale producers face tremendous difficulties in sustaining their livelihoods through agricultural production and have diversified their household income through non-agricultural activities such as tourism, construction and craftsmanship.[39] Çiftçi-Sen was established in 2008 to mobilise small farmers *vis-à-vis* corporations as well as state policies that had been designed to withdraw support from small and family farmers with the intention of rendering agriculture more efficient and corporatised. Çiftçi-Sen brings together seven producers' unions and attempts to protect farmers' rights with respect to diverse issues such as prices, environmental protection, legal frameworks and social protection. Çiftçi-Sen is also active at the transnational level and a part of La Via Campesina, an organisation that works to secure farmers' rights at the global level.

Alternative Food Initiatives in Turkey

In Turkey, the search for alternative agricultural practices and alternative lifestyles has been ongoing since the early 1990s. Although initially confined to a very small group, interest has grown significantly over time. As one of the first ideologues and practitioners of ecological living in Turkey, Victor Ananias began his activities in the early 1990s and founded the Buğday Association. The Buğday Association is one of the pioneers of AFIs in Turkey with its BAHÇE (garden) project – a consumer-supported agricultural undertaking that began in 2005 in Istanbul and lasted for several years. Buğday also established organic farmers' markets in Turkey in 2006, which have since then increased in number. Today, there is a plethora of different kinds of organisations and platforms that are concerned with food and agriculture in Turkey.

To evaluate whether AFIs do indeed constitute an alternative modality of life, we examined 55 food initiatives[40] and found that AFIs tend to emerge as part of or as a result of three processes in Turkey: environmental struggles such as anti-mining social movements, union activism such as labour unions or farmers' unions and individual or collective demand and search for healthy and affordable food. Needless to say, these processes are not mutually exclusive and may simultaneously play a role in the emergence of certain initiatives, whereas only one factor is effective in others.

The wide variety of food initiatives in Turkey are organised by different types of actors: consumers, producers and intermediaries. Some consumer and producer groups actively seek to raise awareness about food-related issues, while others, formed to raise awareness, engage in production for a variety of reasons; hence, there are AFIs where the spheres intersect in Figure 9.1 as well. Although AFIs in general attempt to eliminate intermediaries, there are intermediary-like commercial projects that open up marketing channels for small farmers or traditional or organic products. They are depicted outside the three spheres in Figure 9.1. In producer, consumer and awareness-raising AFIs, the initial stimulus to form a cooperative or collective emerges from individuals with prior experience in

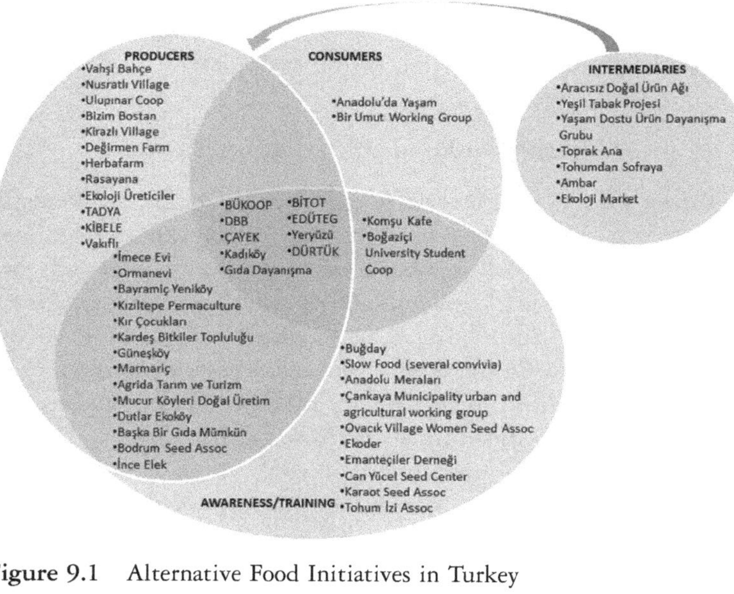

Figure 9.1 Alternative Food Initiatives in Turkey

political and/or civil society activism. Their political engagement and the skills they acquired elsewhere serve to mobilise them in attempts to find alternative ways to market and sell their products instead of being subsumed under the price-determining game that intermediaries play. People who have relocated from urban to rural areas also have a strong impact on mobilising other farmers or women in the village to start a producers' collective or cooperative. Furthermore, although these organisations are usually spearheaded by well-educated, middle class urbanites, there is a tendency in rural areas to mobilise farmers in villages surrounding their sites of production, and in urban areas, these groups try to be as inclusive as possible in order to attract lower-income groups. However, the price barrier involved usually prevents such inclusiveness in the urban context.

Some AFIs are solely concerned with raising awareness about the food issue, while others mobilise around issues such as conserving and disseminating heirloom seeds, permaculture and establishing eco-villages. Overall, producers, consumers and intermediaries try to organise all processes related to food production, from its monitoring, certification and collection to the transmission and distribution of orders and consumption. Orders are usually collected and transmitted through a variety of channels. Some collectives organise weekly, monthly or irregular orders through a webpage or email list. Others engage in consumer-supported agriculture and yet others organise producers' markets, or have a shop where products are delivered and sold. Some collectives require organic certificates whereas others believe this kind of certification is commercialised, very expensive and thus a burden on small farmers. The latter group usually resorts to participatory guarantee systems (PGS) where, with the help of experts and consumers, they fill out forms detailing the production process so as to ensure that the products they get are produced according to certain standards.

Among the AFIs in Turkey there are collectives, cooperatives and associations formed by both producers and consumers. On the consumer and producer side, cooperatives – which have legal status and can engage in the formal exchange of goods – are the most lawful way to organise the distribution of goods. Other types of organisations, such as informal collectives or shopping groups, may face problems of durability and informality. However, the cooperative law in Turkey is not very conducive to the formation of cooperatives by producers or consumers:[41] there are many barriers and difficulties along the way that can deter groups from doing so.

Broadly speaking, AFIs struggle to change our conception of the production, exchange and consumption of food and show that there is an alternative to the corporatised and monopolised food system. However, this does not mean that the alternative to the neoliberal food regime is a state-centred and subsidy-driven form of agricultural production: what AFIs attempt to do is to recuperate and discover what a more just and environmentally sound constellation of food production and consumption may look like. In more concrete terms, what neoliberalism entails for small and family farms manifests itself clearly in the domain of seeds: the gradual decline in seed diversity during the capitalist system accelerated when large multinational corporations developed hybrid and genetically modified seeds in order to increase yields as well as their own profits. The 'global market economy [...] imposes uniformity in production processes for the sake of short-term efficiency based on the dictates of the market'[42] and the traditional farming practice of conserving part of the harvest for future use is made impossible because seeds are sterile, and farmers are forced to buy seeds from corporations.

This not only reduces farmers' revenues, but also makes them dependent on manufactured seeds at the expense of the diversity of traditional seeds. In response to this biodiversity loss, seed associations have emerged that gather, regenerate, store and exchange heirloom seeds at seed exchange festivals. One of them is the Bodrum Seed Association, which not only collects and regenerates seeds, but also distributes regenerated seeds to small family farmers and organises a farmers' market in Bodrum where these producers sell their crops themselves. The association carries out tests to check whether chemical residues remain and verifies that the produce was not only grown from heirloom seeds, but that it was agro-ecologically produced as well.

ÇAYEK (*Çanakkale Ekolojik Yaşam İnisiyatifi*) came about when a number of individuals came together due to concerns over extractive activities in the Ida Mountains, promoted by the state and operated by private enterprises. These individuals were concerned that mining in the area would lead to ecological destruction, and claimed that small family farmers would not oppose mining projects unless they were able to make a living off their land and animals. More concretely, a retired urbanite who had moved to a village to engage in agricultural production collected milk from sheep that belonged to the villagers and produced cheese to be sold in the cities. The villagers received a much higher price for their milk in comparison to when they sold to large producers, and as a result, were no longer willing to sell the milk at a lower price than what the small-scale producer paid. This small producer, who was involved in ÇAYEK and the ecology movement in the Ida Mountains, knew that the only way to convince the locals to stand strong against mining projects was to make sure they could maintain their livelihood through agriculture and animal husbandry. This is very much related to the awareness and willingness of urban consumers to deliberately choose products that come from such initiatives and question the viability of the mainstream food regime.

Different AFIs have different priorities, according to which they determine their goals. Looking at the goals of AFIs in Turkey, it seems possible to categorise them under these headings: agricultural, social, political, economic, environmental and educational (see Table 9.1). Needless to say, no single AFI attempts to achieve all these goals at once and some may have diverging goals. The purpose of the remainder of this section is to highlight the diversity of goals we identified in our research on AFIs in Turkey and the challenges they face. Agriculturally, the main goal of some AFIs in Turkey is to change the nature of agricultural production from conventional production – where commercial hybrid seeds, chemical fertilisers and pesticides are used – to one that employs local or heirloom seeds and practices ecological farming to grow nutrient-dense food. Some begin their efforts solely to gain access to healthy food, but may change in the process and incorporate more trust-based modalities that aim to achieve an alternative food regime; meanwhile, others remain more adamant about getting the lowest price for goods and therefore are not concerned with the core of the problem.

Socially, most food initiatives support small-scale producers and desire to get to know farmers to build personal relationships based on trust. Some of the initiatives favour a return to the land – a kind of reverse migration to rural areas – with the purpose of creating groups in harmony with nature. In some cases, this call to the land is a collective endeavour where eco-villages or communes are created by a group of people; in others, a family or an individual from an urban area may buy up land in a village and begin production – usually after retiring from active employment – and over time mobilise the farmers of the village and surrounding villages to establish a producers' collective to benefit small-scale local farmers.

Table 9.1 Typology of the Concerns and Goals of AFIs in Turkey

Agricultural	• Holistic management – integrate agriculture and animal husbandry • Regenerative agriculture • Grow healthy and nutritious/nutrient-dense food • Safeguard local/heirloom/traditional seeds – the sale of which is forbidden by patent laws and other laws • Natural farming/ecological farming • Conserve and sustain traditional production processes
Social	• Return youth to the land – reverse migration from urban to rural areas • Create a harmonious group • Generate and support local food organisations where there are no intermediaries • Get to know producers on the ground and build trust
Political	• Organise joint activities with producers, universities, civil society organisations and public institutions • Enhance the input of women in village economy • Redefine human needs along with the ecosystem
Economic	• Create self-sufficient villages • Facilitate access to products without intermediaries • Support eco-agro tourism • Organise the exchange of goods between organised producers and organised consumers • Provide a source of livelihood (socio-economic benefits) for local producers
Environmental	• Spread sustainable agricultural methods that harm neither the environment nor human health • Sustainable rural development/sustainable agriculture and animal husbandry • Protect and improve the natural environment and wildlife • Increase natural and agricultural biodiversity • Efficient and responsible use of resources such as water and soil • Make villages harmonious with nature in terms of social, economic, cultural, technological, production and settlement related issues • Localism – low carbon footprint

Educational	• Generate models that can be emulated/reproduced • Create exemplary implementation for villagers regarding water use, resource preservation, composting, mulch, etc. • Analyse problems in rural areas, design projects and implement them • Change the food preferences of urban dwellers

Politically, these initiatives attempt to organise events such as conferences, workshops, seed exchange festivals, field visits to producers and talks in order to disseminate their activities, raise awareness and bolster mobilisation efforts. Seed exchange events have been influential in raising concern over the disappearance of traditional and indigenous heirloom seeds and the dominant use of conventional ones. Furthermore, these events attempt to link AFIs with municipalities, universities, civil society organisations and concerned individuals. Sharing experiences related to the formation and maintenance of AFIs facilitates the emergence and viability of new ones. Economically, the main goal of most producers and consumers in AFIs is to organise transactions without intermediaries and to provide a source of livelihood for local small producers who would otherwise be forced to sell to intermediaries at lower prices. Some AFIs believe it is imperative for consumers and producers to jointly organise in the form of cooperatives or associations, so that producers can protect their interests without having to give in to the pressures of the price determination process run by intermediaries, and consumers can change their relationship to food and consumption and become co-producers or 'prosumers' – consumers who actively engage in the process of food production and consumption.[43]

Environmentally, AFIs have local as well as global concerns, which include instilling ecologically and socially sustainable agricultural practices, increasing natural and agricultural biodiversity, using resources efficiently and responsibly and achieving a low carbon footprint by consuming as locally as possible. More broadly, these initiatives attempt to generate models that can be reproduced and set an example to others. They aim to bring about a transformation by promoting sustainable agriculture and animal husbandry in rural areas, and by changing the consumption patterns of the inhabitants of urban areas.

Our research results indicate that AFIs face many challenges. For urban groups, maintaining the levels of voluntary work required to run a collective is not easy. All duties end up being shouldered by the same small group of individuals, who in the end may experience burn-out. Furthermore, some members of an AFI may have different motivations that conflict with those of others; for instance, while some may prioritise buying products at reasonable prices, others may believe price negotiations must be avoided at all costs since the main motive is to protect the interests of small producers or family farms. In a similar vein, the priority to access healthy and local products may be in conflict with the urge to bring about an initiative that would prioritise solidarity. The size of the consumer group is also a challenge. A small group of about 100 members is probably more manageable in terms of maintaining coherence, but this is also challenging because demand volume may not be enough to sustain the collective in the long run. Furthermore, in cases where organisations are unable to draw new cohorts of members into active involvement, the viability of the collective is challenged. Some of these AFIs organise horizontally without any hierarchy. Most have a core group that may be open to all members who are willing to be more systematically involved. Main operational decisions are made by members of the core group at periodic meetings. Moreover, there is usually a desire to establish a rotation in the duties being performed so that members experience all phases of the process. As for producer cooperatives or collectives, finding outlets for their products, establishing and maintaining communication with prosumers, securing a steady level of demand for their products and deciding on how revenues will be divided constitute important challenges.

Discussion

The previous section provided a snapshot of AFIs in Turkey. Do these initiatives, organised in diverse forms, constitute a real alternative to the existing hegemonic and dominant corporatised food system? How do they impact farmers and consumers? On the farmers' end, have they been able to reverse the depeasantisation trend that began in the post-1980s era and gained unprecedented speed since the early 2000s? On the consumers' end, have attempts to politicise food and agricultural issues and mobilise urban dwellers been successful in bringing about change in awareness and practices? For farmers, AFIs have a positive potential impact, although this is currently limited in terms of the demand volume from these initiatives. Despite the criticism that these are insignificant attempts to provide farmers with a source of livelihood and prevent depeasantisation, we argue that AFIs fulfil important roles: they open up new channels of food transaction by eliminating intermediaries and putting long-separated urban and rural dwellers in touch, modify urban tastes to incorporate local crop varieties into their diets, conserve and promote heirloom and local seeds and demonstrate that old and forgotten techniques of production are being revived and practised to show these methods are viable and efficient in contrast to conventional means of production. For consumers who are active in AFIs, their relationship to food changes as they become involved in its production and exchange. However, if consumers are only interested in accessing healthy food or engaging in individualised ethical behaviour – such as consuming fair-trade or organic produce – but make no attempt to generate collective subjectivities by practising alternative types of organisation, then it is not possible to claim that these initiatives promote a new social fabric that constitutes an alternative to the one constructed upon market imperatives.

Today, a new social category seems to have emerged from the exchange practices within AFIs. Some of the organisations that aim to connect urban consumers with small producers without the involvement of intermediary structures refer to a new actor called a prosumer – *türetici* in Turkish, which is a neologism that integrates the terms consumer (*tüketici*) and producer (*üretici*). A common emphasis on the prosumer made by the consumer and/or producer collectives sheds light on the endeavour to transform the subjectivities that are performed in market relations. As an alternative to the market rationality that assigns detached and indifferent social roles, these collectives suggest that the prosumer, as a new agent arising from experimentation with alternative modes of exchange, plays an important role in the construction of micro-food networks. Here, consumers attain a new understanding about their responsibilities *vis-à-vis* the assorted producers embedded in distinct local economies and in varied social and environmental circumstances.

The model, proposed by the Ormanevi collective (a producers' collective), BÜKOOP and DBB (consumer-led initiatives), aims to transform urban consumers into semi- or co-producers by compelling them to organise, engage in more direct – in some cases even face-to-face – relationships with farmers, gain awareness about the social and economic conditions brought about by the current food regime and arrive at a shared responsibility concerning the livelihoods of small scale farmers. A Slow Food convivium, *Fikir Sahibi Damaklar* (Palates with Opinions), for instance, departs from the objective of using the critical capabilities of agents who are 'considered to be consumers in our everyday practices' and recasts them as 'producer-supporters' who reshape their food preferences in ways that promote the common well-being of humanity, animals and nature through a just, equitable and healthy food regime. From a broader perspective, the transformation in consumer-subjectivity reflects the construction of relations of trust and solidarity between the urban and the rural, the receiver and the supplier, while otherwise isolated and entrenched social positionings are opened to encounters, understanding and transitivity. Therefore, it denotes a new form of life where certain ethical questions that revolve around the production, distribution and consumption of food occupy a prominent space in one's life, considering the centrality of food in everyday practices.

Such transformation should not be taken merely as self-centred or self-regarding ethics, which is restricted to the formation of individual preferences. Instead, it goes beyond an individualistic response to injustices induced by the current food regime, insofar as concrete effects regarding the maintenance of ecological and fair agro-production and exchange are sought; also, seed diversity and locally controlled, self-sustained small-scale industry is protected from the monopolising tendencies of the corporatised, multinational agro-food industry. Thus, the new modality of life mentioned here is based on a constant questioning of all the conditions and consequences pertaining to the processes in which food arrives on the fork from the farm, or at least in certain modesty, it is an orientation to become as informed and influential/transformative as possible. As the Güneşköy Cooperative – another producers' initiative that aims to raise awareness – states among its founding objectives, AFIs, first and foremost, attempt to invent and develop 'life experiences' that are sustainable and amenable to the rural environment and 'to disseminate such accumulated experience'. Drawing on our fieldwork on the AFIs in Turkey over the past two years, we agree with Levkoe's[44] argument that becoming more active in food politics through associations brings about a 'transition to collective subjectivities' because food serves 'as a point of entry for deeper political engagement' for the participants. As individual participants become more exposed to collective social needs, work with a multitude of social agents involved in the food system and develop 'broader and more diverse kinds of relationships', collective subjectivities are established even if participants initially had more individualistic goals and motivations.

An alternative social order also entails a critical approach to market imperatives and at times, their replacement with other ethico-political principles, or the prioritisation/revalorisation of other norms than the ones that govern market relations. AFIs, in their extensive variations in terms of organisation, structure, goals and span, manifest the diversity inherent to any economy 'as a site of decision of ethical praxis'.[45] Thus, they destabilise the capital-centric logic, which blocks social agents' imaginaries by projecting capitalist market relations as the single mode that characterises the form of labour, exchange and organisation in economic bodies. Contrary to such homogenous representation of the food economy, AFIs highlight the mechanisms invented to reverse the exclusionary effects of the capitalist market. For instance, instead of subscribing to the principle of competitive value enhancement in the neoliberal rationale, or capitalising on the authentic asset value of their individuated products in niche markets, women from the village of Nusratlı formed a 'cultural tourism and solidarity association' where the collective body assists small-scale farmers excluded from the market by promoting their products with technical support in marketing, providing online sales opportunities, opening up new channels to increase publicity for local producers across wider regions and other similar forms of assistance. The associative and collaborative approach to individual goods indicates the co-existence of market, non-market and alternative market modes in organising the economy.

As discussed above, in most of the alternative food initiatives examined in this study, members strived to demonstrate that an 'outside' exists and that society is not limited to corporatised, monopolistic and harmful practices that from a neoliberal perspective are promoted as benefiting everyone. They tried to construct a new social fabric and relations based on solidarity, participation and responsibility-sharing. In the case of AFIs, the relationalities that are imagined and forged outside neoliberal hegemonic structures happen in the domain of food – which is a daily need. Therefore, having to step out of one's daily routine is easier than when resistance politics involves organising a demonstration or protest. In other words, members of AFIs enact actions in such a way that a different mode of life is practised to show that an alternative is possible. However, this enactment should take place in a democratically organised setting and should not rest on pre-defined imperatives such as the necessity to ask for organic certificates or providing goods at the lowest possible prices. Consequently, as long as norms, ends, means and processes are open to contestation by all members without resorting to hierarchies in decision making, AFIs can be said to allow space for democratic enactments that attempt to bring about alternative actualised practices.

The members of BÜKOOP (a consumers' cooperative that operates from a public university) or Tarlataban (a collective garden project that belongs to the same university and includes non-university participants) emphasise their preference in making consensus-based decisions while ensuring all weekly (or biweekly) organisational meetings are open to all members, with a genuine investment in inclusionary and participatory deliberation (for instance, without resorting to a hierarchy on the basis of seniority). For sure, not all questions find consensual answers immediately, hence sometimes they are 'taken to rest' and discussed further later, and members do not take action until they persuade one another.[46] In the meantime, those who take part in deliberations learn from one another about technical details or new ethical problematics related to the matter at hand, which they may not have known about earlier. Sometimes, long processes of debate and disagreement certainly can hinder reaching an immediate response that is needed for pressing issues (such as the timely planting of seeds or getting in touch with a farmer for orders), yet participants train themselves in being open, flexible and responsive.

Having provided an overview of the transformative achievements, we should also note that AFIs nevertheless receive significant criticism regarding how effective they are. To put it more clearly, alternative propositions to re-structure food networks are taken with a grain of salt; on the one hand, with reference to the scales within which they operate quantitatively and on the other, to the degree of radicalism that they involve qualitatively *vis-à-vis* the capitalist agrifood market that they challenge. The qualitative dimension can be briefly summarised as remaining 'alternative' rather than 'oppositional', since they do not challenge the current agrifood system explicitly but prefer to work incrementally within existing market structures by creating alternatives while the dominant system stays intact.[47] Here, incrementalism refers to a lack of striving for national policy change, governmental entitlements or any other macro-level institutional restructuring. In parallel, the quantitative aspect underscores that AFIs are limited in scope in terms of economic activity and emphasises the need to 'scale up' and 'scale out'.[48]

The above-stated criticism concludes that AFIs have yet to offer an adequate response to deep-rooted social, economic and environmental injuries that globalised capitalist food-markets have caused. Although we share the main concerns implied in these critiques, we would also like to highlight that the highly local and low-scale operativity of the micro-food networks stems from their attentiveness to contextuality. Unlike the homogenising and totalising inclinations of mainstream economic approaches, the operational logic of AFIs relies on the needs, demands and experiences of the local populations within their respective environments. Therefore, diversification – be it in terms of ethical, ecological, social principles; legal status; organisational structure; or the rules that regulate day-to-day business – needs to take shape according to the particular circumstances specific to how collectivities assess market conditions and its effects, their priorities, primary orientations and the social, economic, environmental problems that they address.

The following statement by a BÜKOOP member illustrates this point quite explicitly: 'We intentionally do not aim to grow, although we constantly receive calls from neighbourhood forums to open up branches in those places. Instead of expanding our scale with new branches and wider networks, we recommend they share our experience, our practical, legal and technical insights, and encourage them to initiate their own associations.'[49] This suggestion is indicative of BÜKOOP's and many other AFIs' preference to multiply (in diversity) over scaling up or growth, owing to their investments in the primacy of autonomous, participatory and collective decision making in terms of questions and principles that do not have predefined formulas and require reflecting on the local context. Following the Gezi movement, which began as an action to protect a public park in Istanbul and escalated into a complex movement of resistance, a number of park fora emerged that attempt to address social, political and environmental issues at the neighbourhood level. In one such park forum, namely Kadıköy – one of the main neighbourhoods in Istanbul – some participants decided to develop a project to establish a neighbourhood cooperative for food provision. Building their model on the experience of BÜKOOP, they managed to create a neighbourhood-level group and have experimented with selling boxes of food directly to interested individuals who had placed an order. Over time, BÜKOOP has shared its experience and information on its producers with initiatives in other universities and neighbourhoods. This is what coop members were referring to when they talked about multiplying rather than scaling up their activities.

Conclusion

Through the survey of AFIs in Turkey, this chapter examined whether AFIs were able to challenge mainstream conventional agricultural production and distribution processes by imagining and creating alternative organisations that connect consumers and producers. We found that AFIs tended to have both common and diverging goals, and that they used different methods to achieve their ends. We argue that AFIs do provide a viable alternative modality in Turkey, but that they need to diversify and multiply in order to be effective and make a more significant impact. The initiatives, which are concerned with enacting solidarity-based and participatory structures that are open to change, are consciously attempting to create an alternative to the all-pervasive neoliberal model.

Further research is needed in this area to observe whether, and to what extent, AFIs are successful in the long run and whether they multiply, which seems to be the crucial point that will enable them to maintain the small farmers and producers on the ground, prevent them from giving up and becoming wage workers in agricultural production, or migrate to cities to be employed in the service or manufacturing industries.

Notes

1. The authors wish to thank Yağmur Aslan and Leyla Kabasakal for their help during the research for this chapter. The usual caveat applies.

2. Patricia Allen, David Goodman, Harriet Friedman and Douglas Warner, 'Shifting plates in the agrifood landscape: The tectonics of alternative agrifood initiatives in California', *Journal of Rural Studies* 19 (2003), pp. 61–75; p. 61.
3. Laura DeLind, 'Organic farming and social context: A challenge for us all', *American Journal of Alternative Agriculture* 9 (1994), pp. 146–7; Kate Clancy, 'Reconnecting farmers and citizens in the food system', in W. Lockeretz (ed.), *Visions of American Agriculture* (Ames, 1997); Jules Pretty, *The Living Land: Agriculture Food and Community Regeneration in Rural Europe* (London, 1998); and William B. Lacy, 'Empowering communities through public work, science, and local food systems: Revisiting democracy and globalisation', *Rural Sociology* 65/1 (2000), pp. 3–26.
4. Lacy, 'Empowering communities'; Julie Guthman, 'Bringing good food to others: investigating the subjects of alternative food practice', *Cultural Geographies* 15 (2008), pp. 431–47; Robert Gottlieb, *Environmentalism Unbound: Exploring New Pathways for Change* (Cambridge, MA, 2001); and Alison Hope Alkon and Teresa Marie Mares, 'Food sovereignty in US food movements: Radical visions and neoliberal constraints', *Agriculture and Human Values* 29 (2012), pp. 347–59.
5. Jenny Cameron and Rhyall Gordon, 'Building sustainable and ethical food futures through economic diversity: Options for a mid-sized city', Paper presented at the Policy Workshop on The Future of Australia's Mid-Sized Cities. Latrobe University, Bendigo, VIC, 28 and 29, September 2010.
6. Charles Z. Levkoe, 'Towards a transformative food politics', *Local Environment: The International Journal of Justice and Sustainability* 16/7 (2011), pp. 687–705; p. 689.
7. David Goodman and E. Melanie DuPuis, 'Knowing food and growing food: Beyond the production-consumption debate in the sociology of agriculture', *Sociologia Ruralis* 42/1 (2002), pp. 5–22.
8. Pretty, *The Living Land.*
9. David Schlosberg, 'Theorising environmental justice: The expanding sphere of a discourse', *Environmental Politics* 22/1 (2013), pp. 37–55; p. 44.
10. Madeleine Fairbairn, 'Framing transformation: The counter-hegemonic potential of food sovereignty in the US context', *Agriculture and Human Values* 29 (2012), pp. 217–30.
11. Ibid.
12. See among others Charles Z. Levkoe and Sarah Wakefield, 'Understanding contemporary networks of environmental and social change: Complex assemblages within Canada's "food movement"', *Environmental Politics* 23/2 (2014), pp. 302–20; Levkoe, 'Towards a transformative food politics'; Guthman, 'Bringing good food to others'; Gottlieb, *Environmentalism*; Neva Hassanein, 'Practicing food democracy: A pragmatic politics of transformation', *Journal of Rural Studies* 19/1 (2003), pp. 77–86; and C. Clare Hinrichs, 'The practice and politics of food system localisation', *Journal of Rural Studies* 19/1 (2003), pp. 33–45.

13. As we will elaborate in the following sections, the term 'form of life' here refers to modes of living, where people extend their ethical orientations and critical practices to the entirety of their everyday lives, whereby these orientations and practices become definitive, inseparable attributes of their self-constitution. For related theories, see Bonnie Honig, *Emergency Politics: Paradox, Law, Democracy* (Princeton, 2009); and 'Surviving: Mere life and more life'; as well as Giorgio Agamben, 'What is a destituent power?', *Environment and Planning D: Society and Space* 32 (2014), pp. 65–74.
14. Ayşe Aslı Öçal, 'Acción Colectiva y Procesos de Reestructuración en la Agricultura: Análisis de nuevas experiencias asociativas en Turquía [Collective Action and Processes of Restructuration in Agticulture: Analisis of new associative experiences in Turkey]', unpublished PhD thesis, Universidad Autonoma de Madrid (Madrid, 2015).
15. Philip Mirowski, *Never Let a Serious Crisis go to Waste: How Neoliberalism Survived the Financial Meltdown* (London, 2013).
16. Michel Foucault, *The Birth of Biopolitics: Lectures at the Collège de France, 1978–1979* (New York, 2008).
17. For a broader examination of neoliberalism's pervasiveness, see Wendy Brown, *Undoing the Demos: Neoliberalism's Stealth Revolution* (New York and Cambridge, MA, 2015); Michel Feher, 'Self appreciation, or the aspirations of human capital', *Public Culture Public Culture* 21/1 (2009), pp. 21–41; and Pierre Dardot and Christian Laval, *The New Way of the World: On Neoliberal Society* (London and New York, 2014).
18. For a broader discussion of Arendtian world-building politics, see Honig, *Emergency Politics*, 'Proximity'; and Hannah Arendt, *On Revolution* (New York, 1963).
19. Honig, *Emergency Politics*, p. 136.
20. Ibid.
21. For an elaborate discussion of performative dimensions of political enactments, see Jason Frank, *Constituent Moments: Enacting the People in Postrevolutionary America* (Durham, 2010).
22. At an ontological level, Agamben pursues a similar political project of replacing 'the ontology of substance with an ontology of how, an ontology of modality', and suggests the term 'form-of-life' to refer to a life that is inseparable from its form, modality and attributes: 'The decisive problem is no longer "what" I am, but "how" I am what I am', Agamben, 'What is a destituent power?', p. 73.
23. Harriet Friedmann, 'Scaling up: Bringing public institutions and food service corporations into the project for a local, sustainable food system in Ontario', *Agriculture and Human Values* 24/3 (2007), pp. 389–98; Josée Johnston and Lauren Baker, 'Eating outside the box: FoodShare's good food box and the challenge of scale', *Agriculture and Human Values* 22/3 (2005), pp. 313–25; and Mary A. Beckie, Emily Huddart Kennedy and Hannah Wittman, 'Scaling up alternative food networks: Farmers' markets and the role of clustering in western Canada', *Agriculture and Human Values* 29 (2012), pp. 333–45.

24. Gülten Kazgan, '1980' lerde Türk Tarımında Yapısal Değişme', in O. Baydar (ed.), *75 Yılda Köylerden Şehirlere* (Istanbul, 1999).
25. Oya Köymen, 'Cumhuriyet Döneminde Tarımsal Yapı ve Tarım Politikaları', in O. Baydar (ed.), *75 Yılda Köylerden Şehirlere* (İstanbul, 1999).
26. İpek İlkkaracan and İnsan Tunalı, 'Agricultural transformation and the rural labor market in Turkey', in B. Karapınar, F. Adaman and G. Özertan (eds), *Rethinking Structural Reform in Turkish Agriculture: Beyond the World Bank's Strategy* (New York, 2010).
27. Köymen, 'Cumhuriyet Döneminde Tarımsal Yapı'.
28. Zühre Aksoy, 'The Conservation of Crop Genetic Diversity in Turkey: An Analysis of the Linkages between Local, National and International Levels', unpublished PhD thesis, University of Massachusetts Amherst, 2005; Zülküf Aydın, 'The World Bank and the Transformation of Turkish Agriculture', in A. Eralp, I. Tunay and B. Yeşilada (eds), *The Political and Socioeconomic Transformation of Turkey* (Westport, 1993).
29. Barış Karapınar, Fikret Adaman and Gökhan Özertan, 'Introduction: Rethinking structural reform in Turkish Agriculture', in B. Karapınar, F. Adaman and G. Özertan (eds), *Rethinking Structural Reform in Turkish Agriculture: Beyond the World Bank's Strategy* (New York, 2010); and Mine Eder, 'Political economy of agricultural reforms in Turkey', in Ahmet İnsel (ed.), *La Turquie et le Developpement {Turkey and Development}* (Paris, 2003).
30. Aydın Zülküf, 'Neoliberal transformation in Turkish Agriculture', *Journal of Agrarian Change* 10/2 (2010), pp. 149–87.
31. Halis Akder, 'How to dilute an agricultural reform: Direct income subsidy experience in Turkey (2001–2008)', in B. Karapınar, F. Adaman and G. Özertan (eds), *Rethinking Structural Reform in Turkish Agriculture: Beyond the World Bank's Strategy* (New York, 2010).
32. Ibid.
33. Ibid.
34. Yıldız Atasoy, 'Supermarket expansion in Turkey: Shifting relations of food provisioning', *Journal of Agrarian Change* 13/4 (2013), pp. 547–70.
35. Ibid.
36. Ibid.
37. Koray Calışkan and Fikret Adaman, 'The logic of neoliberal agricultural reform initiatives: Perspectives and consequences', in B. Karapınar, F. Adaman and G. Özertan (eds), *Rethinking Structural Reform in Turkish Agriculture: Beyond the World Bank's Strategy* (New York, 2010), p. 93.
38. Akder, 'How to Dilute an Agricultural Reform'.
39. Çağlar Keyder and Zafer Yenal, 'Rural transformation trends and social policies in Turkey in the post-developmentalist era', in B. Karapınar, F. Adaman and G. Özertan (eds), *Rethinking Structural Reform in Turkish Agriculture: Beyond the World Bank's Strategy* (New York, 2010).
40. This study is based on a web-based research on the existing AFIs in Turkey. Some of the AFIs were currently active whereas others had ended their active

involvement or were in a dormant phase. Their actual status was not important for the scope of this paper, which aims to provide a survey of the attempts to form AFIs in Turkey.

41. Ziya Gökalp Mülayim, 'The fundamental problems of Turkish co-operatives and proposals for their solution', *New Medit* 9/4 (1998), pp. 14–21.
42. Zühre Aksoy, 'Local-global linkages in environmental governance: The case of crop genetic resources', *Global Environmental Politics* 14/2 (2014), pp. 26–44; p. 32.
43. Bram Büscher and Jim Igoe, '"Prosuming" conservation? Web 2.0, nature and the intensification of value-producing labour in late capitalism', *Journal of Consumer Culture* 13/3 (2013), pp. 283–305; Adina Dumitru, Isabel Lema-Blanco, Iris Kunze and Ricardo García-Mira, 'Transformative social innovation: Slow Food movement', a summary of the case study report on the Slow Food Movement. TRANSIT: EU SSH.2013.3.2–1 Grant agreement no: 613169 (2016).
44. Levkoe, 'Towards a transformative food politics', p. 692.
45. J.K. Gibson-Graham, *A Post-Capitalist Politics* (Minneapolis, MN, 2006), p. 87.
46. Engin Ader, 'BÜKOOP dili, BÜKOOP tipi uzlaşı modeli ve bunlara hayat veren BÜKOOPlular [The language of BÜKOOP, the consensus-building model of BÜKOOP and the members of BÜKOOP who make them all possible]', http://www.BUKOOP.org/?p=872, accessed 15 May 2016.
47. Allen et al., 'Shifting plates', p. 65.
48. Friedmann, 'Scaling up'; Johnston and Baker, 'Eating outside the box'; and Beckie et al., 'Scaling up alternative food networks'.
49. 'Yerel, adil, temiz, sağlıklı gıda: BÜKOOP [Local, fair, clean, healthy food: BÜKOOP]' http://www.bantmag.com/magazine/issue/post/29/246, accessed 15 May 2016.

CHAPTER 10

COMMONS AGAINST THE TIDE: THE PROJECT OF DEMOCRATIC ECONOMY[1]

Bengi Akbulut

Introduction

With the onset of the 2000s, the Kurdish Freedom Movement in Turkey started rearticulating its political project around the notion of 'Democratic Autonomy'. This model envisioned a radical democratisation of (political) decision-making processes across multiple scales through nested communes and councils. Concomitant to the political project of democratic autonomy is the construction of a communal and democratic economy along the principles of gender equality, ecology, democracy and egalitarianism.[2] More specifically, the project of 'Democratic Economy' involves the re-embedding of the economy within social processes, its reorganisation to ensure access of all to means of social reproduction, and its reconfiguration defined by needs.

While significant debate has subsequently taken place on the idea of democratic autonomy and its political feasibility, discussions on articulating the vision of democratic economy started fairly recently. Most notable among these are the eight workshops organised by the Democratic Society Congress (*Demokratik Toplum Kongresi*),[3] throughout the summer of 2014 in different cities with the participation of diverse local actors including activists, academics, officials from municipalities, and representatives from local business associations and labour unions. The workshops were organised under thematic headlines and culminated in the Democratic Economy Conference that took place in early November 2014. The declaration that stemmed out of the Conference substantiated a set of concrete proposals towards organising the economy in a way that prioritises need over profit, ecology over industrialism, local self-government over centralised governance, and that highlights gender egalitarianism in all economic phenomena.

This chapter locates the project of Democratic Economy and the emerging concrete experiences associated with it as an alternative to the paradigm of neoliberal developmentalism that has marked Turkey's contemporary political–economic landscape. Both the neoliberal character of this paradigm and – to a more limited extent – its unquestioned commitment to developmentalism *qua* economic growth have been the object of critical scrutiny.[4] However, imagining, constructing and sustaining alternatives to neoliberal developmentalism at various scales remained to be a more confined area of inquiry. Within this context, the Kurdish Freedom Movement emerges as the main social and political force to initiate a broad-based societal debate on an alternative economic vision and operationalise concrete practices to this end. While this is not to say that the project of Democratic Economy is the only or the essential example of an alternative economic imagination and practice, the parallels it bears with other such (existing and nascent) experiences should be noted. The case of Democratic Economy can thus be taken as a broader locus of discussions around alternative ways of organising economic life.

More specifically, this chapter depicts the vision of democratic economy by operationalising the analytic of the commons/commoning found in the works of Silvia Federici, George Caffentzis and Massimo De Angelis, among others, and defines it as entailing a series of commoning practices. The next section provides a brief critical overview of the literature on the commons and explicates the analytic of commoning. It is followed by an exposition of the vision of democratic economy as it is laid out in the final declaration of the Democratic Economy Conference as well as of the concrete steps taken to materialise this vision. The final section concludes by pointing to a number of challenges and contradictions lying ahead of this project and the commoning practices it entails.

Commons: From Tragedy to Commoning[5]

The literature on the commons has long been influenced, if not dominated, by Garrett Hardin's (in)famous 'tragedy of the commons' framework[6]: the collective use of a resource (e.g. a pasture) by a group of individuals (e.g. herders) will lead to its inevitable overexploitation, as each user will be motivated to increase his/her extraction from the resources without taking the costs associated with such an increase on other users into account. As each and every individual would be acting this way, the inevitable outcome is the tragedy, the depletion of the resource and 'ruin to all'.[7]

However, the empirical validity of this narrative has been forcefully challenged, most notably by the works of Elinor Ostrom,[8] Fikret Berkes[9] and Arun Agrawal,[10] among others, who illustrated that communities can indeed craft their own rules of access and enforce them through mutual monitoring to avert the 'tragedy'. A significant part of this line of work subsequently focused on identifying the conditions under which such successful cases of community management emerge, and highlighted, in particular, the importance of social norms, mutual trust, reciprocity, etc. in inducing sustainable collective use of the commons.

While Ostrom et al.'s work is groundbreaking in the sense that it has replaced Hardin's notion of the *economic* individual with a *social and economic* one – an individual who is responsive not only to economic incentives, but to social norms and rules as well – it hardly incorporates a vision of the social beyond the aggregation of individuals, or of a form of relationship between communities and commons that is not based on extraction of benefits. On the other hand, this approach – much like Hardin's framework – ignores the political–economic contexts within which commons are embedded into and, in a related vein, the way dynamics of accumulation and of power interact with the commons. A radically different, and much older, literature speaks precisely to this lack: Marxian political economy and the notion of primitive accumulation.

In *Capital*'s Volume I, Marx locates the origins of and the conditions that enable capitalist accumulation, i.e. the existence of capital and wage-labour, within the enclosure of the commons.[11] Writing on land enclosures and appropriation of common property in seventeenth-century

England, he illustrates how producers were divorced from their means of production by a variety of means, ranging from individual acts of violence to legal restructuring enabling expropriation. Through enclosures, commons were transformed into capital, and immediate producers were turned into wage-labourers; this process, primitive accumulation, yielded the original surplus that enabled subsequent capitalist production. The concept has later been reworked (e.g. accumulation by extra-economic means, accumulation by dispossession) to show that primitive accumulation is on-going, both in the global North and the global South, in different forms with new twists.[12] In that sense, the Marxian literature has located the notion of commons in relation to the accumulation of capital and revealed the ways in which the commons have served, and continue to support and/or enable, capitalism.

Within the Marxian literature on the commons, a distinct approach epitomised by the works of Caffentzis,[13] Federici,[14] De Angelis[15] and more broadly the Midnight Notes Collective,[16] is particularly noteworthy for the purposes of this chapter. This vein defines the concepts of commons and enclosures in a rather distinct way than the traditional Marxian line, in particular by reference to the set of social relationships around commons. This approach points to the amalgam of social relations and practices that produce and reproduce commons as forms of non-commodified social wealth – i.e. acts of *commoning*.[17] More specifically, commons are defined as sites of social reproduction accessed equally by all, autonomous of the intermediation of the state or the market, where social reproduction takes place under collective labour, equal access to means of (re)production and egalitarian forms of decision making.[18] They thus form modes of social reproduction and of accessing social resources that provide various degrees of protection from both the market and the state. Enclosures, in turn, are acts directed towards the expropriation, fragmentation and destruction of the autonomy of social reproduction by the market and/or the state.

This framework rescues the notion of the commons from fixity and posits it as a processual and relational concept. Seen this way, commons are not limited to shared forms of natural and social wealth, but include forms of relationships, networks, practices and struggles that provide (with varying degrees of) access to means of social reproduction autonomous of the market and the state.[19] Perhaps more importantly, the framework places emphasis on the particular characteristics of social practices that constitute commons. Accordingly, commons are forms of non-commodified wealth to be used by *all*, sites of *collective cooperative labour*, and regulated *non-hierarchically*. Such an approach thus incorporates the bases by which social relationships of commoning are organised (for example, solidarity, collectivity, cooperation, self-governance, egalitarianism, democracy), and reveals forms of relationships between communities and commons that are not limited to utilitarian extraction of benefits from a resource (for example, being self-sufficient, autonomous reproduction of life, guaranteeing subsistence rather than profit-generation).

This perspective helps locate practices like time banks, urban gardens, rural and urban land re-appropriations, food cooperatives, local currencies, 'creative commons' licenses, and bartering practices as existing and proliferating forms of commons and commoning.[20] Urban and rural land occupations, for instance, are commoning practices to the extent that they provide collective access to the means of social reproduction outside of the market and represent non-commodified forms of social wealth. Time banks and local currencies similarly represent ways of organising exchange autonomously of prevailing market forces and enable communities to uphold values other than efficiency (sustainability, fairness, equity) in exchange interactions. Urban community gardens can serve as vehicles for regaining control over food production, regeneration of the environment and provision for subsistence.

Following this line of thought, this chapter understands commons as sets of practices and relationships that provide mechanisms of collective social reproduction that remain (in varying extents) outside of the mediation of the state and the market. It adopts the notion of commoning to point to the diversity of forms that such practices can take as well as to their dynamism, and to open space to address how they are shaped by, and shape, the broader political–economic topography they are embedded in. This understanding is further grounded on the organising axes of the constitutive relations and practices of the commons, such as equal access, collective labour and democratic decision making. The following section operationalises this framework of understanding the commons in the specific case of the democratic economy project of the Kurdish Freedom Movement.

Democratic Economy as a Project of Commoning

As mentioned earlier, the final declaration of the Democratic Economy Conference held in November 2014 had articulated the principles along which to organise the economy, as well as a set of concrete proposals that provide guidance to be acted upon by various actors (municipalities, civil society organisations, commissions, etc.) within the movement.[21] Accordingly, the foundational principles that shape the project of Democratic Economy are gender emancipation, justice, egalitarianism, ecology, democracy and solidarity. It is important to note that these are not understood as separate domains of action but rather the organising tenets in all aspects of the economic field. Democracy, for instance, implies that decision-making processes at every scale and on every aspect of economic life should be democratic, organised through institutional venues such as councils, assemblies and communes. Ecology, on the other hand, denotes the recognition that all non-human nature is the common heritage of human and non-human kind and that all economic activities should be constrained by ecology as well as by society.

More concretised proposals regarding thematic subheadings, such as agriculture, women, trade, industrial production, energy, etc. further substantiate how the democratic economy vision would be operationalised. Below a selected set of them are summarised:

- The precarious and invisible nature of women's unpaid labour should be recognised, and unpaid domestic labour responsibilities should be socialised through appropriate institutional forms such as day-care centres and communal kitchens. Women's participation in all decision-making processes regarding local resources should be ensured and all spheres of democratic economy should be organised by positive discrimination of women.
- Agricultural production should be organised on the basis of need and conservation of local resources (e.g. seeds), rather than on efficiency and profit-orientation. Existing agricultural production units and cooperatives should be gender-democratised. Land should be considered as commons, and access and use of land should be understood as a common right. Land distribution as well as other tools of realising justice in land access should be developed. The uses of highlands, pastures and forests should be defended against commodification.

- Water, land and energy belong to all living and non-living creatures and the society as a whole; they cannot be commodified. Fossil fuel consumption should be minimised. Self-management should be established in the energy sector via decision-making platforms and energy cooperatives. Water management should be socially based, where distribution among different needs will be determined on the basis of social needs, equity and ecology. The right to water for all should be observed in decision making on water use, to be organised through water councils. Local communities should have the decision-making power on all underground and surface resources.
- Raw material production should be based on need. Production organised through cooperatives will prioritise local markets rather than export for processing. Production and consumption cooperatives will be established as a coordinated network. Local production units, artisans and craftspeople will be supported and protected. Social control mechanisms over labour health and safety issues will be established, involving producers, users and consumers.

Democratic economy is explicitly stated to be a non-accumulationist economy where economic relations are not oriented towards growth, but to the fulfilment of the needs of all. In a parallel vein, collective and equal access to the means of social reproduction is posited to be a priority over efficiency and profit-orientation. It thus conveys a vision of the economy geared towards certain values and principles (as opposed to others) and denotes the motives of economic relations as sites of political and ethical decision making.[22] In this sense, the vision of democratic economy notably deconstructs economic imperatives that are otherwise seen as inevitable, such as economic growth and profit-orientation, and re-imagines the economy as a sphere of possibility, which political subjects can decide and act on to shape. More generally, by opening all aspects of economic relations to decision making along the foundational principles of gender emancipation, egalitarianism, justice, ecology, democracy and solidarity, the democratic economy project subjects this field to ecological limits (taken to be binding) and societal control, and entails an effective re-embedding of the economy within the society and the environment in the Polanyian sense.[23] Among the various means of societal control and decision making are the existing communes and councils operating at different scales and themes (neighbourhood, town, city, etc.; youth, women, education, economy, ecology, etc.), as well as specifically cited venues such as energy cooperatives and water councils.

The explicit needs-oriented characterisation of the economy within this vision is buttressed by the prioritisation of use-value over exchange value, ensuring of collective and equal access to assets, and the positing of all non-human nature such as soil, water, energy sources as the non-commodifiable common heritage of all living creatures.[24] The emphasis on fulfilment of the needs of all is coupled with collective rights over water, energy, land and local resources more broadly. Put in different words, the project of democratic economy involves a series of practices to guarantee communities' access to forms of social reproduction (fulfilment of the needs of all, collective/common rights to land, water, energy and other resources) that are autonomous from both the state and the market (non-commodified resources, need-based production), i.e. *commoning*, at multiple and nested scales. Furthermore, these forms of social reproduction, as well as the determination of what constitutes/limits needs themselves, are embedded within participatory and democratic deliberation mechanisms, which will seek equitable access, ecological limits and gender egalitarianism in decision making. Energy and water councils, for instance, are put forward as local democratic platforms where decisions will be made based on fulfilment of needs and equity.

Within this context, the prominence of gender justice within the organisation of all economic relations in general, and in decision making and management of the means of social reproduction in particular, is particularly noteworthy. As stated above, the construction of democratic economy is to ensure women's participation in all decision-making processes that they have traditionally been excluded from. Moreover, this project not only recognises and addresses the issue of unpaid/invisible labour performed by women, but it also calls for socialisation of such labour responsibilities through appropriate institutional forms such as day care centres and communal kitchens. The notion of socialisation operationalised here resonates closely with the commoning of carework discussed by feminist theorists of the commons.[25] Understanding carework as an amalgam of practices and social relations that constitute the fundamental basis of all social life and thus a commons that we all depend on, these discussions shift the issue of social justice in relation to the commons by emphasising who is involved in their production (for example, women in carework commons) from the traditional focus of justice in the commons on who appropriates their benefits.[26] By upholding the principle of collective and egalitarian contribution to the maintenance and reproduction of unpaid production, the democratic economy project is in fact positing a commoning approach to carework.

Although the operationalisation of the democratic economy project at a more comprehensive scale is yet to be initiated, significant steps have been taken especially with the instrumental support of municipalities in the region. A notable example among these is the recent municipal initiatives of providing land access/use rights to landless farmer families who are otherwise forced to take up seasonal (migrant) agricultural labour. Agricultural plots in urban peripheries were opened to collective cultivation of landless families, ranging 10–40 in number, together with municipalities' technical and equipment support. These units are linked to seed/seedling camps, where indigenous seeds are being conserved and developed. While many of these units were mainly oriented towards subsistence production initially, they are now also connected to direct producer–consumer hubs in urban centres for marketing surplus production. A related initiative is the emerging agricultural commune in rural Diyarbakır (Kocaköy), largely led by the efforts of the local commission of agriculture.[27] The commission has conducted extensive field research into identifying a suitable community where land communalisation would be encouraged as well as possible crops to be cultivated, in addition to providing technical and equipment support.

Yet another example is the establishment of numerous women's cooperatives (15 in total as of now, but growing in number) networked in production and distribution activities that the Kurdish women's movement spearheaded. The cooperatives are engaged primarily in textile production and agro-processing, and market their products directly to consumers via the cooperative distribution hubs, *Eko-Jin*. Most of the agro-processing cooperatives have stemmed out of (and are connected to) existing urban agriculture collectives previously formed by the cooperative members and represent linked production-processing units in this sense. The cooperatives are further networked with municipal officials, activists, academics and civil society groups under the broader umbrella of the women's movement, the *Free Women Congress* (KJA), which function as a venue of decision making and debate. They are also connected with neighbourhood communes where both internal-organisational issues and their relationship with other cooperatives are discussed with local communities in which they are embedded. The cooperative members see their primary goal as increasing the number of cooperatives in the network and broaden its field of impact towards the eventual aim of forming an autonomous solidarity economy.[28] Partly in line with this goal, most Eko-Jin cooperatives adopt the principle of incorporating one more member with every 1000 TL (roughly €300) increase in monthly revenue.[29]

These examples are notable as they organise various dimensions of social reproduction based on collective labour and egalitarian access to, and sharing of, social wealth. Although the outputs of the production process in both cases are (at least partially) commodified, commodity production is neither the organising objective of production nor seen as an end in itself. It is rather posited as a necessary means to incorporate more members or to build a protective front for the solidarity economy network in progress. On the other hand, both the urban farming collectives and the Eko-Jin cooperatives are linked with input and raw material providers, which are outside of commodity circuits themselves, as well as with exchange outlets through networks that are largely outside of established markets. Such self-organised sites of exchange open space to incorporate values of reciprocity, mutual aid and solidarity as opposed to market norms of competition between the actors involved, e.g. between Eko-Jin cooperatives, between raw material providers and cooperatives, between seed/equipment providers and urban farmer collectives, between producers and final consumers. These networks in this sense represent acts of commoning as they provide spaces of organising social reproduction in ways that provide degrees of autonomy from the state and the market, and along the principles of collective labour, egalitarian access and democratic decision making. Furthermore, the fact that both the farming collectives and the Eko-Jin cooperatives are embedded within various venues of democratic deliberation and decision making implies the institution of broader social control and deliberation on the social wealth they produce.

Conclusion

The vision of democratic economy and the seemingly scarce yet highly significant practices it inspired and nourished have demonstrated a concrete field of possibility within the seemingly inevitable imperatives of neoliberal developmentalism. Although much remains to be seen in how this project will further concretise, a few notes regarding the opportunities and challenges lying ahead are in order. The concrete practices and initiatives associated with the project of democratic economy are primarily located within the sphere of rural/semi-rural production, and what this vision proposes for urban/metropolitan settings is yet to be developed.[30] Perhaps more importantly, this project is grounded within a social sphere fragmented along the axes of economic inequality, most notably in terms of landownership. Given that the project of democratic economy does not entail a redistribution of existing ownership/tenure of land and other assets, but rather operationalises the principle of collective access in redistributing public/municipal assets, the future implications of existing inequalities on organising the field of social reproduction along commoning practices are uncertain.[31] Another node of contradiction is between the emphasis on needs as the organising principle of democratic economy and its explicit stance to be non-accumulationist and not oriented to economic growth, as well as its embracing of ecology as the limit to economic relations. While what constitutes needs is to be decided by democratic and egalitarian decision making, meeting needs that cannot be fulfilled by self-production will pose a site of conflict. The question then becomes how much of surplus is to be *accumulated* to meet needs beyond self-sufficiency and if such needs are seen legitimate collectively.

The impressive extent to which the Kurdish peoples and the Kurdish Freedom Movement are politically organised certainly provides an opportunity for this project, unmatched by any other social force in Turkey. The fact that capitalist relations are not as deepened as the western parts of the country similarly equips the democratic economy project with a significant space of manoeuvre. Yet, the escalated (armed and political) violence from the side of Turkish state as well as the growing – yet still limited – capitalist–developmentalist bloc in the region, with ties to Turkish and international capital, pose challenges for the democratic economy project.[32] Most notably, the AKP's strategy of shifting labour-intensive industries to the region via state subsidies and tax incentives as a part of its developmental programme implied an intensified diffusion of capitalist relations, partly through the collaboration of Kurdish and Turkish capital.[33] Given that many of the emerging commoning practices associated with this project rely (in various degrees) in their ability to market their products and overcome competition, these two challenges can be seen as obstacles to the extent that they imply a deepening of capitalist relations and markets in the region.[34] Intensified market competition can potentially smother the democratic economy initiatives, and the deepening of the capitalist commodity economy bears the danger of eroding the protective shield provided by the commoning acts described above. The struggle for democratic economy thus seems to be on more than one front.

Notes

1. The author would like to thank Azize Aslan, Yahya M. Madra, Şemsa Özar and Ceren Özselçuk for the stimulating discussions, which developed many of the ideas that found their way into this chapter. The usual caveat applies.
2. Joost Jongerden, 'Radicalising democracy: Power, politics, people and the PKK', 2015, Centre for Policy and Research on Turkey, http://researchturkey.org/?p=8401, accessed 12 July 2016; Ahmet Hamdi Akkaya and Joost Jongerden, 'Reassembling the political: The PKK and the project of Radical Democracy', *European Journal of Turkish Studies* (online), 14 (2012), http://ejts.revues.org/index4615.html, accessed 10 July 2016.
3. Democratic Society Congress is a Kurdistani umbrella organisation that was established in 2007 in order to bring together the diverse civic associations of the Democratic Social Movement (DTH). It functions almost like a national level assembly that aims at the 'socialisation of politics' as well as the 'politicisation of the social' by way of fostering the formation of commissions and the development of programmes and visions in these respects.
4. Bengi Akbulut, 'Development as injustice: An evaluation of Justice and Development Party's development strategies', *Perspectives* 13/15 (2015); Bengi Akbulut and Fikret Adaman, 'The unbearable charm of modernisation: Growth fetishism and the making of state in Turkey', *Perspectives* 5/13 (2013); İsmet Akça, Ahmet Bekmen and Barış Alp Özden (eds), *Turkey Reframed: Constituting Neoliberal Hegemony* (London, 2014); Mine Eder, 'Türk usulü buldozer neoliberalleşmeyi anlamak: AKP'nin politik ekonomisi ve ötesi [To understand the bulldozer neoliberalism: The political economy of the AKP and beyond]', in Y.M. Madra (ed.) *Türkiye'de Yeni İktidar Yeni Direniş: Sermaye-ulus-devlet karşısında ulusötesi müşterekler [New Power New Resistance in Turkey: Supranational commons facing capital-nation-state]* (İstanbul, 2015); Ziya Öniş and Fikret Şenses, 'The new phase of neo- liberal restructuring in Turkey: An overview', in Z. Öniş and F. Şenses (eds), *Turkey and the Global Economy: Neo-liberal Restructuring and Integration in Post-Crisis Era* (London, 2009); and Erinç Yeldan, *Küreselleşme*

Sürecinde Türkiye Ekonomisi {Turkish Economy in the Process of Globalisation} (İstanbul, 2011).

5. The arguments in this section are further developed and discussed in Bengi Akbulut, 'Commons', in Clive L. Spash (ed.), *The Routledge Handbook of Ecological Economics: Nature and Society* (Abingdon, 2017).
6. Garrett Hardin, 'The tragedy of the commons', *Science* 162 (1968), pp. 1243–8.
7. Ibid., p. 1244.
8. Elinor Ostrom, *Governing the Commons: The Evolution of Institutions for Collective Action* (Cambridge, 1990); *Neither Market nor State: Governance of Common-Pool Resources in the Twenty-First Century* (Washington, DC, 1994); 'Coping with the tragedies of the commons', *Annual Review of Political Science* 2 (1999), pp. 493–535.
9. Fikret Berkes, 'Local-level management and the commons problem: A comparative study of Turkish coastal fisheries', *Marine Policy* 10/3 (1986), pp. 215–29; and 'Revising the commons paradigm', *Journal of Natural Resources Policy Research* 3/1 (2009), pp. 261–4.
10. Arun Agrawal, 'Sustainable governance of common-pool resources: Context, methods, politics', *Annual Review of Anthropology* 32 (2003), pp. 243–62.
11. Karl Marx, *Capital* Vol I (London, 1967).
12. Massimo De Angelis, 'Marx and primitive accumulation: The continuous character of capital's "enclosures"', *The Commoner* 2/1 (2001), pp. 1–22; Jim Glassman, 'Primitive accumulation, accumulation by dispossession and accumulation by extra-economic means', *Progress in Human Geography* 30/5 (2006), pp. 608–25; David Harvey, *The New Imperialism* (Oxford, 2003); and Midnight Notes Collective, *The New Enclosures* (Brooklyn, 1990).
13. George Caffentzis, 'The future of the commons: Neoliberalism's "Plan B" or the original disaccumulation of capital?', *New Formations* 69/1 (2010), pp. 23–41.
14. Silvia Federici, 'Feminism and the politics of the commons in an era of primitive accumulation', in S. Federici, *Revolution at Point Zero: Housework, Reproduction and Feminist Struggle* (Oakland, 2012).
15. De Angelis, 'Marx and primitive accumulation'; and Massimo De Angelis and David Harvie, 'The commons', in M. Parker, G. Cheney, V. Fournier and C. Land (eds), *The Routledge Companion to Alternative Organization* (London, 2014).
16. Midnight Notes Collective and Friends, *Promissory Notes: From Crisis to Commons*, http://www.midnightnotes.org/Promissory%20Notes.pdf, accessed 11 July 2016.
17. Peter Linebaugh, *The Magna Carta Manifesto: Liberties and Commons for All* (California, 2008).
18. Silvia Federici and George Caffentzis, 'Commons against and beyond capitalism', *Upping the Anti: A Journal of Theory and Action* 15 (2013), pp. 83–97.
19. That commons provide degrees of autonomy from the state and the market does not imply that they are a completely autonomous sphere from the

market or the state, or that commoning practices take place on a terrain outside of the two. Reclamation of the public sphere where past labour and resources are stored is a form of commoning as access to public resources and services provides a degree of protection from the market. In a parallel vein, this approach does not deny that there is a role for struggles within the sphere of the state to defend, reclaim and construct commons. On the contrary, many forms of access to collective social wealth can be (and is) acquired through such struggles and institutionalised by state legislation. Contemporary examples include the sanctioning of the right of the indigenous people to use the natural resources in their territories by the Venezuelan Constitution in 1999 and the recognition of communal property by the Bolivian Constitution in 2009.

20. Federici and Caffentzis, 'Commons against', p. 87.
21. For the full declaration in Turkish, see JINHA, accessed 28 June, 2015; http://jinha.com.tr/search/content/view/13418?page=1&key=b12d318ef45843944dc05366594a3d01c. For the English translation of the concrete set of proposals put forth in the Declaration, see Yahya M. Madra, 'Democratic economy conference: An introductory note', *South Atlantic Quarterly* 115/1 (2016), pp. 211–22.
22. Yahya M. Madra and Ceren Özselçuk, 'Demokratik özerkliğin iktisadiyatına bir katkı [A contribution to the economics of democratic autonomy]', *Demokratik Modernite* 11 (2015), pp. 104–10. Published a couple of months after the Democratic Economy Conference, this special issue has essays, among others, on the importance of production cooperatives as the centre of alternative economic model, the diverse economy research methodology, the importance of economic planning and the role of municipalities in enacting democratic and communal economies.
23. Karl Polanyi, *The Great Transformation: Economic and Political Origins of our Time*, (Rinehart, 1944); Fikret Adaman, Pat Devine and Begüm Özkaynak, 'Reinstituting the economic process: (Re)embedding the economy in society and nature', *International Review of Sociology/Revue Internationale de Sociologie* 13/2 (2003), pp. 357–74.
24. Azize Aslan, 'Demokratik ekonomi konferansı: Bireyci kapitalist bir ekonomiden, toplumsal komünal bir ekonomiye [Democratic economy conference: From an individualist capitalist economy to a social communal economy]', 2015, http://zanenstitu.org/demokratik-ekonomi-konferansi-bireyci-kapitalist-bir-ekonomiden-toplumsal-komunal-bir-ekonomiye-azize-aslan/, accessed 10 July 2016.
25. For a collection of essays on this issue, see http://www.commoner.org.uk/?p=114.
26. Bengi Akbulut, 'Sofradaki yemeğin ötesi: Gıda müşterekleri ve feminizm üzerine [Beyond the food on the table: On food commons and feminism]', *Feminist Yaklaşımlar* 14 (2015), http://www.feministyaklasimlar.org/sayi-26-haziran-2015-2/sofradaki-yemegin-otesi-gida-musterekleri-ve-feminizm-uzerine/, accessed 9 July 2016.

27. Azize Aslan, 'Demokratik özerklikte ekonomik özyönetim: Bakûr örneği [Economic self-management in democratic autonomy: The example of Bakûr]', *Birikim* 325/May (2016), pp. 93–8.
28. Ibid.
29. Ibid.
30. Ibid.
31. Ibid.
32. Madra, 'Democratic economy conference'.
33. Azize Aslan, 'Kapitalizm Kürdistan'a yayılmak istiyor [Capitalism wants to diffuse into Kurdistan]', interview, 2014, http://alternatifsiyaset.net/2014/11/21/kapitalizm-kurdistana-yayilmak-istiyor/, accessed 12 June 2016.
34. Aslan, 'Demokratik özerklikte'.

CONCLUSION

NEOLIBERAL MODERNISATION CAST IN CONCRETE

Fikret Adaman, Murat Arsel and Bengi Akbulut

The Boom in Energy and Construction Projects under the AKP

This book was built on the premise that the AKP's particular brand of neoliberal modernisation is primarily manifested within the sphere of environment and, more broadly, space. While growth-oriented modernisation and developmentalism have always been fundamental pillars of how the Turkish state has legitimised its power and acquired societal consent for its claim to rule,[1] the specific form they took within the AKP era was marked by the rise of energy and construction projects, and the corresponding reshaping of rural and urban space. While a detailed analysis of the structural reasons underwriting the prominence of energy and construction is beyond the scope of this book, it is possible to identify factors that can together provide an explanation.

Both energy and construction projects on the whole require relatively low levels of human capital and technical know-how, and typically have a quick turnaround on capital outlays. Although the building of a nuclear plant and the construction of a train tunnel under the Bosphorous are certainly exceptions since they both require long-time horizons and sophisticated technologies, the bulk of AKP's projects in these two sectors fall on the low human capital and low technology side. In that sense, they represent venues of capital accumulation that provide a quick answer with a grandiose façade to the ever-present developmental problématique. These sectors are also marked by state control over the required resources, namely capital and natural inputs (especially land). Energy and construction thus represent fields of investment where the state can most effectively and relatively costlessly mediate and accelerate capital accumulation.

The book demonstrates that the AKP has implemented the necessary legal and administrative changes 'better' and faster than previous administrations. These have enabled economic agents to more easily acquire and mobilise resources for energy and construction investments, including urban space, water bodies, land and various forms of protected areas. This easing of the conditions of accumulation was also coupled and helped along further by the employment generation potential of these sectors. Albeit precarious and short-term, the fact that such employment could absorb much of the reserve of the low-skilled labour cemented their desirability economically and politically.

Moreover, the rise of energy and construction opened a much-welcome venue to absorb the short-term foreign investment spurred by financial liberalisation engineered by the AKP. These sectors have a distinct ability to create effective demand for the cheap credit that became available in the mid-2000s since the size of some of the energy and construction projects 'naturally' pointed to the need to secure foreign financing. The available cheap credit found its way also into the consumer (housing) debt market, which partly ensured that demand for the expanded housing stock remained robust.[2] In other words, the rise of energy and construction could provide channels of financial inclusion and expansion that was needed for Turkey's integration with global financial markets in a more effective way than other sectors. While we do not imply that the rise of energy and construction sectors is tied causally to the imperatives of the financial sector, the evidence presented here suggests that these sectors are especially well positioned to receive flows of 'hot money'.

Construction and energy also reproduce the existence of the state, imbuing the very ideals of modernisation and development more concretely than any other economic sector. The uniqueness of these sectors lies in the particular products they deliver, products that will be directly and immediately consumed by the masses, including those that were dispossessed by them. Furthermore, dams, bridges, highways, power plants and other monumental construction and energy investments resonate closely with modernisation in the social imaginary.

It is of course important to remember that modernisation has long been justified not for its own sake but to help elevate (and return) Turkey to its rightful place amongst great nations.[3] To that end, construction and energy projects – even when they are built by foreign states and corporations as is the case with nuclear power plants – find general, if at times grudging, support and admiration from different groups within society.

Political Economy of Development in the Post-15 July Era

The idea of this book was conceived and the chapters comprising it were written before the attempted *coup d'état* that shook Turkey on 15 July 2016. Although it was well-known that the AKP was a coalition of conservative religious political networks that were prone to tensions and conflicts, the coup attempt was beyond imagination, especially since it was thought that the Turkish army had decisively lost its political hegemony to the AKP. While the dust has still not fully settled, all signs point to the already weakening Fethullan Gülen fraction as the major force behind the plot to overthrow the Erdoğan bloc. The political conjecture since the coup was put down has been defined by the attempts of this latter bloc to reconsolidate its grip on power, restore its damaged legitimacy and to advance a number of agendas that could not be pursued in more peaceful times.

More broadly, beyond the coup, Turkish politics have been dominated by the escalation of the conflict with the Kurdish movement and the government's use of intensified use of violence, repercussions of the Syrian war, and deterioration of relations with the EU. This, however, does not indicate that the issues lying at the heart of this book are no longer significant or relevant, or that they are unconnected to these more visible issues shaping the political agenda. On the contrary, the dynamics and conflicts that the book sheds light on are structurally linked to the core of the political economy of the AKP era. Within this context, it is not surprising that Erdoğan regularly references the still pending plans to build over Gezi Park in the same context as the attempted coup. He has also promised to deliver two additional prestige projects in Taksim Square, an opera and a mosque.[4]

Furthermore, reading the political economy of the AKP era through the transformations expressed by the rise of construction and energy offers additional insight into contemporary Turkish politics. On the one hand, the Gülen movement, as the fundamental partner in the ruling bloc cemented by the AKP, had been crucial for the neoliberal modernisation project that rested on energy and construction. While clearly delineating the movement's role within this context is impossible, the fact that the economic sphere is known to be among the movement's main fields of organisation, together with education and judiciary, is telling. The corruption probe against the AKP in December 2013 that was sparked by tape recordings allegedly held and revealed by the followers of Gülen is also indicative of the movement's intricate involvement in the rise of construction and energy. This probe, which resulted in the investigations of top party officials, can be read as one of the early signal of fractures within the AKP. While the reasons underlying this fracture are likely to be manifold, tensions and limits inherent to the AKP's model of neoliberal modernisation must have played a significant role. The fact that the above mentioned corruption probe was sparked by construction contracts is not only ironic but indicative of the complexity of the AKP's internal power struggles. On the other hand, it is becoming obvious that the post-coup context is far from being an obstruction on this model, but rather paving its way further and deeper. Most notably, the infamous Article 80 of a state of emergency decree, which was recently approved by the parliament (on 19 August 2016), introduces drastic measures to support investments in fields of developmental priority, such as up to 100 per cent corporate tax breaks and income tax subsidies for investors, up to 200 per cent state contribution to investment costs, and transfer of use rights of land for 49 years at no cost (with the possible transfer of all property rights in the future) for investments to be made on Treasury estates. The analytical perspective of this book can also offer additional insights on the recent escalation of the Kurdish conflict.

Notwithstanding the fact that the Kurdish issue is deeply rooted in the historical construction of the Turkish state and thus cannot be reduced to AKP's policies, a critical reading of recent developments in the region enables us to locate the Kurdish movement's political and economic vision as an alternative to the AKP's neoliberal modernisation project. The peace process advanced by the AKP had cast the Kurdish movement's demands for equality and democratisation in a liberal mold, reducing them to individual rights and liberties to be accessed within the sphere of the market (as in the case of the right to education in one's mother tongue).[5] The response of the Peoples' Democratic Party (HDP in its Turkish acronym) to this approach was to formulate an alternative paradigm and discourse that combined elements of radical democracy, decentralisation and community economies. This vision was fundamentally at odds with the project of neoliberal modernisation and the AKP's aggression towards the autonomous cantons of Rojava and its supporters in Turkey can be best apprehended in this light.

Authoritarian Developmentalism around the World

While the empirical focus of the book is on Turkey, its analytical approach has broad contemporary relevance in terms of the rising wave of authoritarianism around the world. While Fukuyama's argument that the fall of the Berlin Wall essentially symbolised the 'end of history' was commonly accepted as far-fetched, there was indeed widespread optimism that the ensuing decades would unleash another wave of democratisation in the developing world. This belief was built upon the assumption that economic liberalisation could not advance beyond a certain point without matching political as well as sociocultural liberalisation. The latter two were assumed to be in a symbiotic relationship with economic liberalisation, benefiting from a climate of 'free enterprise' as well as creating the conditions for further capital accumulation. There were signs in Turkey and beyond that this script was playing out more or less as predicted throughout the 1990s and 2000s.

A spate of political movements did indeed come to power with strong electoral support in many developing countries and implemented a combination of economic and political liberalisation policies. It is notable that the latter, in many cases, aimed especially at addressing the concerns of hitherto marginalised and disenfranchised communities. For instance, as discussed in the introduction, the rise of the AKP government of Erdoğan came hand-in-hand with not only strict adherence to the policies recommended by the IMF but also moves to relax decades-old restrictions on Islamic practice in the public sphere as well to recognise, albeit to a limited extent, the cultural rights of the Kurds. In other contexts, economic liberalisation took a less overt form at the national level, though connections between national economies and global markets were strengthened as was the case in Ecuador.

The latter for instance 'nationalised' its oil industry while opening itself up for increased foreign capital to deepen its oil extraction activities and jump start its large-scale mining investment. Once again, political liberalisation was an integral part of this transition: not only indigenous values were explicitly integrated into national development goals, the rights of nature were enshrined into the new constitution of Ecuador.[6]

However, more recently, recent regional and global crises of capitalism have had a transformative impact. In countries such as Russia and Egypt, political freedoms have been curtailed to a very large extent and most previously accepted acts of dissent have been criminalised. In other countries such as Turkey and Ecuador, there have also been a certain degree of regress, with the freedom of the press as well as the ability of certain groups and their allies in national politics to campaign have been curtailed significantly. Economic liberalisation has not necessarily been reversed in most of such contexts but has been advancing more unevenly than before. Overall, signs point to the emergence of a model of not just neoliberal but also authoritarian developmentalism, as epitomised by the Turkish experience.

Thus, the contributions in this volume further illustrate how variegated geographies of neoliberalism are produced and reproduced.[7] Although the predominance of state-led projects has been replaced with private capital initiatives in this period, the state has been pivotal in reconstructing, shaping and participating in energy and construction sectors. By founding the energy and construction markets, participating in and mediating the market processes proactively and providing private actors with appropriate incentives, it has effectively mobilised a state-led developmental regime. It has, however, shifted to deploying market-based mechanisms in bringing about desired developmental outcomes, rather than directly intervening in the economic sphere. Quite unlike the dominant images of the neoliberal state, the Turkish state emerges as the actor who mobilises capital with specific motivations rather than being the passive instrument of capital accumulation. It is, however, distinguished from the stylised developmental state in that it governs the developmental process through economic incentives and market-based mechanisms, i.e. the logic of neoliberalism.

While we characterise the AKP's project of modernisation as neoliberal, it would be too simplistic to claim that neoliberalism alone explicates the dynamics that shape Turkey's political economy. This project has been operationalised within and through a context molded by the (historical) making of the state-society relationships, class relations and the management of tensions therein, and cultural specificities. This calls for complicating the analyses of neoliberalism with analytical frameworks regarding such different aspects of political economy. In that sense, focusing on the case of Turkey goes beyond making an empirical contribution to the vast literature on varieties of neoliberalism, as the peculiar character of the state-society relationships in Turkey carries lessons for scholars of critical environmental studies (including, but not limited to, political ecology, peasant studies, development studies and economic geography).

On the other hand, our book illustrates the ways in which the AKP's neoliberal modernisation paradigm has sparked contradictory dynamics of generating dissent and reproducing consent on the side of the society (not to mention how unstable the governing coalition happened to be, as the attempted coup of 15 July demonstrated). In particular, the contributions to the volume reveal the diversity of the motivations, discourses and trajectories of environmental mobilisations that often elude existing categories of environmentalism. Not only do we witness the significance of motivations that go beyond livelihood-based concerns (or feeling of belonging, health, spiritual value) and the mobilisation of broader social discontent through environmental politics, but the class composition of the actors are also more complicated. In addition, cases of non-mobilisation emerge to be equally important in understanding how this neoliberal modernisation model is worked through the sphere of the social. In that sense, this book points to the need for critical environmental studies to complicate its understanding of how the environment and its transformations become politicised.

Notes

1. Bengi Akbulut, 'State Hegemony and Sustainable Development: A Political Economy Analysis of Two Local Experiences in Turkey', unpublished PhD thesis, University of Massachusetts, Amherst, 2011.
2. İsmet Akçay, Ahmet Bekmen and Barış Özden (eds), *Turkey Reframed: Constituting Neoliberal Hegemony* (London, 2014).
3. Murat Arsel 'Reflexive developmentalism? Toward an environmental critique of modernisation', in F. Adaman and M. Arsel (eds), *Environmentalism in Turkey: Between Democracy and Development?* (Aldershot, 2005).

4. 'Erdoğan'ın Gezi Parkı inadı sürüyor: Taksim'e kışlayı yapacağız! [Erdoğan's insistence continues: We will construct the mall complex at Gezi park]', *Bir Gün*, 19 July 2016, http://www.birgun.net/haber-detay/erdogan-in-gezi-parki-inadi-suruyor-taksim-e-kislayi-yapacagiz-120542.html, accessed on 10 September 2016.
5. Bülent Küçük, 'Demokratikleşme maketi neye yarar? [What is the purpose of the democratisation model]', *Bianet*, 13 October 2013, http://bianet.org/bianet/toplum/150617-demokratiklesme-maketi-neye-yarar, accessed 29 August 2016; Bülent Küçük and Ceren Özselçuk, '"Mesafeli" devletten "hizmetkâr" devlete: AKP'nin kısmi tanıma siyaseti [From the state of "distance" to the state of "service": AKP's policy of partial recognition]', *Toplum ve Bilim* 132 (2015), pp. 162–90.
6. Murat Arsel, Barbara Hogenboom and Lorenzo Pellegrini, 'Extractive imperative in Latin America', *Extractive Industries and Society* (forthcoming).
7. Neil Brenner, Jamie Peck and Nik Theodore, 'Variegated neoliberalisation: Geographies, modalities, pathways', *Global Networks* 10/2 (2010), pp. 182–222.

EPILOGUE

POST-TRUTH AND THE POLITICS OF AUTOCRATIC NEOLIBERALISATION

Erik Swyngedouw

The Oxford Dictionaries elected the word 'Post-Truth' as the 2016 word of the year. Indeed, 'Post-Truth Politics' (PTP) have become something of a buzz in the recent past. PTP refers to an increasingly hegemonic situation whereby emotion, affect and personal feelings trump fact, reasoning and the search for truth in political debate and practice, and is now customarily associated with the rising prominence and success of nationalist and populist movements, and their particular penchant for 'spinning' information and distorting facts. PTP as a catchword is particularly popular with the liberal elite and their disdain for the presumed idiocy of the poor, underprivileged and excluded who fall prey so easily to the populist call of the Donald Trumps, Nigel Farages, Marine Le Pens or Recep Erdoğans of this world. However, and what the collection of essays in this book amply demonstrates, this condescending contempt of the liberal left (and not so left) elite of the post-truth antics of populist discourses woefully disavows or ignores that post-truth inflected 'facts' and 'arguments' underpinned precisely part of the success of the neoliberal fantasy that was so ruthlessly pursued at all geographical scale ever since Pinochet, Reagan and Thatcher set both tone and content to their class mission to change the face of the world; a project further solidified by the 'spinned' Third

Way politics of Tony Blair (remember Saddam's weapons of mass destruction?) or Bill Clinton. It is precisely the discursive and policy success of neoliberalisation that nurtured a form of reasoning whereby truth and fact mattered less than the affective pull of the message.

As Slavoj Žižek has argued repeatedly, glimpsing the truth of the situation requires a parallax view, a slant perspective that looks in from a partial outside, an outside that is nonetheless an integral part of the constellation we are in.[1] This book in its narration and dissection of Turkey's torturous political-economic trajectory of geographically and historically specific 'neoliberal' (although the term may not in fact capture the Turkish condition well) transformation within a wider patterning of the uneven and heterogeneous trajectories of neoliberalisation over the past two decades or so exquisitely demonstrates at least some of the core truths of neoliberalisation; truths that are customarily ignored, if not radically disavowed, by the very architects of its inauguration. It takes indeed a view from the margins of the situation the world is in to glimpse some of its actual core dynamics. The universality of the 'neoliberal' universe simmers through the particular manners by which it unfolds at its outer margins and frontiers. In the way Chile was the founding marker of textbook neoliberalisation in the early 1980s, Turkey seems to fulfil that role in an exemplary manner for our present post-millennial times. PTP, in sum, is not the prerogative of populism; it is the cosmopolitan neoliberal elite that first experimented with it and subsequently elevated it to the dignity of a political and ideological strategy. It takes a book like this to strip the post-fact narratives of the ideologues of the market of their fallacies. In the remainder of this epilogue, I shall explore some of these truths that lurk beneath the surface of the mythical promises of neoliberal Walhalla.

A few years back, Slavoj Žižek infamously stated that capitalism is increasingly infused with 'Asian' values. With this ethno-geographical signifier he referred primarily to the extraordinary accumulation success in strictly capitalist terms of countries as diverse as China, Singapore or South Korea, while none of them excel very much in nurturing the lofty art of liberal multicultural tolerance and pluralistic democracy.[2] On the contrary, these countries re-confirmed what Marxists and a coterie of others have insisted on for a long time, namely that capitalist social relations and associated repressive legal regimes thrive best – and possibly inevitably so – in the context of an autocratic and centralised state that is tightly controlled by an elite who seamlessly fuses the internally contradictory promises of nurturing 'national' development within a practice of unbridled global integration. While Europe and the US could wallow for a while in the mirage of an end-of-history liberal democratic idyll, and maintain that global capitalist integration would sound the death-knell of authoritarian and autocratic regimes in those parts of the world that had not yet registered that 'history was over', the political-economic aftermath of the 2010 financial crisis and the shockwaves that the various urban insurgencies – from Tahrir to Taksim via Occupy! – sent through the ranks of the outflanked elites relegated this fantasy to the dustbin of history. Of course, the contours of a centralised imposition of market rule combined with the repression of many forms of social and class action, were already clearly identifiable from the early days of neoliberalism in the 1980s, but post-crisis techno-managerial state control and the top-down implementation of austerity rule has propelled the repressive class character of the state to new heights, not only in Turkey but in Europe and elsewhere as well. It is truly ironic that the EU's elite self-congratulatory attacks on Erdogan's authoritarian rule – correct as it may be – masks the increasingly autocratic financial-economic rule imposed by the EU's ruling elites on countries like Greece and Spain, the increasingly repressive – if not racist – response to the refugee crisis, the unrelenting support for the new dictatorship in Egypt after the failed democratising revolution, and so on. Turkey's political-economic dynamics, as presented in this book, indeed both foreshadow and reflect the fractured mirror image of the rest of the West's own condition.

Of course, populist-nationalist developmentalism, while transforming rapidly as the book documents so thoroughly, has always been at the core of Turkey's modernisation trajectory, but populist-capitalist developmentalism has now begun to universalise as the dominant Zombie-neoliberal successor of the failed neoliberal globalisation project. Indeed, neoliberalisation marches forward as an undead Zombie corpse.[3] While the crisis of 2010 and after announced the death-knell of neoliberalism as a thriving ideological project and few still believe in its prophylactic qualities to heal the world's economic woes, neoliberalisation's recipes – appropriately adjusted with the injection of a solid dose of authoritarianism – keep lunging forward as a Zombie spectre.

Indeed, I could not be other than struck by the similarities between Turkey, the US, the UK and indeed France over the past few months. While the success of Trump, the BREXIT melodrama, or the rise of Le Pen's Front National are generally staged and reported as the result of the combination of the idiocy of misguided and ignorant idiots that uncritically follow the racist-populist-nationalist post-truth one-liners of self-defined anti-establishment pundits who are just out there to massage their considerable egos and bank accounts, they are just as much seen as an integral – albeit perhaps regrettable – outcome of a democratic political system. As Claude Lefort insisted already 20 years ago – and echoing Plato – totalitarianism is indeed the unacknowledged but insistent underbelly of a pluralist representative democratic configuration.[4] What is nonetheless radically disavowed, if not repressed completely, is the enduring nagging presence of a constitutive outsider. Indeed, the condition of possibility of the rise of authoritarian rule – as Walter Benjamin did not tire to point out – is nothing but a symptom of a failed and disavowed progressive project. Indeed, authoritarianism is predicated upon a constitutive censored outsider, the traumatic core that threatens to disrupt the fake tensions between nationalism and internationalism so dear to the liberal elites. It is the one that aspires to cutting through this 'glocal' deadlock by staging and actively performing an interruptive politics that point towards a democratic and socio-ecologically inclusive horizon beyond the present state of affairs. While in the US the liberals lament the demise of Clinton, in the UK Brexiters are looked at as a strangely misguided and misogynistic troupe of little Englanders, and the French contemplate having to chose between an ultranationalist Marine Le Pen or arch-conservative François Fillon in the upcoming elections, the media, political commentators and liberal observers are systematically silent about the extraordinary appeal and political performativity of socialist Bernie Sanders in the US, of the surprising rise of Jeremy Corbyn in the UK, of the insurgent practices of Nuits Debouts across French cities, of the success of the progressive HDP (The Peoples' Democratic Party) in Turkey or PODEMOS in Spain, just to name a few examples. These are of course the true enemy for the elites. They constitute the Real dangerous classes that indeed threaten the order that is and have their gaze firmly fixed on transforming the state of the situation and replacing the elite coalitions that keep quarrelling impotently while making sure that nothing really changes. Their aspirations point to a horizon beyond the present, one that prefigures the real possibility of a more egalitarian, radically democratic and socially inclusive society. It is precisely these transformative movements that remain un-symbolised outsiders in the eye of both liberal and illiberal elites, and that need to be repressed, if necessary by all means possible. While the nationalist right is still considered to be and portrayed as an integral part of the instituted and legitimate democratic order, the radical left and other democratising movements are customarily relegated to a zone beyond the acceptable, to the site of the rabble, to a censored place that evades symbolisation and integration within the horizon of really existing possibilities.

***

Of course, the political deadlock of the present is intimately related with the infernal dialectics of accumulation and profit making under state-orchestrated Zombie neoliberalism. While in the helicon early days of neoliberalisation, the IT revolution and the mythical garage-economies of the Bill Gates-ses and Steve Jobs-es, combined with an accelerated globalisation of capital circulation, generated new forms of accumulation and self-expansion of value, this sort of technology and innovation-induced growth (combined with a ruthless exploitation of the global South proletarians in the mega-factories of the global IT gadget assembly companies) has turned in recent years increasingly to forms of amassing value and wealth from outside the capital circulation process. It is precisely this that Marx called 'original' or 'primitive' accumulation, and more recently dubbed by David Harvey as 'Accumulation by Dispossession'.[5] The recent political economy of Turkey is indeed precisely marked by the extraordinary acceleration of accumulation by dispossession through both the land/finance and the resource/finance nexus. This book's analysis of agricultural transformation, spiralling urban speculative development, and the state-orchestrated and state-led production of large-scale urban development projects have indeed been pivotal to fuel Turkey's growth while the economic-financial and political interests were tightly woven together in what cannot be termed other than a symbiotic state-capital oligarchy, leading to the accelerated making of a plutocratic kleptocracy basking in a crony network of extended family ties and nepotistic relations.

Here again, the key and autocratic (if not authoritarian) role of the state in opening space, dispossession land and natures, imposing or changing land-use, etc., points at how the political terrain and its top-down imposition of market rule is absolutely vital for the 'free market' to operate. As Karl Marx pointed out a long time ago, the process of accumulation by dispossession sweats blood and dirt from every pore in a violent spiral of state-led and state-based repression and dispossession. Accumulation by dispossession through the land-finance nexus injects a continuing flow of value and assets that hitherto remained outside the capital circulation process into the self-expansion of value. This accelerating dance of capital-in-flow of course produces a frenetic over-expansion of value and the inevitable ballooning of fictitious capital formation desperately searching for new places and times to invest for further expansion.

This mobilisation of assets that originate from outside the capital circulation process within the frenzy of capital accumulation and self-expansion of value points at what arguably is one of the key dynamics of both dispossession and accumulation is without any doubt the rent relationship.[6] Indeed, the mobilisation of both urban space and non-human resources – whether in agricultural, through nuclear fissure material or by mobilising land for the construction of a new airport – offers lucrative new niches for rent extraction and value transfers to the owners of such assets. The analysis in the book conclusively demonstrates how the production and appropriation of rent, the incessant creation of new property regimes and their associated possibilities for generating rent and the continuous flow of wealth from the dispossessed to a rentier class that sees its wealth balloon incessantly have become key drivers of Turkey's political economy in recent times, producing a speculative bubble that is at risk of being punctured at any time. Here too, the Turkish example demonstrates in Technicolor clarity what has been the phantasmagorical base that nurtured the spasmodic neoliberal accumulation strategies pursued by 'core' capitalist economies over the past two decades or so.

Sustaining the continuous production of rent crucially depends on what Neil Smith theorised a long time ago as 'the production of nature'.[7] Indeed, the enrolling of the non-human, whether in the form of formerly ecologically sensitive but now prime developable land, redeveloping urban space, damming water, splitting nuclear material or transforming agricultural production within capital circulation processes not only alters property relations and associated power dynamics, but also opens up new possibilities to transfer wealth between social groups and classes. In the process, entirely new socio-ecological landscapes are produced that rhyme with and express in geographically concrete ways the dynamics of Turkey's particular neoliberalising trajectory.

However, the blatant contradictions of the nationalist-global project pursued by the ruling Turkish elites are marked by all manner of fissures, tensions and conflicts. The recent string of upheavals, varying dramatically from the Taksim Square insurgency to the botched *coup d'état* and interspersed with a spade of bloody terrorist attacks, demonstrate that the populist-national discourse of national cohesion and inclusive development promised by the Erdoğan clan is fragile at its core and fracturing in its effects, requiring increasingly more draconian authoritarian measures to maintain a semblance of coherence. In the process, the Post-Truth rhetoric of the Turkish government scales new heights.

It is precisely the 2013 Taksim Square revolt that marked a watershed in the unfolding of Turkey-style neoliberalisation. What originally sparked off as a social movement resisting the cutting down of a few trees in an emblematic park and the planned construction of an Ottoman style shopping centre quickly turned into a mass insurgency, bringing together a wide range of people from often very different class, gender, religious or other backgrounds, demanding nothing less than a democratisation of the state and more inclusive and egalitarian modes of public decision making.[8] Very little of the present escalating conflicting situation can be grasped without placing Taksim as an important quilting point in the chain of events. The Taksim insurgency, together with a wide range of existing and new social movements and progressive forces, nurtured, among others, the formation and electoral success of the HDP, a political movement that brings together all manner of radical democratic forces within an eco-feminist-left programme. Alongside, a wide range of other grass-roots movements, activist organisations and progressive alliances emerged and spread as resistance to authoritarian neoliberalisation intensified.

Perhaps most importantly and beyond the narrow confines of the theatrics of party politics, the Taksim movement and its associated social mobilisations signalled a clear political discontent with respect to rampant processes of dispossession, rising inequality and intensifying crony-authoritarianism. It also cuts through a simplistic populist-nationalist discourse. Indeed, what glues together these often very different activists and heterogeneous social movements is their fight against dispossession and privatisation, and their myriad ways of experimenting with new forms of both re-claiming the commons and organising the commons along democratic principles. In doing so, they both demonstrate the relentless process of erosion of the commons and foreground the pivotal importance of reclaiming urban, rural, ecological and other commons spaces as the basis for new forms of democratic, egalitarian and solidarity-based life-in-common. These are the movements that try to revive democratic politicisation and point towards a horizon of the possible beyond the present condition of post-truth authoritarian and nationalist neoliberalisation. These emancipatory movements in Turkey present also in this respect a glimpse of what might be or is already possible elsewhere too. This book is indeed a key pointer on route not only to demystify the post-truth regimes of the present but to welcoming budding forms of commonism and its practices of egalitarian and socio-ecologically sensible inclusion, a place where once we shall all meet.

Notes

1. Slavoj Žižek, *The Parallax View* (Cambridge, MA, 2006).
2. Slavoj Žižek, *Living in the End Times* (London, 2010).
3. Jamie Peck, 'Zombie Neoliberalism and the Ambidextrous State', *Theoretical Criminology* 14/1 (2010), pp. 104–10.
4. Claude Lefort, *Democracy and Political Theory* (Minneapolis, 1989).
5. David Harvey, *The New Imperialism* (Oxford, 2003).
6. Diego Andreucci, Melissa García-Lamarca, Jonah Wedekind and Erik Swyngedouw, '"Value Grabbing": A Political Ecology of Rent', *Capitalism Nature, Socialism* (forthcoming, 2017).
7. Neil Smith, *Uneven Development: Nature, Capital and the Production of Space* (Oxford, 1984).
8. Japhy Wilson and Erik Swyngedouw (eds), *The Post-Political and its Discontents: Spectres of Radical Politics Today* (Edinburgh, 2014).

LIST OF CONTRIBUTORS

Fikret Adaman (BA and MA in Economics at Boğaziçi University; PhD in Economics at the University of Manchester) is currently Professor of Economics at Boğaziçi University. His interests include political ecology, political economy of Turkey and methodology of economics. His recent work has been published in the *Journal of Peasant Studies, Development and Change, Antipode, Social Science and Medicine*, and *Conservation Letters*.

Bengi Akbulut (BA in Economics at Boğaziçi University; PhD in Economics at the University of Massachusetts, Amherst) is Assistant Professor of Ecological Economics in the Department of Geography, Environment and Planning at Concordia University. Her work focuses on political economy of development, political ecology, state-society relationships, and feminist economics. With Fikret Adaman she runs a biweekly radio programme, 'The End of Economics as We Know It', criticising the growth paradigm that disregards social and ecological costs. Her recent work has been published in the *Journal of Peasant Studies, Development and Change,* and *Cambridge Journal of Economics*.

Murat Arsel (BA in Economics and Government at Clark University, MA in Politics of the World Economy at the LSE, MPhil in Environment and Development and PhD in Human Geography at the University of Cambridge) is Associate Professor of Environment and Development at the International Institute of Social Studies (ISS) of Erasmus University

Rotterdam. He is currently co-chair of the editorial board of *Development and Change* and held the Keyman Family Visiting Professorship in Modern Turkish Studies at Northwestern University in 2014. His recent work has been published in the *Journal of Peasant Studies*, the *European Journal of Development Research, Extractive Industries and Society,* and *Conservation Letters*.

Ali Çarkoğlu (BA and MA in Economics at Boğaziçi University; PhD in Political Science at the State University of New York at Binghamton) is currently a professor of political science and the dean of the College of Administrative Sciences and Economics at Koç University, Istanbul. His areas of research interest include voting behaviour, public opinion and party politics in Turkey. His recent contributions have appeared in *Democratization*, *European Journal of Political Research*, *Electoral Studies*, *Turkish Studies*, *New Perspectives on Turkey*, and *Political Studies.*

Sinan Erensü (BA in Social and Political Sciences at Sabancı University; MPhil in Sociology at the University of Cambridge; PhD in Sociology at the University of Minnesota) is Keyman Postdoctoral Fellow at the Buffett Institute for Global Change, Northwestern University. His research and teaching interests include political ecology and political economy, urban and rural studies, energy infrastructures, and the politics of dispossession. Titled as 'Fragile Energy: Power, Nature and Politics of Infrastructure in the "New Turkey"', his dissertation research explores the political work that energy infrastructures do in twenty-first-century Turkey.

Huri İslamoğlu (BS in Economics at the University of Chicago; MA and PhD in Economic History at the University of Wisconsin, Madison) is currently a senior fellow at the Institut d'Études Avancées de Nantes, France, and Professor of Eeconomic History in the History Department at Boğaziçi University. Her research interests include economic history, global history, political economy and property law. She is the editor of *Shared Histories of Modernity in China, India and the Ottoman Empire* (2009), *Constituting Modernity: Private Property in the East and West* (I.B.Tauris, 2004), and *Ottoman Empire and the World Economy* (1987), and author of *State and Peasant in the Ottoman Empire* (1994).

Zeynep Kadirbeyoğlu (BA and MA in Economics at Boğaziçi University; MPhil in Social and Political Sciences at the University of Cambridge; PhD in Political Science at McGill University) is an assistant professor in the Department of Political Science and International Relations at Boğaziçi University. Her research interests include globalisation, transnational networks, democratisation, decentralisation, citizenship, environmental change and forced migration. Her articles have been published in, among others, *Environmental Policy and Governance, Environmental Politics*, and *Mediterranean Politics.*

Nazlı Konya (BA in Political Science and International Relations at Boğaziçi University) is currently a PhD candidate in Political Theory at Cornell University.

Tuna Kuyucu (BA in Sociology at Boğaziçi University; PhD in Sociology at the University of Washington) is an assistant professor in the Department of Sociology at Boğaziçi University. His research interests include economic sociology and urban sociology. His publications include articles in *Urban Affairs Review*, *Urban Studies*, *International Journal of Urban and Regional Research*, and *Nations and Nationalism.*

Hande Paker (BA in Economics at Boğaziçi University; PhD in Sociology at McGill University) is a political sociologist who works on political ecology, civil society, state and the transformation of citizenship. She has carried out research and published on modes of civil society-state relations, politics of the environment at the local-global nexus and grounded cosmopolitan citizenship, with a particular focus on environmental struggles and women's rights. Her articles have appeared in *Environmental Politics*, *Theory and Society*, and *Middle Eastern Studies.* Her latest research project carried out as part of the Mercator-IPC Fellowship (2015–16) focuses on local and transnational environmental spaces of action to analyse how environmental civil society actors engage the issue of climate change.

Erik Swyngedouw is Professor of Geography at the University of Manchester. He was previously Professor of Human Geography at the University of Oxford. He is a member of the Academia Europeae. His latest books include *The Post-Political and its Discontents* (with Japhy Wilson) and *Liquid Power.*

Z. Umut Türem (BA in Political Science at Boğaziçi University; MA in Sociology at Boğaziçi University; PhD in Law and Society at New York University, Institute for Law and Society) is an assistant professor at the Atatürk Institute for Modern Turkish History at Boğaziçi University. His research interests include neoliberalism, globalisation, and political economy of law and regulation. He recently edited (along with three other colleagues) a volume entitled *The Making of Neoliberal Turkey* (2016) and his recent articles have appeared in a number of journals: *A Journal of Feminist Cultural Studies*, *Indiana Journal of Global Legal Studies*, and *Journal of International Relations and Development.*

INDEX